Christ
and the
Christian
Life

Christ
and the
Christian
Life

TWO ESSAYS FROM
CHRISTIAN DOGMATICS

Gerhard O. Forde

Fortress Press
Minneapolis

CHRIST AND THE CHRISTIAN LIFE
Two Essays from *Christian Dogmatics*

Cover design and illustration: Brad Norr Design

Print ISBN: 978-1-5064-8810-3
eBook ISBN: 978-1-5064-8811-0

Contents

Publisher's Note

Originally published in 1984, the landmark two-volume *Christian Dogmatics* became a touchstone reference volume for generations of seminarians, pastors, and scholars. The present volume collects two major essays by Gerhard O. Forde from that project in the hope of reintroducing them to a new generation of readers.

Part I

The Work of Christ

Introduction

Therefore, if any one is in Christ, he is a new creation; the old has passed away, behold, the new has come. All this is from God, who through Christ reconciled us to himself and gave us the ministry of reconciliation; that is, in Christ God was reconciling the world to himself, not counting their trespasses against them, and entrusting to us the message of reconciliation. So we are ambassadors for Christ, God making his appeal through us. We beseech you on behalf of Christ, be reconciled to God. For our sake he made him to be sin who knew no sin, so that in him we might become the righteousness of God. (2 Cor. 5:17–21)

So reads a central New Testament passage on the work of Christ which can stand as a theme for this *locus*. We are concerned here with what God did in Jesus Christ, with the *work* rather than the person of Christ. The distinction cannot be made absolutely. In the broadest sense, Christ is what he does and does what he is. Dogmatic convention has made the distinction, however, and it is useful to continue it, if for no other reason than that so much curiosity and effort are invested usually in the dogma of Christ's person that his work would be shunted off into a few remarks and footnotes were the two doctrines treated together. So with the caveat that person and work should not and cannot ultimately be separated, we treat here that part of the dogmatic tradition which has dealt with the work of Christ.

There is no official dogma of the work of Christ—not in the sense in which one could speak of the dogmas of the Trinity, of the person of Christ, or even of justification in the churches of the Reformation. At best, one can speak of certain dominant doctrines, views, or motifs in different epochs. Yet the tradition bears witness to the tenacity with which the church has accorded a central place to Christ's work. The churches of the Reformation, for instance, have looked on that work as the "chief article" on which everything rests,[1] no doubt because of its importance for the doctrine of justification. To the Augsburg Confession, Christ "was crucified, died and was buried in order to be a sacrifice not only for original sin but also for all other sins and to propitiate God's wrath."[2]

The statement from the Augsburg Confession points to the major question for this *locus: Cur deus homo?* Why did God become a human person in the particular way manifest in the actual story of Jesus? What is accomplished thereby? What does Jesus do? We are concerned about the action and the passion of Jesus and what results from them, as distinguished from his being. Why must he be crucified and raised? If it is a doing, a work of Christ, and not just a being with which we are concerned, then it must have some result, some effect. What is that effect, and why is there just this form of doing to achieve it?

Central throughout the discussion is the question of God's relation to the doing. Does God in Jesus do it for us, or does Jesus do it for God on our behalf? Is God propitiated, satisfied, or in some way altered by the event? Is God wrathful? Does God "need" Christ's work to become merciful? Or does God act on us through the event, changing us or the situation in which we find ourselves? Does God need the cross, or do we? Who is the real obstacle to reconciliation? God? Humans? Or some others—demons, perhaps?

The dogmatic tradition of the church has attempted to answer the question posed by Christ's work by means of various "theories," "pictures," "models," or "motifs" of atonement. The very proliferation of such patterns of thought has itself become a problem for dogmatics and poses a second question for this *locus*: What is or should be the relationship between these patterns and the thing itself, the actual story of Jesus? It seems fair to say that considerable confusion reigns. Since the time of Anselm the dominant theory in the West has been some version of "vicarious satisfaction"—the so-called objective view, also called the "Latin," or "penal" view. Christ satisfies what is demanded for salvation instead of us, thus "objectively" changing God. Yet such a view enjoys at best an uneasy dominance. Whenever it is propounded, opponents protest. Anselm had Abelard. Protestant orthodoxy had Socinus. Revivalism and biblicism in the nineteenth century had liberal theology. Opponents press the central question already stated: Does God have to be satisfied? Is God not always a God of love and mercy?

For at least a century and a half there has been a sustained polemic against vicarious satisfaction. Yet also the various subjective theories usually fail to convince. Termed "subjective" because they propose that we, the subjects, are changed rather than God, such theories are usually charged with failure to take divine judgment and human sin seriously, so that they succumb to mere moralism. The God of mercy and love sends Christ to teach by his example, inspiring us to follow in the way of love. "A God without wrath brought men without sin into a kingdom without judgment through the ministrations of a Christ without a cross"—so H. Richard Niebuhr characterized popular nineteenth-century liberalism.[3]

When the objective and subjective views were fighting to a standoff, Gustaf Aulén's *Christus Victor* (1931) seemed to offer an alternative.[4] Aulén broadened the question by maintaining that neither theory was part of the classic Christian faith, both being later rationalizations. The classic view was rather that of "victory" over sin, death, and demonic forces through Christ. Christ's work brings not a change in God or merely in God's subjects, but a changed *situation*. In many ways, *Christus Victor* was epoch-making, especially in Scandinavia and the English-speaking world, because it raised the level of argument to a new plane. Yet it too was not able to satisfy everyone. Proponents of the objective view charge it with slighting the problem of guilt, justice, and divine holiness.[5] Subjectivists find the idea of victory over demonic forces too mythological and archaic to carry much weight.

The argument over theories and motifs, while stimulating and broadening, seems to have brought more rather than less confusion. Multiplying theories, models, and pictures seems to have become a theological hobby. The inability to settle the dispute among them leads to the attempt to make a virtue of the vice, under the auspices of the platitude that no one view or theory can do justice to the profound mystery of Christ's work. Each theory is supposed to convey an aspect of the truth. J. W. C. Wand, for instance, counts as many as seven different pictures and likens atonement to "a precious jewel, which is so large that you can only see properly one facet at a time." One has to turn it around in one's hand to see each facet in turn.[6] Almost every writer on atonement now appears obligated to play this game.

In spite of the broadening of perspective that development of such facets may bring, there is something profoundly unsatisfactory about the underlying presupposition and thus about the eventual outcome of the approach. We refer to this here as the problem of the relationship between the dogmatic construction and "the thing itself." Carved up into so many bits and pieces, the work of Christ becomes the plaything of human need. One is confronted with a cafeteria of ideas about Christ to which one pays lip service, but one's own taste then settles the matter. Left to one's own devices, one usually opts for the least offensive view, or at least that which supposedly meets what we consider to be our needs. Indeed, Wand betrays this when he says, "Our conception of the Atonement is likely to prove the more complete and satisfying the more it is able to meet all the manifold needs of the human personality."[7] Theologians seem to have forgotten that the work of Christ in atonement is one event and not several different ones. The Roman Catholic scholar Hans Kessler makes the same observation in reviewing Catholic dogmatic textbooks.

> They explain the—by them assumed—decisive meaning of the death of Jesus by a collection of categories—satisfaction, sacrifice, merit, redemption, etc., which they more or less throw together paratactically and at best bring into external order by means of conceptual analysis. But thereby it is neither clear what material connection there is among the categories nor is it apparent whether they have a common internal intent. Much rather one gets the impression it is as though one unified living process were split into an impenetrable multiplicity of concepts and the intended phenomenon lost at the outset.[8]

The multiplicity of more or less unrelated views in the tradition is itself a problem for dogmatics. There seems to be a kind of "embarrassment at the center" when we come to the work of Christ. The doctrine seems to falter, as though, to use Barth's words, it were tripping over some invisible object. We need to ask why. Is it because, as the platitude has it, dogmatics is not completely adequate to the task? That our subject is a mystery or paradox too elusive for us? Or is language inherently too limited to convey transcendent truth? Must we content ourselves with partial, pictorial, parabolic or symbolic utterances and try to overcome the limitation as best we can by sheer multiplication? But that is just the linguistic justification for pluralism and relativism.

Dogmatics has, in various ways, always been aware of its limitations, and will, one hopes, remain so. But we must press the question: Does that general caveat cover the embarrassment here? Can we in this case invoke such modesty to mask our ineptitude? Could it not be that the difficulty is of quite a different order? Martin Hengel concludes his recent study of crucifixion in the world of Jesus' time with these words:

> The theological reasoning of our time shows very clearly that the particular form of the death of Jesus, the man and the Messiah, represents a scandal which people like to blunt, remove, or domesticate in any way possible. We shall have to guarantee the truth of our theological thinking at this point.[9]

Indeed. We shall have to ask whether dogmatics itself is immune from this particular error: not that the blaze of transcendent truth dazzles, but that we are unwilling to face what stands quite clearly before our eyes.

> Who has believed what we have heard?
>   And to whom has the arm of the Lord been revealed?
> For he grew up before him like a young plant,
>   and like a root out of dry ground;
> he had no form or comeliness that we should look at him
>   and no beauty that we should desire him.
> He was despised and rejected by men;
>   a man of sorrows, and acquainted with grief;
> and as one from whom men hide their faces
>   he was despised, and we esteemed him not.
>
>   (ISA. 53:1–3)

The question we face in considering the work of Christ is whether and to what extent our very attempts to find meaning for ourselves in the tragedy and horror of Golgotha are attempts to insulate against the offense. H. J. Iwand says:

We have made the bitterness of the cross, the revelation of God in the cross of Jesus Christ, tolerable to ourselves by learning to understand it as a necessity for the process of salvation. . . . As a result the cross loses its contingent and incomprehensible character.[10]

We have surrounded the scandal of the cross with roses. We have made a theory of salvation out of it. But that is not the cross. That is not the bleakness inherent in it, placed in it by God.[11]

The question is whether our very attempts to understand the cross in our conventional ways may not simply put roses on the cross, and just so blunt the actual work of Christ on us through his cross and resurrection. The question is whether this itself may not be the secret reason for the failure of all our theories. For theories do not reconcile. If dogmatics covers the offense with its theories, it cannot serve a proclamation that actually *is* a ministry of reconciliation.

The questions we have put set for us the procedure to follow: first, investigation and evaluation of the tradition; second, an attempt at reconstruction which seeks to avoid the hazards and to state the work of Christ in a form true to Scripture and viable today. Obviously we cannot rehearse the whole tradition. Our purpose is dogmatic and not historical. Dogmatic rather than historical considerations govern, for the most part, the selection of representatives from the tradition. After a preliminary consideration of the New Testament materials, chapter 1 deals with central figures representing the major theories: objective, subjective, and classic. Chapter 2 is a transitional piece preparatory to attempted reconstruction in chapters 3 and 4.

CHAPTER ONE

The Shape of the Tradition

The dogmatic tradition strives to understand and present Jesus' work in his life and death in a way that stresses his historical act for us rather than his being as such. The various theories of the atonement have this aim. Insofar, however, as they attempt to capture the significance of the event in theories, they tend to defeat their own purpose and obscure the offense with roses.

The Scriptural Tradition

The basic material relevant to the work of Christ is simply the biblical story as it culminates in the cross and resurrection of Jesus, and some ad hoc attempts to interpret the significance of that story for its first hearers.

The story is simple enough and well known. Jesus, the carpenter's son from Nazareth, came declaring the imminent coming of the kingdom of God in connection with his own person and ministry, preaching repentance, forgiving sins, and performing signs and wonders. Those whom he encountered were confronted with a finality, with an ultimate judgment that could not be avoided. He opened a new vision of God for those who accepted him, a vision of the God whom he called his Father. In Jesus' being for them, this God was there for them. He brought new life and freedom. He did not demand, he gave; he did not crush, he raised up; he did not judge, he

removed burdens and let people breathe freely. He broke and
transcended the bounds of convention and tradition and advo-
cated the poor, the downtrodden, the outcast, the oppressed.
He gave hope. Jesus manifested the love of God.

But he was not accepted. Perhaps he could not be—here.
One cannot forgive sins here. It destroys all account books. One
cannot run roughshod over the laws and traditions that keep
earthly life and community in shape. The radical and unconditional love of God the Father could not go unchallenged—not
when there is important business to attend to. He had to go.
He was handed over to the Roman authorities and crucified,
apparently as a messianic pretender. His life ended in an ago-
nizing cacophony of voices.

> "Shall I crucify your King?" "We have no king but Caesar"
>   (John 19:15).
> "Do not weep for me, but weep for yourselves and for your
>   children" (Luke 23:28).
> And the inscription of the charge against him read, "The King
>   of the Jews" (Mark 15:26).
> "Aha! You who would destroy the temple and build it in three
>   days, save yourself, and come down from the cross!" . . .
>   "He saved others; he cannot save himself. Let the Christ,
>   the King of Israel, come down now from the cross, that we
>   may see and believe" (Mark 15:29–32).
> "My God, my God, why hast thou forsaken me?" (Mark 15:34).

His death was not pretty. It is easy to forget that, when centuries
of worship and art have made of the cross a beautiful cult sym-
bol. Martin Hengel's *Crucifixion in the Ancient World* reminds
us not only that the cross was excruciatingly painful, humiliating, and degrading—a death reserved for the public humiliation of slaves and political outcasts to deter further crime—but
also that precisely that kind of death is the culmination of the
story, an ineradicable part of the historical deposit with which

the theology itself must grapple.[1] The very folly and offense of it is the stuff from which the theology must start.

But the story does not end with the cross. There are other voices that write the end—and a new beginning!—to the story:

> He has risen, he is not here (Mark 16:6).
> Why do you seek the living among the dead? (Luke 24:5).

God raised Jesus from the dead. God vindicated the one rejected by all. God put the stamp of approval on the one humiliated and degraded. God ratified the action of the one who had the audacity to forgive sins here.

Such, in brief, is the story. What does it tell us about the work of Christ? What does this Jesus and his story do? It is amazing, when one takes the New Testament as a whole, how little is explicitly said which gives what could be called a dogmatic explanation of the work of Christ—at least of the sort that has become so dominant in the tradition. The earliest layers of the New Testament Gospel sources, the sayings sources such as Q, indicate no particular reflection on or view of Jesus' work or his fate. Jesus' death was no doubt a mighty shock, but it seems mostly to have been understood in terms of the usual fate of God's prophets: they were rejected and came to a bad end. Such rejection, of course, unmasks the unrepentant, unbelieving, and guilty stance of God's people. This early view of the life and death of Jesus is reflected also in some of the speeches in Acts, such as Peter's speech in Acts 2, and even in some of Paul's earlier writings (see, e.g., 1 Thess. 2:14ff.). Jesus himself, though he might have and quite possibly did reckon with a violent death at the hands of his adversaries, seems not to have understood or interpreted his own death as a sacrifice for others or ransom for sin. Such interpretation apparently came as the result of later reflection.[2] Even in their final redaction the synoptic Gospels contain little direct or explicit interpretation of Jesus' work. Mark 10:45 has Jesus say that the Son of Man came to give his life "as a ransom for many," and the accounts of the Last Supper speak of Jesus' blood as his "blood of the covenant, which is poured out for many" (Mark 14:24) and "my blood of the covenant, which is poured out for many for the forgiveness of sins" (Matt. 26:28). Such passages, in their present form at least, are usually regarded as having come not from Jesus himself but from later interpretative traditions. The same is true of the instances where Jesus predicts his own death and resurrection, such as Mark 8:31ff. and 9:31, and parallels in the other Synoptics. They are interpretations attributed to Jesus after the fact. But aside from such scanty references, the Synoptics even in their final form afford little explicit interpretation of Jesus' work.

There is, however, a great deal of interpretation implicit in the presentation of Jesus' life and death. This is no doubt more important than the few explicit passages. The passion predictions placed on Jesus' lips show that already in the earliest days there was an attempt to come to grips with the terrible tragedy and offense of his death by seeing it as part of the divine will. Jesus' death was not the result of mere human caprice; it happened "according to the Scriptures," just as the Scriptures reveal—especially in the psalms of lament and suffering. The drama is played out according to the apocalyptic timetable. The ultimate reason for it lies in the hidden counsel of God which is now being revealed. The interpretation given Jesus' life could also be extended to his death: It was part of the apocalyptic drama.

The apocalyptic setting leads almost naturally to a second and deeper level of interpretation also implicit in the Gospels: Jesus' life and death have eschatological import. They are an end-time event—above all one through which final judgment is exercised. It means judgment pronounced over the old ways, over godlessness, over holding on to the old cultic rituals and

laws as ways of salvation. The apocalyptic judgment is anticipated. The Son of Man, rejected by humans, is revealed para-
doxically as the hidden judge of all. This understanding is
especially evident in the many controversies between Jesus and
his adversaries.

The concept of judgment also brings with it a new element:
Jesus' life and death have soteriological significance. He brings
salvation. The night is past, the light shines. God has drawn
near to all people. In the earliest layers of the tradition, there
was apparently no special emphasis put on his death as the saving event. Jesus as a whole brought salvation. Mark, in the first
Gospel, apparently took this kind of material and interpreted
the whole in the light of the crucifixion as its *telos* and climax.
Thus, following Mark, the Gospels in their present form are
predominantly passion narratives, with the other material
organized to lead inexorably to the cross. The cross assumes
a paramount position for interpreting the work of Jesus, the
risen Christ.

But how can a humiliating and offensive death on a cross be
of soteriological significance? This is the question with which
the entire Christian tradition has wrestled ever since. The materials in the New Testament indicate that beyond the kind of
interpretation given in the synoptic Gospels there was from the
earliest days, most probably in circles influenced by Hellenistic
Judaism, a tradition that interpreted Jesus' death as in some
sense an atonement or expiation for sin. Just exactly what that
sense is seems to be a matter for debate among current scholars.
At any rate, this tradition drew on cultic materials, the concept
of sacrifice, covenant sacrifice, Passover, the concept of the suffering servant (Isaiah 53), and so forth, to interpret the significance of Jesus' life and death. Although this tradition seems to
have intruded only quite late into the synoptic materials (Mark
10:45 and pars, plus 14:24 and pars, being the only instances),
it was apparently a very early tradition. It is generally held that

Paul in Romans 3:25–26 and also in 4:25 is drawing on this earlier tradition, quoting hymnic and confessional material from Hellenistic Jewish-Christian circles. But this indicates that the tradition is already well established before Paul's writing. Romans 3:25–26 speaks of Christ as one "whom God put forward as an expiation by his blood . . . to show God's righteousness, because in his divine forbearance he had passed over former sins." Romans 4:25 speaks of Jesus as "put to death for our trespasses and raised for our justification"—perhaps part of an early Jewish-Christian confessional statement. Echoes of this tradition interpreting Jesus' death as in some sense a sacrifice or expiation for sin are to be found quite regularly in the writings related to or dependent on Paul (though not so much in Paul himself) and in the Johannine literature (see, e.g., John 1:29; 6:51; 1 John 1:7; 2:2; 3:5–6; 4:10; Rev. 5:8–9; 7:14; 12:11). Such a view comes to most sustained expression in the Epistle to the Hebrews, where Jesus' sacrifice is interpreted against the background of the rite for the Day of Atonement. Jesus' sacrifice is better and more perfect, fulfilling and thus ending "once and for all" the need for cultic sacrifices. He has opened up a "new and living way" through his flesh, accomplishing in actuality what the old rite could only foreshadow.

But what is the import of this tradition? The history of interpretation shows that it has been easy to move from this kind of material to an understanding of Christ's work as a vicarious satisfaction of divine honor (justice, wrath, etc.) akin to that usually associated with Anselm. Put in its most crass form, this view would hold that Jesus' death is a sacrifice in which he is a substitute for us who pays the divine justice what is due for human sin and/or appeases the divine wrath. As we shall see, there is a long tradition, especially among Western conservative Christians, which has taken this line. There seems to be a virtual consensus among contemporary biblical scholars, however, that this tradition finds little support in the Scriptures, either in the Old or New Testament. Scripture never speaks of God as one who has to be satisfied or propitiated before being merciful or forgiving. God is always the *subject* of the action, not the object.

Yet even if Jesus' death is not to be thought of as propitiating God, the New Testament quite clearly insists that it was substitutionary, or at least representative. The many "for you," "for us," "for our sins," "for many" formulas certify that. What the "for our sins" or "for us" formulas mean exactly, however, has been and continues to be a subject of debate. Some, following more traditional lines, would insist that such formulas mean *substitution*: "For us" means "instead of us." Those following this line usually like to insist that the idea of one person's sacrificial death having propitiatory or expiatory efficacy for others belongs to a firm biblical and Jewish tradition current and well known in Jesus' time. Such interpretation draws on various strands of the Old Testament materials, the sacrificial cult, and especially the suffering servant motif of Isaiah 53, as well as later accounts of the vicarious efficacy of the sufferings of the "just man" and the martyrs of the Maccabean era.[3] In light of this material, it has been common among New Testament scholars until quite recently to hold that the idea of a death having vicarious or even atoning significance was a firmly held biblical and Jewish view. Some (most notably Oscar Cullmann) have asserted that Jesus quite probably understood his own life and coming fate in this fashion, combining the "Son of Man" concept with the "suffering servant" of Isaiah.

Recent scholarship, however, has begun to cast doubt on these "received" positions. The most telling argument is that there simply seems to be no literary evidence that such interpretation was present in Jewish circles in Jesus' time. There seems to be no concept of a death having vicarious significance in Jewish circles in the sense given it by later Christian interpretation.[4] Even though such passages as Isaiah 53 seem most explicitly to point in that direction, it is apparent that no Jewish tradition of the time of Jesus (prior to A.D. 70) understood it as indicating a vicarious death. Furthermore, there seems to be no evidence that "Son of Man" or "suffering servant" materials were current or combined in the fashion suggested by scholars like Oscar Cullmann.[5] The literary evidence, therefore, just does not seem to support what has been a widely held view among New Testament exegetes. The idea of a death having vicarious significance was not a commonly held tradition. Persuasive arguments can be made that the idea came not from Jewish but from Christian sources, Christians "thoroughly at home in the Greek-Hellenistic thought world."[6] Even the interpretation of the death of the martyrs in 4 Maccabees is most likely quite late and influenced by the same sort of thought.

Such recent scholarship casts considerable doubt on the right of the "vicarious death" strand to claim preeminence in interpreting the death of Christ and the "for us." At the least one could not claim that it is *the* biblical and Jewish tradition which could pretend once and for all to settle the metaphysics of the matter. At the most it could claim to be only one of the ways the early Christians sought to come to terms with Jesus' death.

The line of interpretation that draws on the cultic materials, the idea of sacrifice, and the suffering servant is no doubt an attempt to deal with the stark offensiveness of the cross with the biblical materials themselves: Where Jewish thought had almost insurmountable difficulties, one used Jewish means to try to overcome them (the Epistle to the Hebrews is a prime example of that). But it is doubtful that one could press these materials into a hard-and-fast theory of atonement, as was later done. In essence, perhaps little more is being said through such materials than was said in the synoptic Gospels: In Jesus' life and death, God turns toward the lost, the sinners, the outcast, and accepts them. Jesus' death is what it cost God to do that. But we shall have to say more about that in the reconstructive part of our *locus*.

For now, the point is that the "for us," while it does certainly mean a sacrificial death on our behalf, cannot be systematized into a hard-and-fast theory. The "for us" formulas should be interpreted more in the sense of "on our behalf," "for our good," or "for our benefit," rather than "instead of us." Indeed, one could argue that the "instead of us" runs the danger of missing the point altogether, for then it seems primarily the *hindrances* to salvation that necessitate the death. The act is oriented solely toward the past. But Jesus' work "for us" in the New Testament is oriented also toward the future. He died not only to repair past damage but to open a new future "for us."

If one interprets the "for us" in the sense of also opening a new future, it is more possible to combine—as the New Testament repeatedly does—an understanding of Jesus' death as atonement with the concept of example. Many of the central New Testament passages on atonement do this very thing. First Peter 2:21–24 is an excellent illustration:

> For to this you have been called, because Christ also suffered for you, leaving you an example, that you should follow in his steps. He committed no sin; no guile was found on his lips. When he was reviled, he did not revile in return; when he suffered, he did not threaten; but he trusted to him who judges justly. He himself bore our sins in his body on the tree, that we might die to sin and live to righteousness. By his wounds you have been healed.

Even the only two passages in the New Testament which speak directly of Jesus' sacrifice as offered "to God," Eph. 5:2 and Heb. 9:14, seem more concerned with the exemplary nature of that sacrifice than with any sort of propitiatory machinery. In the Ephesians passage we are exhorted to be "imitators of God, as beloved children. And walk in love, as Christ loved us and gave himself up for us, a fragrant offering and sacrifice to God." The Hebrews passage makes a similar point. The cultic sacrifice is limited, purifying only the "flesh," that is, effecting only a ritual purification. Jesus' sacrifice, however, "without blemish to God" should "much more" purify the conscience from dead works to serve the living God. The cultic type of sacrifice, that is, is directed toward the past, dealing with the ritual impurities incurred by past actions. Jesus' sacrifice "for all," "for us," opens up a new future: One might serve the living God from the heart, no longer concerned about "dead works"! If one interprets the "for you" as opening that new future, one no longer has to tear apart what so often has been sundered in the tradition: the atoning work and the example.

But it is to the writings of Paul that one must look for the most concentrated and sustained exposition of the significance of the cross and the resurrection of Jesus. Paul's writings are gripped by a sense for the utter folly and offense of the cruelty and humiliation of the crucifixion and the startling nature of the reversal in the resurrection. He holds this tirelessly before his hearers and readers. Paul was well aware of the reality of it all and found this to be of the essence. Martin Hengel has put it well:

> When Paul speaks of the "folly" of the message of the crucified Jesus, he is therefore not speaking in riddles or using an abstract cipher. He is expressing the harsh experience of his missionary preaching and the offence that it caused, in particular the experience of his preaching among non-Jews, with whom his apostolate was particularly concerned. The reason why in his letters he talks about the cross above all in a polemical context is that he deliberately wants to provoke his opponents, who are attempting to water down the offence caused by the cross. Thus in a way the "word of the cross" is the spearhead of his message. And because Paul still understands the cross as the real, cruel instrument of execution, as the

instrument of the bloody execution of Jesus, it is impossible to dissociate talk of the atoning death of Jesus or the blood of Jesus from this "word of the cross." The spearhead cannot be broken off the spear. Rather, the complex of the death of Jesus is a single entity for the apostle, in which he never forgets the fact that Jesus did not die a gentle death like Socrates, with his cup of hemlock, much less passing on "old and full of years" like the Patriarchs of the Old Testament. Rather he died like a slave or a common criminal, in torment, on the tree of shame. Paul's Jesus did not die just any death; he was "given up for us all" on the cross, in a cruel and a contemptible way.[7]

For Paul the proclamation of the cross is crisis, the eschatological crisis, the absolute end and the new beginning. In his own constructions Paul does not seem to speak so much of Jesus' death as a sacrifice for sin or a ransom. Nor does he dwell on the concept of guilt and forgiveness coming from the cross. As already noted, he quotes the already existing traditions with apparent approval in this regard, but does not pursue it in his own thinking. Rather, for him the cross is total crisis, the end of the old, the breaking of the demonic powers and the opening of something new, the life of love and freedom. The "for us" means "on our behalf," the new life "in Christ," "in the Spirit." It has to do with the future, the new age.

Paul is thus adamantly opposed to every attempt to avoid, stop short of, leap over, or detour around the cross in its reality and offensiveness. When he is dealing with a Jewish-Christian legalism that stops short of the cross (Galatians), he will preach the gospel of the utter freedom the cross brings, the cross as the end of the law. Jesus has borne the curse of the law in his own accursed death—actually. Now all that is over; faith has come; all distinctions are abolished and freedom is given.

If in another instance Paul is confronted with perfectionism or arrogant enthusiasm that thinks it has surpassed or leaped over the cross to a resurrected life already in the present

(1 Corinthians), Paul will preach the utter folly of "Christ and him crucified" to judge and destroy all such premature presumption. Christians cannot be better than their crucified Lord. One cannot leap over the cross. Jesus indeed brings the new, but through the cross, not around it. The perfection is not yet, and the world is in travail until the eschatological fulfillment.

Or if, still further, there are those who want to look on the earthly Jesus as a kind of "divine man" of Greek provenance, a charismatic hero and wonderworker whose charismatic power one can possess and use to one's own advantage and glory (2 Corinthians), Paul will again preach the lowly and despised Christ and speak of a power manifest in weakness and folly.

No avoidance, no detour, no leaping over the cross to premature fulfillment is possible. The cross is ultimate judgment and grace. The new comes through it, not around it. To be a beneficiary, an heir, of the work of Christ is to be "in Christ," by faith, to be "baptized into his death," in order to share the hope of his resurrection.

When Paul wants, therefore, to describe the new flowing from the work of Christ, he can simply say that faith has come, faith born out of the shame, offense, and weakness of the cross, where the love of God for all is hidden from the wise of this age, but revealed to those who believe. It is perhaps not inaccurate to say that Paul sees Christ as placing humans in the same eschatological crisis manifest in the Gospel accounts, but that (at least in the extant letters of Paul) the crisis comes predominantly in the cross, not so much in the life of the historical Jesus as such. Paul apparently could not escape the shock of the cross and its offense. He could not easily write off the fact that this crucified one was the one approved and vindicated by God. The willingness and capacity of theology or of the Christian life to be transformed by the "*logos* of the cross" is the test of its viability. The shattering fact, for Paul, was that all God's history with Israel had led to the hill of Golgotha. The "custodian" (Gal. 3:24) had led them to that awful place. It was the end—and the possibility of a new beginning.

In summary, we can safely say that the New Testament materials give evidence of several strands of interpretation. One strand, perhaps the earliest (as evidenced by the sayings sources), interprets Jesus' work much as that of a prophet or teacher who met the same fate as all genuine prophets among God's people: he was rejected and killed. Already implicit in that, however, is the element of judgment on the people who refuse to accept him. The judges are judged in Jesus. This forms the basis for what could be called the next strand, or layer, of the tradition: Jesus' life and death have apocalyptic or eschatological significance. The resurrection makes that evident. His death is not just historical accident, it is a part of the apocalyptic drama of the end-times: In him and in his message the ultimate judgment has been revealed. This would mean also that his life and death have soteriological significance: Those who accept him will be able to stand in the day of judgment. A third strand of the tradition speaks of Jesus' work more directly in sacrificial terms. Jesus' death is a sacrifice, an expiation, a ransom, "for us," "for our sins." This strand no doubt attempts to overcome the almost insurmountable antipathy to the shame and offense of the cross by drawing on traditional biblical material (the cultic ritual, the suffering servant, the Psalms, and so on) to show that Jesus died "according to the Scriptures." He fulfilled and ended "once for all" the sacrificial rite. It is this strand that has enjoyed most extensive development in the subsequent dogmatic tradition, fourth, we must point to the Pauline "*logos* of the cross." In the weakness, folly, shame, and offense of the painful and humiliating death of Jesus on the cross, God has reached the end and ultimate judgment on humanity, the world, the demons, the "elemental spirits," the entire creation. Those who die with Jesus and receive him in his hiddenness, humiliation, and weakness shall be raised in him to newness of life. The way lies through the cross to the resurrection in him. He is ultimate judgment and grace. Such, in brief summary, are the New Testament materials. Now we turn to see what the subsequent dogmatic tradition has done with them.

Vicarious Satisfaction of Divine Justice

The closest thing to a dogma of the atonement through the years in the West has been the doctrine of vicarious satisfaction. First worked out by Anselm of Canterbury (1033–1109), and refined through the years, it became standard for the great systems of medieval scholasticism and Protestant orthodoxy and has remained so for most of conservative Christianity. Its "inner solidity" has made it the "seed of crystallization" for atonement thinking;[8] it seems presupposed both by Reformation confessional documents and by the Council of Trent, and it was almost raised to the level of formal dogma by Vatican I.[9]

Prior to Anselm soteriology was defined mostly in terms of knowledge: Christ gives true knowledge of the "eternal *logos*" in contrast to the false knowledge and speculation of the gnostics. Knowledge, however, proves to be an inadequate model for taking account of the actual historical life and fate of Jesus. One can too easily develop a split vision in which the history becomes a mere allegory or appearance of the transcendent gnosis. The actual history, the offense of the cross, can become an embarrassment. The gnostics, of course, spiritualized altogether—some, such as Basilides, holding that the "gnostic redeemer" departed from Jesus, leaving only "the man" to be crucified.

Christian theologians were concerned to press beyond gnosticism and give the actual history theological import. The knowledge model, however, caused difficulties. Three possibilities seemed to suggest themselves. The first was to make the historical life a "pattern" or "way." If one conforms to the pattern, especially to the extent of martyrdom, one will see God as the martyr Stephen saw God. Early martyr theology, the apologists, and to some extent later Antiochene theology were influenced by this option. A second tendency was to substantialize the model and see the incarnation as the joining of the "eternal *logos*" and the historical flesh, so that by participating sacramentally in the "God-man," we receive "the medicine of immortality." A third possibility was to read a kind of inner logical order out of—or into!—the historical facts themselves, so as to arrive at the "true gnosis." Here we think of Irenaeus.

The problem with all these attempts to give significance to the history itself is that the split vision is not cured. One still sees through the history to the ideal. The emphasis tends to shift from the action, the history, to the being of the God-man, the "union of the two natures." Even in Irenaeus and the theology of recapitulation—Jesus repeats the stages of human growth, overcoming where Adam succumbed to the tempter—the history is seen through. All events mean the same thing.[10] When one systematizes the history, one sees through the scandal of the cross, and history is in fact transcended by gnosis.[11]

There were also the various pictures of atonement, such as that of ransom paid to the devil or reconciliation through sacrifice. But these received no solid dogmatic treatment and did not explain the necessity for the work of Christ.[12] Origen, for instance, fecund source of many such ideas, regarded them more as instructive pictures for the simple than as doctrine for the accomplished gnostic.[13]

Anselm was the first to pose the question about the necessity for the actual event of the cross, and thus the first to pose the soteriological question as a specific theme in itself. His question is "Why?" *Cur deus homo* (why the God-man?), his major treatise on the atonement, relentlessly pursues the question of necessity—not just the *a posteriori* necessity of previous pictures, but a rationally deduced *a priori* necessity.[14] He claims to demonstrate both the absolute reasons for the necessity of a God-man and the necessity for salvation to take place in exactly the way it did.[15] He wants to demonstrate that atonement had to take place the way it did.[16]

Anselm dismisses both the theory of recapitulation and the idea of a ransom paid to the devil as insufficient (though not wrong). A recapitulation theology, working with contrapuntal pictures, has aesthetic appeal but does not give substantial reasons for the cross. It is like painting "on clouds or in water" (*Cur Deus Homo*, i, 4). Talk about the deception and defeat of Satan is equally insufficient, because it does not explain why the Almighty had to go to such trouble to defeat enemies. Could not God simply have crushed Satan and released the captives by divine decree (ibid., 1, 1, 5, 6, 7)?

The answer to the question "Why?" must therefore lie in God, in a necessity laid on God in relation to the fallen creation. The basic contours of Anselm's argument are simple enough. No doubt the simplicity has commended it to dogmatics through the years. The rational creature owes God the Creator the debt of total response. Sin is a withholding of this response and thus a dishonoring of God, a disruption of the order of creation. Furthermore, since total obedience is owed, a simple return to obedience will not be able to pay for past sins. Restitution can be made to the divine honor only by giving back more than the total obedience owed.[17] The situation seems hopeless.

But what of God? Can God not simply forgive? If that were so, there would be no necessity for the God-man. Hence Anselm insists that it is not possible or fitting for God simply to forgive. Such mercy would cancel justice and order by its arbitrariness; sin and justice would be on the same level, and chaos would result. To protect the divine honor and created order, some other way must be found.[18]

Thus Anselm arrives at his great either-or: "*aut poena aut satisfaction*" (either punishment or satisfaction). God could, of course, punish the sinner. But punishment would mean destruction and thus frustrate God's hope for creation—there would be no one left to replace the fallen angels in paradise. So if the creature is not to be punished, satisfaction must be rendered to the divine honor.[19] The creature must do this but cannot; God could do it but must not; hence the only solution is the God-man. Only one who is sinless can render to God a satisfaction more than the sinner is obligated to give. It is a necessity.

The necessity is met by Jesus Christ. As sinless God-man it is not incumbent on him to die. Since he voluntarily gives himself up to death, he gives more than was required. His death is worth more than anything that is not God. So great a sacrifice deserves a reward. But as God-man he needs no reward. Therefore he can give it to those for whom he became incarnate. Those who receive his merits shall be saved.

Such is the vicarious satisfaction of the divine honor. The major question bequeathed to the subsequent dogmatic tradition by Anselm's construction—and one should bear in mind that Anselm was perfectly aware of it, since it is repeatedly pressed by the interlocutor, Boso—is the question of mercy. If God is satisfied, how is it mercy? Before going on to press the question, we must let Anselm have the word. He concludes by telling Boso:

> Now we have found the compassion of God which appeared lost to you when we were considering God's holiness and man's sin; we have found it, I say, so great and so consistent with his holiness, as to be incomparably above anything that can be conceived. For what compassion can excel these words of the Father, addressed to the sinner doomed to eternal torments and having no way of escape: "Take my only begotten Son and make him an offering for yourself"; or these words of

the Son: "Take me and ransom your souls." For these are the voices they utter, when inviting and leading us to faith in the gospel.[20]

Note how Anselm's words reflect the sacrifice of the mass.

Anselm's doctrine represents an acute juridicizing of Christ's work—some call it a Latinizing.[21] To give the actual history rational necessity, Anselm is driven to call on ideas from the realm of law and justice.[22] The relationship between God and God's creatures comes to be understood in terms of legal order, a *iustitia commutativa*.[23] Sin is not so much a personal matter as it is an objective and legal matter. God's relation to it is not so much wrath—Anselm never speaks of God's wrath—as one determined by the logic of order. So the possibility of atonement comes to hinge on making equivalent restitution; the payment must equal the debt. "The order permeated by the *iustitia commutativa* becomes in this fashion a merciless law, in which—without the satisfier furnished by God—no remedy appears possible."[24]

Does Anselm successfully answer the why of the terrible event of the historical cross? Can the necessity be demonstrated in this fashion? It is possible, of course, to point to holes in Anselm's logic.[25] How could Christ's death be necessary and at the same time a free and voluntary sacrifice? Anselm sputters and seems never quite able to put the question to rest. How can the equivalence between Christ's death and the demand of the divine honor be demonstrated? Anselm tries to argue that because the evil of destroying the Son of God is greater than the evil of allowing the whole human race to be destroyed, his life is an incomparably greater good than the mass of all human sin and evil and can hence be offered as an equivalent satisfaction.[26] But the logic will not work. It is like the attempt to prove the worth of something by asking how great an evil it would be to destroy it; one assumes the worth to begin with. Equivalence cannot be demonstrated in that fashion.

Logical problems in Anselm's doctrine led later theology to surrender his insistence on an absolute or *a priori* necessity for atonement and to speak rather of a relative necessity. God could have done it differently, but the way God actually did it was most appropriate to give an example and awaken our hope.[27] It is dangerous, however, to retain the idea of vicarious satisfaction without Anselm's argument for its necessity. The cruel death of Jesus is a costly example. The protest Anselm puts in the mouth of Boso comes back to haunt: "that the Most High should stoop to things so lowly, that the Almighty should do a thing with such toil."[28] Anselm may have ventured too far, but he was at least correct in his attempt to insist that the history, the concrete life and death of Christ, was more than a mere picture or example of truths already known. Anselm was right in insisting that something vital happened to the God-creature relationship in the death of Jesus.

The more serious problems with Anselm's doctrine are theological rather than logical. The most persistent one is the question of justice versus mercy and its consequences for the doctrine of God. The attempt to prove the necessity of satisfaction leads to the idea that mercy can be exercised only when the demands of justice have been fulfilled. But if God has to be paid and has been paid, how is God merciful? Why cannot God, the almighty, simply forgive? Indeed, we are enjoined to forgive our debtors; why cannot God? Anselm is aware of the questions, since Boso constantly nags about them. Anselm's answer is basically that God cannot use divine freedom in a manner that is unfitting. Just as it is unfitting for God to lie, it is also unfitting to let sin go unpunished.[29] But the reasoning is questionable. To lie is indeed wrong and would be unfitting for God. But is it wrong to have mercy? Mercy is of a different order from lying. The result of the attempt to prove necessity is inevitably the elevation of justice over mercy. The question remains: If God has been satisfied, where is God's mercy?

It was Abelard (1079–1142) who sensed the vulnerable spots in Anselm's argument and gained the historical reputation of being Anselm's great antagonist, even though he did not work out a complete or consistent alternative. Abelard does not see why justice must be satisfied before God can be merciful. Did not Jesus forgive before his death? Does not the cruel death on the cross increase human sin rather than compensate for it? What can possibly atone for the murder of Christ? Is it not cruel and unjust that anyone should demand innocent blood as a ransom or be in any way delighted with the death of the innocent, that God should find the death of the Son so acceptable that through it God should be reconciled to the world?[30]

Abelard shows clearly how the vicarious satisfaction doctrine recoils on God. It restricts the freedom of God and leads to a gruesome and forbidding picture of the deity. This remarkable outcome of the dogmatic enterprise must be noted carefully. The very attempt to construct a neat theory about reconciliation to God leads to the exact opposite: It alienates from God by creating a forbidding picture of God.

Abelard's attack was picked up and broadened by the Socinians at the time of the Reformation and after. Divine freedom and love were raised above justice. "For God can, especially since He is Lord of all, abandon as much of His rights as He pleases."[31] Satisfaction is superfluous, indeed, senseless. Why should God pay God? Furthermore, the account does not balance. How can the suffering of one man outweigh the punishment due the whole race? The sufferings of Jesus are finite, not eternal. What was demanded was eternal death, but Jesus was dead only three days. And so on. The theory does not deliver what it promises: the necessity for just this life and death.

The Socinians also exposed what even staunch contemporary advocates of the doctrine admit is its Achilles' heel: the idea of substitution.[32] The transfer of someone else's sin to the innocent is absurd and improper, just as in reverse the transfer of someone else's righteousness to the unrighteous.[33]

A final fault, common to both sides, is the neglect of the resurrection. Anselm hardly mentions it and can develop his entire doctrine virtually without it. For the Socinians, too, resurrection does not really function except as a kind of promotion of Jesus as teacher-revealer to divine worthiness and power.

The doctrine of vicarious satisfaction, or more accurately, of vicarious punishment, acquired its final shape in the great systems of seventeenth-century Protestant orthodoxy. While the Reformation itself did not need to pay specific attention to the question of atonement, since the doctrine was not explicitly controversial, the theologians of the late sixteenth and the seventeenth centuries had to work out the implications of the doctrine of justification and contend with the Socinians. This led to a final shaping of the doctrine begun by Anselm.

The development of the doctrine of justification as a forensic decree drove to a juridicizing of the atonement even more stringent than Anselm's. The concept of law as a fixed, eternal way of salvation takes the place of the more aesthetically tinged Augustinian concept of order. Law is understood as an objective schema of commands and prohibitions, a checklist of what must be done and not done to be saved.[34]

Once this occurs it is easier to make the logic of substitution work: someone might fulfill the checklist for someone else. Christ as the substitute fulfills the law instead of us. This takes place "objectively," entirely and exclusively outside of us, and thus is the presupposition for forensic justification. Jesus satisfies the demands of the divine law, the wrath and justice of God, the utterly strict judge.[35] This construction also enabled these theologians to insist even more adamantly than Anselm on the absolute necessity for the satisfaction and thus confute the Socinians. Since God threatened Adam and Eve with death in the garden, he would have lied had he not carried out this sentence.[36] God, many insisted, could not forgive without satisfaction. His love and mercy are not "absolute" but "ordinate," that is, possible only within the bounds established by Christ's satisfaction.

> God indeed loved already from all eternity the whole human race, yet not absolutely and unconditionally, but ordinately; namely, in His beloved Son. . . . Therefore, this ordinate affection or love of God necessarily presupposes His wrath, so that this love in God could not have a place, unless, likewise from all eternity, satisfaction had been made to this divine wrath or justice through the Son, who from eternity, offered Himself as mediator between God and man.[37]

God is the most just judge who requires, "according to the rigor of his infinite justice," an infinite price of satisfaction.[38]

Orthodox Protestantism also went beyond Anselm in surrendering the distinction between satisfaction and punishment. Christ suffers the punishment due us under divine wrath. Punishment and satisfaction are more or less equated. Here too the Anselmian view is legalized, simplified, and made more penal in character—at the same time it is deepened. These theologians do not need Anselm's idea of satisfaction by means of the voluntary sacrifice of something more than the sinner is obligated to give, and are not so troubled about the contradiction between the voluntary versus the necessary in the sacrifice.[39] They can simply say that Jesus suffers the punishment due and that since he is also divine, his suffering is of infinite worth.[40]

Nothing new is said, however, about the problems of substitution: how the suffering and obedience of one can be transferred to another. They simply content themselves with the biblical witness that it was "for us." Substitution remained the Achilles' heel of the doctrine.

The most original contribution of Protestant orthodox teaching was the distinction between the passive and the active suffering and obedience of Christ. Christ's work was not only a passive suffering under the law and wrath, but also an active doing of the law for us in his life.[41] While this was a step in the right direction, since it was an attempt to give soteriological significance to Jesus' life as well as to his death, it had the unfortunate effect of legalizing his life as well.

The full-blown soteriology of Protestant orthodoxy was finally codified in the doctrine of the threefold office of Christ: Prophet, High Priest, and King. This doctrine became the common property of virtually all Protestant and Roman Catholic dogmatics, though Catholics usually spoke of Shepherd rather than King. As Prophet, Christ proclaims salvation; as Priest, he offers himself and intercedes eternally; as King, he governs, preserves, and rules all things. The doctrine of the threefold office shows also an attempt to extend soteriology beyond the death of Christ. Yet the main emphasis remained on the priestly office, and it is doubtful that the doctrine is ultimately of much help.[42]

The Triumph of Divine Love

The doctrine of vicarious satisfaction or punishment has always been vigorously resisted in the tradition, in the name of divine love and mercy. Yet the protest always has difficulty assuming convincing positive shape. If God can forgive before the death of Jesus, what is the point of it? The difficulty is to avoid reducing the Christ-event to a mere example, an illustration of a generally known truth. When Jesus becomes just another teacher, no matter how impressive, there is nothing new about the New Testament. Jesus does not do anything someone else could not do. The criticism of vicarious satisfaction can just as well recoil on this view: God must be particularly heartless to go to such lengths just to provide an example, especially when everyone already knows what is being taught.

The earliest attempts at this so-called "moral influence" theory of atonement already suffer from this difficulty. Abelard spoke of Christ as one who persevered unto death in instructing in the way of love, binding us to himself in the way of love so we too should fear nothing in the exercise of love. God is not changed; we are.[43]

The Socinians did not take matters much further. Christ is the confirmation of the will of God to save. His life manifests the will of God to forgive, and his death certifies what is promised under the New Covenant. He is the prophet, the divine legate, who proclaims the gospel in God's name and in God's stead, the Logos who reveals the will of the Father. The resurrection shows how God delivers those who trust in God, and Christ is elevated to virtual divine dignity and power even though he remains a man. Faith is obedience to and imitation of Christ in the hope of eternal life as a reward.[44]

Such reconstructions involve a complete moralization of Christ's work. The basic structure remains a legal one. The ironic fact is that, for all their opposition, the antagonists in this great debate are usually brothers and sisters under the skin. For both sides the basic scheme is law and reward. The only argument is about human ability to fulfill what is demanded. For the conservative, the fallen creature cannot do it and so needs a substitute. For the liberal or "moral influence" theologian, the creature needs only guidance and encouragement. The argument is a standoff. A new departure is needed.

The great nineteenth-century theologians such as Friedrich Schleiermacher and Albrecht Ritschl tried to provide a new departure by describing Christ's work as the establishment of a new historical community in which the redeeming influence of Christ could be experienced, raising us above the fate of merely natural and empirical life. Schleiermacher sought a mean between the kind of theology represented by vicarious satisfaction and that of the moral-influence type.[45] This could be done, he thought, by seeing the redeeming activity of Christ as establishing a new life common to us and to him—original in him, new and derived in us. The historical activity of Jesus is not mere example, it is the establishment of a new corporate life in an actual historical community.

To avoid both moralism and vicarious satisfaction, Schleiermacher depends on a view of religion based on something other than legal or moral categories: the religion of "the feeling of absolute dependence" and the idea of God-consciousness. Sin is that which arrests the free development of God-consciousness, the proper relationship between self, world, and God. Sin is the arresting of the power of the spirit by the flesh. In the new historical community, redemption is effected by the communication of Jesus' sinless perfection. This is not to mean that Jesus is recognized, in Kantian fashion, as a person of exceptional moral excellence by those who already have the moral ideal within them. The communication of sinless perfection is Jesus' own work. He communicates it. It is perfection, not mere moral improvement. He works on his followers in such a way that they are drawn into the sphere of his sinless perfection. This faith is passed on through history from him under the power of his personal influence. In ordinary circumstances the power and influence of historical figures diminish with time. Not so here. Christian faith depends on the communication of the absolutely potent God-consciousness in Christ as something inward yet derived from without in history.[46] The sinless perfection of Jesus, the absolutely potent God-consciousness radiating from his historical life, is the *Urbild*, the productive ideal, manifest in time, creating something new. Jesus does not merely enhance the moral impulses we already have. The perfection radiating from him convicts of sin at the same time it draws under his influence. "Grace" is received only in the community.

What does Jesus do? It seems fair to say that Jesus' significance does not lie in anything particular that he does. Rather, everything he does serves to illustrate one thing: his sinless perfection and potent God-consciousness. Somewhat in the fashion of Irenaeus, Christ succeeds at every point where fallen beings fail. The acts point to the peculiar character of his being.

Schleiermacher's masterful work shows the difficulty of steering between the Scylla of vicarious satisfaction and the Charybdis of moral influence. The idea of the new historical community (the kingdom of God) is a fruitful one, and in this Schleiermacher is a founder of the age to come in theology. But the interpretation of Christ's work in terms of feeling, God-consciousness, and sinless perfection results in a Jesus who is a religious virtuoso, the hero-artist romantics admired so much. In spite of Schleiermacher's passion for a Christ who communicates himself to us in an historical, human, and non-docetic fashion, it is difficult not to suspect at least a tinge of docetism. Jesus dies a protected death. He manifests the power and constancy of his God-consciousness to the end, maintaining his divine dignity. The cry of dereliction from the cross cannot be real. The death does not establish anything new, it merely illustrates the truth of the system. Even here the orthodox system and its antagonists are brothers and sisters under the skin. The orthodox speak of a divine nature that guarantees the infinite worth of Jesus' sacrifice. Jesus "offers" his sacrifice knowing the "system." He dies knowing why, and does not need to ask. He is protected from the terror and disaster of his own death by the system. The cross is covered with roses. Schleiermacher may reject talk of a divine "nature" and prefer "God-consciousness" and "divine dignity," but the result is the same. Jesus does not really die; he demonstrates his God-consciousness. This too is to put roses on the cross. Just as in the orthodox system, a resurrection is superfluous.

Albrecht Ritschl, the most influential of those who tried to redefine the work of Christ in terms of the new historical community, represents a synthesis between the kind of thinking found in Schleiermacher and the emerging *heilsgeschichtliche* theology of the later nineteenth century. He approved of the emphasis on the historical community (the kingdom of God) but rejected the religion of absolute dependence and its abstract monotheism as being too metaphysical and impersonal. The kingdom, for Ritschl, must be understood in more biblical, historical, actual, and practical terms. To get at this, Ritschl tried a variety of distinctions to set off the kingdom from false alternatives. Most prominent for our purposes was the Kantian distinction between the theoretical and the practical. Theology has to do with the practical knowledge of God gained in the historical community and the manner in which this relates one to the world, not with "theoretical," "scientific," "abstract," "objective," or "disinterested" knowledge. Practical knowledge is "religious," "ethical," and "moral," a knowledge that involves the whole person and one's way of life.[47]

Religion is concerned with rising above mere "nature" to "spirit," above subjection to the sway of death, the "flesh," the "world," time, and decay, to the position of *dominion*.[48] In Jesus, God takes the last, decisive, and concrete historical step with humankind in establishing the kingdom, God's true dominion. Everything flows from the practical influence of Jesus as an historical person. Jesus reveals God as Father, the God of love to whom we can draw near with confidence. Wrath is replaced by love; wrath pertains only to life outside the kingdom. Christ draws people into this community of confidence and trust in the God of love who in creation and redemption has set the true *telos* for human existence: a kingdom where all are united to God in love in spite of all hindrances of a natural, physical, or metaphysical sort. One is saved from false conceptions of God by being drawn into the community of love by Jesus.[49]

What then does Jesus *do*? Vicarious satisfaction must be rejected as a prime example of the way natural theology intrudes into and distorts theology.[50] At the same time, Ritschl attacks the idea that Jesus is a mere teacher or example. The forgiveness he brings is not a matter of course, nor can it be a simple deduction from the love of God. If so, then the new community would be a school, not a church, and one would not get beyond theoretical knowledge. Forgiveness and reconciliation must be dependent on and flow from Jesus' actual work, his life, suffering, and death, the practical effect of the historical person.

The point is similar to Schleiermacher's. Sin—resistance to God's sovereign and moral rule—forms a kingdom of evil opposition. Because of sin, humans feel guilt and experience the world and God as hostile, interpreting natural vicissitudes as the result of guilt. The approach to God is therefore distorted, a confusion of nature and spirit. Outside the kingdom, humans are unreconciled to God. Jesus enters this world and suffers all the antagonisms to God's rule operative in the unreconciled. He is true to his calling to the end. He suffers and dies without giving in and thus triumphs over all that stands against God's true rule and *telos*.

The key idea is Jesus' "faithfulness to his calling" (*Berufstreue*). In his faithfulness Jesus rises above all natural, national, and political limitations, even those of the Old Testament, transcending the expectation of mere material well-being, and introduces a new religion "by advancing its significance for mankind to a spiritual and ethical union, which at once corresponds to the spirituality of God and denotes the supramundane end of spiritual creatures."[51] In his faithfulness to his calling, Jesus exercises a double role. He is the revealer of God in taking up a position that "corresponds to the idea of the one

God and to the worth of God's spiritual Kingdom."[52] He also
reveals true man in being one who according to this knowledge
of God worships and serves God to the end without giving in to
the opposition of the world.

Jesus' sacrifice is thus not vicarious in the traditional sense,
but it is a death in faithfulness to his calling.

> It is not the mere fate of dying that determines the values of
> Christ's death as a sacrifice; what renders this issue of His life
> significant for others is His willing acceptance of the death
> inflicted on Him by his adversaries as a dispensation of God,
> and the highest proof of faithfulness to his vocation. Thus it
> is impossible to accept an interpretation of Christ's sacrifi-
> cial death, which, under the head of satisfaction, combines in
> a superficial manner His death and His active life, while at
> bottom it ascribes to the death of Christ quite a different
> meaning, namely, that of substitutionary punishment.[53]

By his faithfulness, Jesus establishes a community of communion with God in spite of human sin and feelings of guilt.
Indeed, in this new relationship we first come really to recognize our sin—our ignorance of God and God's true dominion.
The sense of guilt is not simply removed but is rather intensi-
fied. But the power of sin and guilt to separate us from God is
overcome in the Jesus who reveals the Father as love and draws
us into communion with God. Since it is only in the actual historical community that this relationship is realized, it must be
seen as rooted and grounded in the action of Christ as founder
of that community. In his faithfulness, Jesus Christ is the
perfect revealer, the founder of a new and perfect religion,
the triumph of the spirit of love over nature and the world. He
secures life even against the power of death.[54]

Ritschl, more conservative biblically than many liberals, does
not seem to brush aside the resurrection or to have any problems
with its miraculous nature. At the same time, his insistence on

the "spiritual" and "ethical" nature of Jesus' "religion" prohibits giving too much theological importance to such miracles. The resurrection appearances have only the function of freeing the disciples from the "erroneous first impression" that he was subject to the fate of death. Resurrection does not bring anything new to light; it only reinforces the idea of spirit's victory over nature and receives little treatment or mention in Ritschl's development of the work of Christ.[55]

What is to be said of Ritschl's treatment? On the positive side, it represents the recovery of many important biblical themes: the centrality of the kingdom, the rejection of juridical hegemony in understanding divine righteousness, the passion for the actual rather than the theoretical in considering reconciliation. Ritschl did recover much that had been sacrificed to the gods of metaphysics. Negatively, however, his reconstruction is plagued by much the same problems as Schleiermacher's. The concern for the actual and the practical leads him to interpret atonement in terms of the religion of "practical reason" and "ethical religion" gleaned largely from Immanuel Kant and Hermann Lotze. The result is a Jesus who turns out to be the hero of this religion, whose influence is communicated through the subjective experience of the community.

Several consequences then follow. Since Jesus dies in "faithfulness to his calling," he must be different from all others in that for him no vacillation, no profound disruption or temptation, no *Anfechtung*, is possible. He must die a hero's death, the hero of religion. The cry from the cross does not represent a serious disturbance. Subtle exegesis can put it aside. The lament of the psalmist, from which it is taken, is only of a hypothetical sort, the psalmist is not to be taken as actually suffering the wrath of God, since at the same time the psalmist cries to God for deliverance. The same is true of Jesus. Whoever calls on God as "my God" is not far from God and certainly not subject to God's wrath.[56] So the hero does not really die, but carries out a vocation. The roses remain on the cross.

Further, there is no way to deal with the wrath of God. Wrath must be banished by the system, not by the cross and resurrection. Ritschl's theology thus becomes just another that attempts to remove wrath by theological erasure. He removes it from *the system* and thus conducts the battle against natural theology and metaphysics on the wrong front. The love of God threatens to turn into a mere banality.

All this is the result of Ritschl's attempt to solve the problems of justification and reconciliation by equating Luther's "*pro me*" (for me) with Kantian practical religion.[57] The "I" of the Reformation *pro me* is not the "I" of Kant's practical reason. It is rather the "I" of the divine election which encounters me "from without" in the proclamation. The *pro me* does not belong in the *fides qua creditur* (the faith which believes) but rather in the *fides quae creditur* (the faith which is believed). Any *pro me* apart from the radical *extra nos* (outside us) is mistaken and a fatal methodological error. All christological assertions are indeed *pro me* assertions, but also all *pro me* assertions must be christologically interpreted.[58]

Schleiermacher's and Ritschl's attempts at reconstruction are highly instructive for dogmatics. The attempt to grasp Christ's work as the *historical* triumph of divine love is important in its stress on concreteness and actuality. But it will fail if we simply accommodate such love to *religious* possibilities immanent in this age. The eschatological dimension is lost, and Jesus becomes the hero of religion. The bleakness and disaster of the cross are covered by all the theological roses. Jesus is rescued from death by *theology*, so any further resurrection is largely superfluous.

Theologians who appreciated the liberals' stress on the love of God and the critique of vicarious satisfaction, but still found that view wanting, often took the tack of deepening the idea of love to include divine holiness. The love of God, they insisted, is not banal sentimentality; it is *holy* love, a love shaped by morality and justice, a revulsion against sin. God's wrath cannot simply be erased from the system. The necessity for the cross cannot be based only in the divine will to love; it must also be based in the need to meet the demands of divine holiness.

P. T. Forsyth's thought is a good example of this move. Inheritor, on the one hand, of the vast British literature on the atonement (no group of theologians has been so concerned with the atonement as the British through the eighteenth, nineteenth, and twentieth centuries)[59] and, on the other hand, a student of Ritschl, Forsyth set out to combat the sentimentalizing and aestheticizing he detected in his liberal teachers. He repeatedly makes a sharp distinction between the "liberal Jesus" and the "real theological Christ."[60] To realize his program, Forsyth proposed what he called the "moralization" of dogma. He apparently saw this as a remedy to both the abstract metaphysicalizing complained of by Ritschl and the aestheticizing or sentimentalizing of the liberals themselves. What is needed, he insisted, was not mere criticism of ancient dogma but recasting it in a new form to recapture its moral seriousness and depth. The juridical element in older doctrines of atonement had been lost due to rejection, in many ways legitimate, of vicarious satisfaction. The baby had been thrown out with the bath water. To carry out the program of "moralization," Forsyth employed the concept of the divine holiness: God's personal self-identity and unchangeable faithfulness to the divine self as the Holy One. Everything depends on this. "We have to stir the interest of our congregations," he says, "as much with the holiness of God as the church was stirred—first with the justice and then latterly with the love of God."[61]

Even the omnipotence of God is limited by God's holiness: God's love cannot negate that holiness.[62] The holiness of God dictates the character of theology and finds its echo in the moral order of the universe and the conscience of humans. "The incarnation, being for a moral and not a metaphysical purpose, must be in its nature moral. . . . It is the moral experience alone which can and must dictate the shape of theology. What Christ does is to bring about a new moral creation, a new creation of the moral soul."[63] The unity of the human race (an important idea for Forsyth) is a moral unity, a unity of conscience. "What makes the world God's world is the action and unity of God's moral order of which our conscience speaks."[64] The changeless order of the moral world, manifest in conscience, makes humankind universal.

The "moralization of dogma" leads Forsyth to cast the work of Christ as a work of *redemptive holiness* and to reintroduce the juristic dimension lost in liberalism.[65] But this cannot mean a simple return to ideas about vicarious or equivalent payment and punishment. God is not paid off. Grace is not procured. There can be no transfer of guilt or suffering or punishment.[66] What is needed, for Forsyth, is a reconstruction that retains the moral seriousness of the older views but purges them of commercialism.

In summary, Forsyth's view is as follows. Vital is the Pauline passage "God was in Christ reconciling the world unto himself." What occurs in Christ is the justification of God's holiness. Christ, though sinless, enters into the world of sin, and in solidarity with it renders perfect obedience to and confession of divine holiness. God, as holy, is bound to his own personal will, which he cannot change or relax. But since he is also love, God desires reconciliation. This can be accomplished only in such a way that divine holiness be perfectly maintained, confessed, and satisfied. Christ, by his own consent and obedience, is "made to be sin for us" so that the treatment due sin actually falls on him. Being found among sinners, he accepts the judgment, and in going to his death he bears witness to and confesses the divine holiness in the world of sin. The event of the cross therefore actually establishes and reveals in this world the holiness of God as a *redeeming* holiness, a holy love, because it is revealed in such a way that it can have a sanctifying effect. The cross gives holiness its due, and when humans see this they are made new creatures, drawn into the actual kingdom of holiness in Christ.

In effect, the structure of Forsyth's argument is much the same as Ritschl's. The difference is that holiness tends to replace love as the decisive factor, so that "the moral" replaces sentiment. Christ's sacrifice is obedience unto death in identification with human sin, so as to render compelling confession to the holiness of God and draw the world into this confession. What is of atoning value in Jesus' death is not vicarious suffering as such, but his obedience as the summation of his life, or, as Ritschl would have said, his "faithfulness to his calling" to the end.[67] But what Jesus is obedient to is not love but the vision of the holiness of God which must be confessed among humankind. In this sense, Christ's death can even be said to "satisfy" God. God is satisfied when God's holiness is confessed. Indeed, God must be satisfied. "For an unsatisfied God, a dissatisfied God, would be no God."[68] What makes satisfaction also love is that *God* does it. God sends Jesus to do this for us and for the world and to reconcile us to himself.

The problem of substitution, the Achilles' heel of the older views, is handled by Forsyth through his concept of the "solidary" character of Christ's work, as he likes to call it. Christ's work is not a vicarious substitution in the sense that he was a third party in an individualistically conceived relationship. Indeed, the Gospels show that God can forgive repentant individuals on the basis of divine freedom and mercy without the cross. But such repentance is insecure as long as it does not rest on something of more universal scope. What Christ must do is reconcile the world to God universally, bring the world to its knees before God to be forgiven. Christ's work is solidary in that it has to do with the pardon of the world, with solidary sin. The cross alone can effect that.[69] The necessity for an atonement of an objective sort rests in Forsyth's conception of the moral order of the world. Something must be done to repair and change that moral order and bring the world to confess its solidary sin.[70]

Christ's work is therefore not that of a substitute for individuals, but is representative, creative of a new order.[71] Even the idea of "representation" is too weak. "Surety" is more accurate for Forsyth; Christ is surety for the fallen race, creating the holiness that is lacking.[72] The moral foundation of the world is altered by his act; and as one is *in him*—not just taught *by* him—one is made part of the new moral order in which God's holy love is confessed. Christ's work means a new stage in the history of creation.[73]

A remarkable passage sums up Forsyth's view:

> The work of Christ was thus in the same act triumphant over evil, satisfying to the heart of God, and creative to the conscience of man by virtue of his solidarity with God on the one side, and on the other with the race. He subdued Satan, rejoiced the Father, and set up in humanity the kingdom—all in one supreme and consummate act of his one person. He destroyed the kingdom of evil, not by way of preparation for the kingdom of God, but by actually establishing God's kingdom in the heart of it. And he rejoiced, filled, and satisfied the heart of God, not by a statutory obedience, or by one private to himself, which spectacle disposed God to bless and sanctify man; but by presenting in the compendious compass of his own person a humanity presanctified by the irresistible power of his own creative and timeless work.[74]

Forsyth explicitly saw Christ's work as bringing together all the aspects later separated by the various theories. The atoning work of Christ is "objective" since it is creative of the new kingdom of holiness. It is "victorious" because this kingdom is the conquest of evil on a cosmic scale. It is also "subjective" in creating in us the sanctity pleasing to God. In Christ the God who is always love sanctifies us by creative holiness so we can be treated differently.[75]

In many ways Forsyth's work is a remarkable achievement—reasserting essential dimensions of Christ's work without resorting to the more objectionable features of the older views. His insistence that Christ's work must be creative of a *new* order, that something must actually be done in and for the "race," is a helpful advance. The creation of a new order also helps bring together the various dimensions of atonement: the "objective," the "victory," and the "subjective."

Yet for all that, there is something disconcerting about Forsyth's reconstruction. No doubt it lies in the nature of the program itself: the moralization of dogma. This leads to employing holiness as a moral category that qualifies love. It is difficult to escape suspicion that the long shadow of the "great and sublime Kant" still broods over the enterprise. Can holiness be thus moralized? Rudolf Otto taught us to look with suspicion on such a move.[76] Moralization always involves a narrowing and perhaps trivialization of "the Holy."[77] Further, when the love of God is qualified by moralized holiness there is a pronounced loss of New Testament eschatology. Forsyth does not seem able to make much of the fact that Christ is the end of the law to those who believe, or of the idea that love conquers wrath. The result is a "new order" that still tends to look like Kant's moral kingdom, blurring the distinction between the eschatological kingdom and a this-worldly kingdom of law and morality. In this regard, Forsyth was more captive to liberalism than he would like to admit. The relatively minor role played by the resurrection indicates this. Forsyth does not fail to speak of the resurrection and give it more prominence than his predecessors did. Nevertheless, he can explain the work of Christ largely without it. As in other systems, *theology* rescues Jesus from death. Christ dies in obedience, quite conscious of the system. The cry of dereliction is not what it seems: not the anguished cry of a dying man but the concrete confession of the holy God's repulsion of sin. It is doubtful that the New Testament would sustain such an interpretation. Jesus dies too much like a good Kantian. There are still too many roses on the cross.

Emil Brunner, in his classic work *The Mediator*, affords another example of the attempt to qualify love by holiness.[78] Like Forsyth, Brunner rejects the idea that God is changed by an "equivalent payment." Yet Brunner too insists that atonement has indispensable juristic and forensic aspects. God's love cannot be mere sentimentality. Hence the insistence on holy love. The points at which traditional ideas of vicarious satisfaction went astray are that they were too much fettered by primitive religious conceptions that see God as the object rather than the subject of atonement, and that atonement thinking has been taken captive to general revelation rather than special revelation.[79] This latter point is Brunner's most significant contribution to the argument. Aspects of the truth have been obscured or lost, he says, because we have transformed them into "general religious or moral truth." The problem with penal aspects in atonement thinking is not that they are not true but rather that, taken as general truth, they are never the truth.[80] Taken as special revelation, however, they find their true place.

Brunner's construction differs from Forsyth's in that it comes after the full impact of the rediscovery of biblical eschatology and of the consequent neoorthodox vision of God. The need for atonement roots not in God's need to be paid but rather in the need for a *special* revelation, a special act of deliverance on the part of the God who is holy love. We cannot be saved by general truth. God's wrathful holiness stands and cannot be mitigated or synthesized with love. Love must conquer wrath concretely in the cross *for us*. Brunner's view is therefore more dialectical than Forsyth's. The moral law indeed stands: "The law is the backbone, the skeleton, the granite foundation of the world of thought."[81] But it is "natural knowledge" and as such can never become fully personal. The dialectical counter-part is the special revelation, the act of love in which God claims us as his own. The necessity for atonement, for the cross, rests for Brunner in the need for a revelation that actually changes the situation. God comes, in Christ, into an alien reality, that of sin under divine wrath, and reveals God in such a way that we perceive that both God's holiness and God's love are infinite. But everything depends on the actual coming of God to us. It cannot be just an idea. If ideas could help, we would not be so badly off. The wrath of God is overcome only to faith in the special revelation. The cross is therefore the event in which wrath is broken through; it is the "expiatory" and "penal" sacrifice of the Son of God because he enters under wrath and suffers to reveal God as holy love. In God's nearness his distance is revealed; in God's holiness his mercy is revealed; in God's grace his judgment is revealed; and so on.

Thus Brunner can conclude that special revelation and atonement are intimately associated—"indeed, rightly under-stood, they are one."[82] Apart from the actual event of the cross, God is wrath. In the cross God is revealed as holy love to faith.

Like Forsyth, Brunner is right in insisting on the place of biblical concepts such as judgment, condemnation, expiation, and so on, which had been shunted aside by liberalism. Yet one wonders again whether the whole has not been too stringently moralized. Strangely absent once again is reference to the res-urrection in connection with atonement and death. Of course, Brunner talks about it at length elsewhere; but his system of atonement seems to work without it. The emphasis on special revelation is a step in the right direction, but it alone cannot carry the burden and is distorted when made to do so. A theological distinction is once again made to do the work of the eschatology itself and threatens therefore even to displace the cross and resurrection. One fears once again that the construction reconciles more to the moral order and holiness of God than it leads to the proclamation of the love of God which really brings a new creation.

Victory over the Tyrants

In 1930 the Swedish theologian Gustaf Aulén published *Den kristna forsoningstanken* (English translation: *Christus Victor*, 1931).[83] This book became a theological event, especially in Scandinavian and English-speaking circles. By claiming that the idea of victory over demonic forces was the classic Christian view of atonement, it had the effect of breaking the deadlock between "objective" and "subjective" views. What had been considered merely a crude pictorial and imaginative curiosity was raised to the level of dogmatic respectability. The victory motif seemed to offer a fresh alternative.

Aulén did not claim to set forth a new theory (only vicarious satisfaction and moral influence, for him, are theories), but simply to bring to light a motif which had governed the thinking and liturgical practice of the church in the early centuries and which was revived by Luther. The motif is that of a dramatic and cosmic battle rather than a logical argument: "Christus Victor" triumphs over the powers of evil in a dramatic battle and releases enslaved humankind. In this victory, God reconciles the world to himself by winning it back, not by being "satisfied." Aulén insists that this is a doctrine of atonement, against nineteenth-century interpreters who often referred to it rather as a doctrine of redemption or salvation, of release from captivity rather than expiation for sin.[84] God is reconciled in the very act in which God reconciles the world.

The background is dualistic and the action is dramatic: God in Christ does battle against the demonic forces. The dualism is not absolute and metaphysical, however, but rather of the sort found in Scripture: radical opposition between the forces of evil and the creator God, even though evil does not have eternal existence.[85] The scriptural roots of the motif are the synoptic picture of Jesus' battle with the demons and tyrants.

The proof that the victory motif is a discreet doctrine that cannot be reduced to other views is provided by a series of contrasts. In vicarious satisfaction God's action is discontinuous: God sends Christ, but then must be satisfied by the act of the God-man. In the victory motif the action is continuous: God sends Christ and works through and in him to defeat the demonic powers. The contrast with the subjective view is also evident. There is not simply a change in the subject. There is rather a complete change of cosmic scope, in the *situation*, and a change in the *relation* between God and the world, including a change in God's own attitude. The classic view, Aulén insists, is if anything more objective than the so-called objective view, because it deals not only with individuals but with the whole world.

The essential features of this view are to be found in Irenaeus' theology of "recapitulation." Christ recapitulates human history by overcoming at every step where Adam succumbed to demonic temptation. The work of Christ is battle and victory over powers that hold humans in bondage: sin, death, and the devil. The victory creates a new situation, bringing the rule of hostile forces to an end, setting humans free. There is no cleavage between incarnation and atonement. It is God who accomplishes the work throughout.

Aulén considers the double-sidedness of the view to be one of its characteristic features: God is both reconciler and reconciled; God both gives and receives the sacrifice. Aulén, far from being worried about this duplicity, seems to find it an advantage, a mark of the dramatic nature of the view that defies enclosure in a rational scheme.

The victory motif leads to an emphasis on the resurrection conspicuously absent from other views. The resurrection is the manifestation of the decisive victory over the powers of evil and death, the starting point for the new dispensation, the new "situation," the gift of the Spirit.

Aulén insists that the classic view was the dominant and basic view in the church for a thousand years, in both East and West, until Anselm's Latin view intruded in the West. It was also, for Aulén, the basic view of the New Testament. Only with the development of the idea of penance in Tertullian and later thinkers did the Latin view gain prominence. Luther revived the victory motif, adding the law and the wrath of God as principal among the tyrants to be defeated. Argument about Luther's views on atonement will concern us later.

The troublesome dogmatic question for the victory motif is the one we have been encountering all along: wherein lies the necessity for Christ's death and resurrection? Anselm, we recall, put the basic question: If defeat of demonic powers is all that is necessary, why could not the almighty God have done it some other way? Why subject the Son to such torture?

As Aulén points out, the Greek fathers did wrestle with just this question. Generally they seem to say that God's true nature, God's righteousness and love, and so on, would not have come to light if God had just used force. Sometimes there is the suggestion that the devil has gained rights over fallen creatures and God must respect them to show the divine righteousness.[86] Most frequently, however, the deepest reason cited is the inner necessity of the divine love. God shows love most clearly by coming and taking the suffering of our bondage on the divine self.[87] Gregory of Nyssa takes this thought even further by saying that divine power and invincibility is not shown by acts of force, by the vastness of the heavens, the orderliness of the universe, and so on, but precisely by condescension to the weakness of human nature, there to do battle and overcome.[88] The early fathers were striving to say something vital in all this, but for the moment their ideas seem to lack coherent persuasive power. At least they were not, apparently, persuasive enough to stave off the logical demands of Anselm and his followers.

The dogmatic tentativeness is also evident in the treatment of the devil and his "rights." The fathers could not agree. They believed that the devil had been rightly and reasonably overcome, but they were uncertain as to whether the devil had gained rights over fallen creatures or was simply a usurper. The idea that the devil had gained rights and deserved proper ransom seems most common.[89] The religious motive behind such language, Aulén insists, is to assert the guilt of humankind and the judgment of God on human sin.[90] One might say that the stress is not so much on the rights of the devil, but that since the "wages of sin is death," the devil has the job, the "right," to execute the sinner, thus carrying out God's judgment. At the same time, however, it can be said that the devil is a deceiver since his dominion of death is contrary to God's ultimate will for humankind. The devil receives the ransom price to which he has a right. To this point the inner logic is virtually the same as with vicarious satisfaction; the difference is who is paid. Not all could accept the logic, however. Gregory of Nazianzus denied the idea of the devil's rights, insisting he was a usurper who gained power by deception and thus deserved only to be despoiled and forced to surrender.[91]

The argument about the devil's rights indicates the difficulty in answering the question of necessity, in consistent fashion, for the victory motif. Perhaps the reason is that just as with vicarious satisfaction the logic tends to falter. A law that cannot give life takes the center of the stage. The devil may have the power to inflict death, but the devil cannot give life—just as the law cannot. The devil cannot release the captives and give freedom. No doubt that is why the idea of the rights of the devil had to be augmented by the thought that the devil exceeded his rights in the case of Christ and thus was deceived and despoiled. By attacking the innocent one the devil lost his rights and his dominion.[92] Instead of saying the devil is satisfied, one has to say he is defeated. The point is that something new has to be brought to light in the death and resurrection of Christ.

Thus there is a proliferation of pictures having to do with the *deception* of the devil. The basic idea is that Christ appears incognito among humans; the devil, thinking him an easy prey, attacks, and is defeated by the divinity hidden in the flesh. The image of the devil being deceived like a fish taking the worm but not seeing the hook becomes a favorite.[93]

All this, however, does not answer Anselm's question about necessity very clearly. The logic repeatedly leads one into blind alleys in which God and the devil threaten to change places, in a sort of dizzying tail-chase. If one says the cross was necessary to pay the devil, one risks making the devil a god with rights to the creation. Thus the protest: the devil is a usurper. If, on the other hand, one presses the idea of the deception of the devil, one makes God a deceiver—precisely the devil's art. Thus the insistence that God acts righteously even with the devil.

Aulén contents himself with the assertion that the view is not a rational theory but a dramatic picture defying systematization. But even he is constrained to give some orderly account of what the pictures are supposed to convey and to insist that we penetrate beneath the surface to the "religious values" that lie concealed there. They are, Aulén says, as follows. First, God does not use force but enters into the drama to gain his purpose by giving himself. Second, the idea of rights expresses

God's fair play even in dealing with evil powers. Third, the alternation between the devil as one with rights, carrying out the divine judgment, and as a usurper serves to convey both the dualistic outlook and the limitations of dualism. The devil is the embodiment of evil, the dark protagonist, but even so the devil is not equal to God and can derive power only from God. This is a way of asserting both the responsibility of the creature for sin and the justice of the judgment. Fourth, the idea of the deception of the devil means that evil ultimately overreaches itself when it comes into conflict with good and loses the battle at the moment it seems most victorious. The ultimate evil act, the cross, is the victory.[94]

The double-sidedness of the view must stand, in Aulén's opinion. "For theology lives and has its being in these combinations of seemingly incompatible opposites."[95] The very incompatibility of the opposites, Aulén says, stood in the early days as a barrier against transforming theology into speculative metaphysics. The drama is of the essence.

How shall one assess the victory motif? One cannot deny its positive importance for dogmatics. Aulén has succeeded in isolating a distinct view of atonement, which had gotten lost through the years. Historians may complain that he has over-simplified or misrepresented the history of the matter, but that does not detract from its dogmatic importance. The single most important advance is the manner in which the resurrection regains its proper place in atonement doctrine. The dramatic-dualistic background facilitates understanding the breaking in of a new age through the death and resurrection of Christ and forestalls any return to moralism. This is an advance of great significance and must be developed further.

But it is questionable whether the motif in its mythological form can make sustained appeal to the modern mind. The "cosmic-dualistic battle" tends to appear extraneous to us and lends itself easily to a kind of triumphalism that says nothing to the despairing, the losers of the world. A way must be found to assert the reality of the victory that retains its cosmic scope and still makes it concrete and viable existentially.

Perhaps this is the reason for the persistent criticism that the victory motif tends to overlook sin and guilt and to shift the emphasis to mortality, finitude, and death. Aulén struggles to overcome this criticism, but it sticks nevertheless.[96] When the basic presupposition is that the major obstacle to salvation is finitude and death, one is not far from gnosticism. Sin recedes into the background as a prehistoric miscarriage in the emanation of the cosmos. Then also it is difficult to maintain the necessity for the cruel death on the cross. Simply to save us from *death*, the redeemer could impart life in some other way. The gnostic teacher liberated from death by imparting knowledge. Irenaeus' Christ "recapitulates" human history: the power of immortal life wins over temptation at every step, and the cross, though the supreme instance of victory, is relativized. One event is as important as another. The point is always the same: the victory of immortality over mortality. The imagery of ransom paid to the devil demonstrates the confusion. Since the one who is to die is immortal, the devil is deceived. The one who is to die could not die. One comes perilously close to the gnostic idea that the cross was a "seeming" to die—the gnostic redeemer escapes before the crucifixion. If the redeemer's death is a deception of the devil, how much is there to choose between the two?

In sum, the dramatic-dualistic imagery can also misdirect our attention away from the Jesus who was crucified for us under Pontius Pilate to a mythic figure who was paying a ransom to the devil and deceiving the devil at the same time. Why the cross? Could the redeemer not just as well have died in bed after a full and saintly life, or perhaps even in battle leading a Zealot crusade or a popular revolution? Or would it not have been better, after having won the victory at every step where Adam succumbed, to turn the tables on death by not dying at all? The "victorious" Jesus can all too easily be portrayed as one who does not finally die. The roses still obscure the truth.

Before moving on, we must assess the importance of the victory motif for dogmatics. It must be seen in context. It arose and gained credence in an age when old optimisms and structures were being destroyed by dark tyrannical forces. Its revival in Reformation times and in our day can also be seen as a protest against any legalistic rationalization that oversimplifies the human problem and ends with a God who is either a vindictive bookkeeper or an overindulgent lover. The dramatic imagery interjects a note of desperate conflict that is more true to actual experience. There is danger and darkness, and God is not uninvolved in or even untainted by the darkness. The demonic forces execute his judgment on sin. Yet once unleashed, they threaten to exceed their prerogatives and usurp those of divinity. It is God who must deal with the problem properly. The victory imagery is helpful in that it restores drama, action, and life where there had been only legalistic bookkeeping.

Yet we must question whether revival of the victory motif has been entirely fortunate for dogmatics. While it rightfully challenged the hegemony of previous views, the alternative it suggests does not seem equal to the task. Aulén himself speaks of it as a series of images with glaring contrasts, and intimates that any attempt to put it into consistent rational shape would rob it of its depth and frustrate the purpose of theology. There may be some truth in this, but it is not clearly specified enough to be convincing.

The inconclusive outcome of the debate has had a relativizing effect. Where one motif becomes "just an image" or "picture," *all* tend to become so, each representing some aspect of the truth. Atonement becomes a theory, a projection in thought, and one can easily lose confidence that anything meaningful is being said at all about *God* and *God's* activity. No doubt it is necessary for dogmatics to go through this crisis in confidence;

after all, it had exceeded its proper limits. But merely to relativize a collection of such excessive images is hardly an advance. The cross loses its overagainstness. The roses are not removed; one only changes them now and then. Willy-nilly the cross becomes even more the object of our speculation, something we look at and assign meaning with our images, models, and theories. The relativization leads to the platitude that no one view does justice to the profound mystery of the atonement.[97] Theologians can then revel in the art of multiplying theories and models—apparently on the assumption that the more one discovers the more truth one will uncover. Thus we arrive at the view quoted above, likening atonement to a precious jewel with many facets which one turns around in one's hand because one can only see one facet at a time. The analogy is itself a damaging one. Imagine looking at the terrible event at Golgotha as though it were a precious jewel one examines at leisure to discern its facets. Instead of judging us, the cross becomes the object of our curiosity, our search for "religious values." We continue the search for roses.

CHAPTER TWO

Luther's Theology of the Cross

A theology of the cross provides material for reconstruction by positing a reversal in direction: God comes to us; we do not mount up to God. Atonement occurs when God succeeds in getting through to us who live under wrath and law. God is satisfied, placated, when his move toward us issues in faith. A "happy exchange" takes place: Jesus takes our sinful nature and gives us his righteous and immortal life.

The Debate over Luther's View

About the time Aulén's *Christus Victor* appeared, Luther's theology of the cross was rediscovered.[1] Both events have contributed to a ferment in reflection on the atonement which makes consideration of Luther's views an important transition to contemporary reconstruction. Aulén's attempt to claim Luther for the "classic" motif sparked a lively debate, which has continued to the present and sheds new light on the contribution of Luther and the Reformation to atonement thinking. Rediscovery of a theology of the cross likewise furnishes new direction for a post-Reformation restatement.

One can say with justification that the views considered so far are all essentially pre-Reformation in structure, or at least have their roots in pre-Reformation formulations of the problems. The "classic" view is a return to a patristic age; the "Latin" view goes back to Anselm's medieval understanding. Even the "subjective" view, which could lay claim to being the most modern, is usually credited to Anselm's medieval contemporary Abelard. The basic structure of the views, however disparate, remains the same. The aim is to escape, to ascend toward God, whether by law and moral improvement or by victory over the tyrants who chain us to our mortality and finitude. Atonement occurs when the ascent to God succeeds. The discussions about Luther's theology raise fundamental questions about the propriety of such views for a truly post-Reformation understanding.

So to the debate. Aulén's claim that Luther espoused the classic view was based on solid evidence.[2] Luther's writings abound in the imagery characteristic of the view, and he had a special love for those most disliked by its opponents. He repeatedly uses the picture of the devil taking the bait of the incarnate Christ and getting caught on the unseen hook of the divinity.[3] The vocabulary he prefers when speaking of Christ's work against human sin is almost invariably that of strife, conquest, destruction, killing, and devouring, rather than satisfaction, payment, sacrifice, and propitiation.

Interpreters had noted Luther's love for the classic imagery before, but mostly they had treated it as linguistic or poetic embroidery, or perhaps a hangover from medieval folklore. The basic dogmatic structure of Luther's thought, it was maintained, remained that of vicarious satisfaction. Aulén disputed that, claiming that Luther's thought manifests the classic pattern: there is a continuity in the divine action throughout; atonement is closely connected with incarnation; and there is no thought of an offering made to God from the side of the human. It is God who overcomes the tyrants by divine omnipotence; there is a stupendous, dramatic conflict, a *mirabile duellum*, in which Christ prevails over sin, the law, death, wrath, and the devil.[4]

Aulén maintains, moreover, that the patristic view not only returns in Luther but is deepened on several counts. Luther sees more clearly that the law is one of the tyrants over fallen humanity. The law demands not merely obedience to external commands but also the spontaneous obedience and love of the heart. This makes the legalistic way impossible and turns the law into a tyrant. Likewise, Luther sees more clearly how this places fallen humanity under the wrath of God. Without spontaneous obedience, the love of the heart, one stands under the wrath of God. No mere payment in an abstract legalistic sense will do. The wrath of God will be stilled only when the love is there. The wrath therefore cannot be bought off at a particular point in time. A battle is fought in which the love of God *breaks through* the wrath. A victory must be won which is effective *in the present* for the believer.[5]

The Latin view dies hard, however. Several interpreters disagree that the basic structure of Luther's view is "classic," or at least that Luther can be claimed for that view without qualification or remainder. Paul Althaus is a prominent example.[6] Althaus maintains that Aulén does not see clearly enough that the powers Christ defeats have a just place as executors of the righteous wrath of God and that Luther constantly emphasizes the right of such powers. The connecting link between the victory motif and a more juridical view for Luther comes in the idea that the devil is the accuser of sinners. His accusation has force only because it exposes actual transgression of divine law, our failure to meet the demands of the divine righteousness. Thus, "The satisfaction which God's righteousness demands constitutes the primary and decisive significance of Christ's work and particularly of his death. Everything else depends on this satisfaction, including the destruction of the might and the authority of the demonic powers."[7]

Althaus resists all attempts to put aside this juridical element and its priority. It will not do, he says, to claim that the victory motif expresses Luther's own view and that he uses the juridical terminology only as a concession to traditional formulations. For Luther, he insists, we must be freed first and foremost from the wrath of the righteous God. The satisfaction made by Christ's death accomplishes this, and all other victory over the demonic powers is a consequence. "God," Althaus insists, "cannot simply forget about his wrath and show his mercy to sinners if his righteousness is not satisfied."[8]

It is not difficult to find quotations from all periods of Luther's career which at least appear to substantiate the claim made by Althaus and like-minded critics of Aulén, even though they may not be so numerous as those of the classic sort.[9] Yet even such critics have to admit the picture is by no means unambiguous, for Luther often and explicitly attacks the idea of satisfaction as at best too weak and at worst an abomination and the source of all error.

> Even if one wants to retain the word satisfaction and say thereby that Christ has made satisfaction for our sins, nevertheless it is too weak and says too little about the grace of Christ and does not sufficiently honor Christ's suffering. One must give them higher honor because he did not only make satisfaction for sin but also redeemed us from death, the devil, and the power of hell, and guarantees us an eternal kingdom of grace as well as the daily forgiveness of subsequent sins, and so becomes for us (as St. Paul, 1 Cor. 1:1 says) an eternal redemption and sanctification.[10]

Satisfaction is not only too weak a term for Luther, but it is also spoken of as the "beginning, origin, door and entrance to all the abominations" of the medieval system.[11] Usually such discussion comes in the context of an attack on the medieval penitential system, in which penance is understood as satisfaction for sin. Luther was keen enough to see that the whole medieval edifice with its doctrine of atonement grew out of and drew its strength from the ideas of penance, which had begun as early as Tertullian.

The Reversal of Direction

How is one to account for this confusing state of affairs? Is Luther simply inconsistent or, to put a better construction on it, too rich and varied in his thought and expression to be pressed into a unified scheme? There have been many attempts to explain or resolve the matter. But the arguments are largely sterile, because they end only by claiming Luther for previously existing views.[12] If Luther can be claimed merely as a representative of one or another of the pre-Reformation theories already expounded, he has no particular significance for dogmatics. If, however, in his own thinking he had somehow transcended the differences so as to point the way to something quite different, enabling him freely to use the various terms without contradiction, that would be significant and might point in new directions for restatement of the doctrine. This is the perspective from which dogmatics should investigate his teaching on atonement. When this is done, it becomes clear that to understand Luther's utterances one must begin quite differently than the debate has done. Luther sought to be "a theologian of the cross." This involves a great reversal. A theologian of glory, he said, calls the bad good and the good bad. A theologian of the cross says what a thing is. To be a theologian of the cross, one has to learn to see things as they are.[13]

Who are the enemies? What is the wrath under which we suffer? It is the alienation, the guilt, the lostness, the antipathy toward the gods, which we actually feel and experience. The voice of the law which we hear is not an abstract ideal but the terror of the darkness, the demand arising from anything and everything that we do something to fulfill our being and secure our destiny in the face of death. In such a strait, atonement theories do little good. Their explanations do not placate the actual wrath under which we live. They do not end it. They do not end it because there is no reversal of direction. Their assumption is still that payment must be made to God or "the gods" or even to "the demons." But who can ever see or know that payment has in fact taken place, or that it is sufficient? Even if it is, I am left with the task of mustering up the ability really to believe it, on pain of death. How can I do that? I am still under wrath, actual wrath.

Luther saw that it makes little difference for the lost creature whether one says that payment is made to God or says it is made to the devil. So long as the basic structure is payment of a debt on pain of death, nothing new breaks in. Wrath remains. If nothing new happens, one is still under the law. When that is the case, God and the devil are virtually interchangeable and merge into one confusing picture.

For atonement and reconciliation to occur, there must be a reversal of direction. Something must happen, something quite new and different, to end the wrath and defeat the enemies in actuality. If one thinks in terms of an actual end to wrath, an actual stop to the accusing voice of the law, then satisfaction and victory mean the same thing. If the God from whom we are alienated could actually put an end to the separation, then the wrath under which we live would be ended. If we could actually receive this God and trust this God's self-giving, then the divine wrath would be satisfied, and God would win the victory. The key lies in the reversal: not that something is given to God, but that God gives something to us.

This is Luther's concern in speaking of atonement. Atonement occurs when God gives himself in such fashion as to create a people pleasing to God, a people no longer under law or wrath, a people who love and trust God. When God succeeds in that, God is "satisfied." Atonement occurs, that is to say, exactly in that God was in Christ reconciling the world unto himself. The question for atonement is whether God can succeed in doing this. The question is not whether there is blood precious enough to pay God, or even the devil, but whether God has acted decisively to win us. The question is whether God can actually give himself in such a way as to save us. For God is not the problem, we are. Can God actually deliver us from wrath, save us from sin and embittered hostility and bring something new? What Luther has to say centers around the question of *the way things are*. Can wrath be ended? But that is a question of what God gives and not what God gets, for it is, one should not forget, *God's* wrath, and only God can end it.

The reversal is responsible for our puzzlement over Luther's statements about satisfaction or placation of God's wrath. That God's wrath must be placated if we are to be saved is self-evident when dealing with actuality. It is a tautology. But wrath cannot be placated in the abstract by heavenly transactions between Jesus and God. Nothing is accomplished for us by that. God's wrath against us is placated only when God's self-giving makes us his own, when God succeeds in creating faith, love, and hope. Thus the following remarkable statement (concerning the Lord's Supper):

> God's majesty is greater than the blood of the whole world and the merits of all the angels are able to placate. The Body of Christ *is given* and his blood *is shed* and just so is it placated. Indeed it is given and shed *for you*, just as it is said, "for us." Why "for us" except to placate the wrath of God which threatens our sins? Moreover, *the wrath of God is placated when sins are forgiven*. That is, as it is said, "Given and shed for the remission of sins." *For unless it is given and poured out the wrath will be retained*. So you see that the work of satisfaction or sacrificial placation are *worth nothing except by faith alone*.[14]

When one is dealing with the way things are, wrath cannot be placated in the abstract—say at the moment of Christ's death when payment is supposedly made. Wrath is placated when the body and blood are given *to us* and are received in faith. It is in the giving and the receiving that wrath is placated.

Statements about satisfaction made in criticism of penance indicate the same reversal of direction. The following is a good example, in which Luther says that a distinction should have been made in using the concept:

> . . . namely, that it should be done to humans but not to God, as Christ shows in Matt. 7 and 18 and also St. Peter did . . . , *otherwise Christ would have stayed with his entire satisfaction for us in heaven.* Then all the traffic to God in memorials and cloisters and indulgences would not have happened and the great god belly be so well served. But it was all mixed up and finally sent up to God alone. . . . For this error is the most ancient from the beginning of the world and will remain also the latest until the end of the world.[15]

If God were the object of satisfaction, there would be no need for incarnation or the cross.

The question for Luther's doctrine of atonement is thus not that of abstract payment to God but rather how God can succeed in giving himself to us so as actually to take away our sin, to destroy the barrier between us and God. This is the reason for the prominence in Luther's thought of "the happy exchange." Christ, through his actual coming, his cross and resurrection, takes away our sinful and lost nature and gives us his sinless and righteous nature. This cannot be an abstract metaphysical transaction. We must, through the cross of Christ, his terrible suffering and death, be actually purchased and won, indeed, killed and made alive. If it is to be a "happy" exchange, our hearts must be captured by it.

The exchange can take place, therefore, only if Christ actually takes our place, takes our sinful nature, "has and bears" our sins. He cannot just take human nature; he must take sinful human nature and come under the curse of the wrath of God. To give us his life he must take our death. Satisfaction cannot be, as for Anselm, a substitution for punishment. Christ suffers the punishment and destruction of death in our place, our nature, in order to give us his. He must take our sins and destroy them, devour them.

This is made explicit in what is perhaps the classic statement of Luther's doctrine of atonement in his commentary on Gal. 3:13 ("Christ redeemed us from the curse of the law, having become a curse for us—for it is written, 'Cursed be every one who hangs on a tree'" [in the 1535 Galatians commentary, *LW* 26:276ff.]). The type of thinking—in this case, of the medieval scholastics—that posits payment to God cannot, Luther says, abide this kind of passage: "They strive anxiously with what they think is godly zeal not to permit the insult of being called a curse or an execration to come to Christ" (*LW* 26:176). Such thinking would rather have, no doubt, an unambiguously spotless Lamb, a sinless Christ to offer God as a substitutionary payment. But Luther will have none of that. Christ must be one who has and bears our sins; he must actually become a curse for us to set us free from the curse of the law. If not, Christ merely becomes an example of purity or of patience in suffering to be imitated. That simply puts roses on the cross and turns Christ into a new law. The "sophists" deprive us of the most "delightful comfort"

> When they segregate Christ from sins and from sinners and set him forth to us only as an example to be imitated. In this way they make Christ not only useless to us but also a judge and a tyrant who is angry because of our sins and who damns

> sinners. But just as Christ is wrapped up in our flesh and
> blood, so we must wrap him and know him to be wrapped
> up in our sins, our curse, our death and everything evil.
> (ibid., 278).

If we are to deny that Christ is a sinner and a curse, we should also deny that he suffered, was crucified, and was buried (ibid., 278). A Christ who is unwrapped from our sins and offered to God as payment and who all the while is privy to this celestial machinery does not die any more than the gnostic redeemer died. In Luther's view, if there is to be redemption, Christ must become, as Paul says, a curse for us—and that really and truly. There must be a real exchange—and for Luther that was the point of the *communication idiomatum.* "Whatever sins I, you, and all of us have committed or may commit in the future, they are as much Christ's own as if he himself had committed them. In short, our sin must be Christ's own sin, or we shall perish eternally" (ibid., 278).

To be sure, Christ "in his own person" as the Son of God does not commit sins, but by entering into our place he takes them really and truly on himself. In our place, here on this earth among us, he no longer acts in his own person, but he is now a sinner and takes the sins committed by us "upon his own body" (ibid., 277).

> When the merciful Father saw that we were being oppressed
> through the Law, that we were being held under a curse, and
> that we should not be liberated from it by anything, He sent
> his Son into the world, heaped all the sins of all men upon
> him and said to him: "Be Peter the denier, Paul the persecutor,
> blasphemer and assaulter, David the adulterer; the sinner who
> ate the apple in Paradise; the thief on the cross. In short be
> the person of all men, the one who has committed the sins of
> all men. And see to it that you pay and make satisfaction for
> them." (ibid., 280)

One should note well: the merciful Father saw that we could not be liberated from the law by anything, so the Father sends the Son to be a sinner cursed by the law so as to pay and make satisfaction.

But how does such payment and satisfaction come about? How can he *be* a sinner? Luther uses concrete imagery indicating that it comes about because of Christ's entry into this place, our place, fully and totally, of his own will. He comes under the law. The curse of the law against everyone who hangs on a tree was obviously meant, Luther says, for criminals.

> Therefore this general Law of Moses included him, although he was innocent so far as his own person was concerned; for it found him among sinners and thieves. Thus a magistrate regards someone as a criminal and punishes him if he catches him among thieves, even though the man has never committed anything evil or worthy of death. (ibid., 227–78)

One might protest that such is simply a miscarriage of justice—the magistrate punishes for guilt by association. The point, however, is that Jesus put himself there willingly. Before the judge he said nothing—other than that these criminals are his friends.

> Christ was not only *found* among sinners; but *of his own free will and by the will of the Father he wanted to be an associate of sinners and thieves* and those who were immersed in all sorts of sin. Therefore when the Law found him among thieves, it condemned and executed him as a thief. (ibid., 278; emphasis added)

And this occurs by full right. "Because he took upon himself our sins, not by compulsion but of his own free will, *it was right* for him to bear the punishment and the wrath of God—not for his own person, which was righteous and invincible and therefore could not become guilty, but for our person" (ibid., 284; emphasis added). His great love, one might say, got him in trouble, and he could not get out—for *he did not want to.* Or, as Luther put it, "Therefore Christ not only was crucified and died, but by divine love sin was laid upon him" (ibid., 279).

The payment or satisfaction takes place, however, not by some machinery of compensatory reckoning vis-à-vis God, but rather in that the law and sin attack him and damn him but cannot succeed and are in turn conquered by his invincible righteousness.

> The law . . . says: "I find him a sinner, who takes upon him-self the sins of all men. I do not see any other sins than those in him. Therefore let him die on the cross!" And so it attacks him and kills him. By this deed the whole world is purged and expiated from all sins, and thus it is set free from death and from every evil. But when sin and death have been abol-ished by this one man, God does not want to see anything else in the whole world, especially if it were to believe, except sheer cleansing and righteousness. (ibid., 280)

But Luther can also speak in interesting fashion of *sin* attacking Christ:

> Not only my sins and yours, but the sins of the entire world, past, present and future, attack him, try to damn him, and do in fact damn him. But because in the same person, who is the highest, the greatest and *the only sinner,* there is also eternal and invincible righteousness, therefore these two converge: the highest, the greatest and the only sin; and the highest, the greatest, and the only righteousness. Here one of them must yield and be conquered, since they come together and collide with such a powerful impact. . . . Sin is a great and powerful god who devours the whole human race, all the learned, holy, powerful, wise, and unlearned men. He, I say, attacks Christ and wants to devour him as he has devoured all the rest. (ibid., 281, emphasis added)

Atonement takes place when Christ has absolutely entered our place and is attacked by the law, by sin, by death and the devil. Being found actually clothed in our sins, he is the object of the just and terrifying onslaught of the curse. He could not protest his own innocence. He was one of us. To claim his own innocence in any way would be to desert us and to leave us in our sins. But he came to be for us and so must enter into death and destruction.

The cry of dereliction from the cross is real. One cannot, for Luther, look on the cross as though it were simply the apex of a life of high moral purpose in which Jesus now remains true to the end and actively offers himself to God on our behalf. That would fit the picture of the heavenward traffic but not Luther's reversal of direction. The tradition pictured Christ's sacrifice as an active offering of self to God. Strictly speaking, the death of Christ was not necessary absolutely but only concomitantly, since it so pleased God.[16] Thus the tradition taught that Christ enjoyed the beatific vision at the moment of abandonment on the cross.[17] That is akin to more recent views that shy away from the cry of dereliction and speak of Jesus' perseverance in the face of tragedy. Not so Luther. Christ feels himself in his conscience to be cursed by God and really and truly enters into eternal damnation from God the Father for us.[18] Christ's death is not an active offering according to some available scheme of recompense. There *is* no such. His death can therefore only be a passive suffering, a "passion" in the strict sense of the word. There is nothing to do under wrath, death, and so on but to suffer it and to die. Christ, clothed in our sin, can only suffer himself to be attacked. The event must be a real one, and the outcome hangs in the balance.

This is the reason for the dramatic imagery and language in Luther. It is not a matter of imaginative embroidery or of using various pictures, where one conceptuality could just as well be substituted for another. It was, again, an attempt to say what a thing is, to speak of what is actually the case. The law, sin, death, and the curse over human existence attack Jesus. If there is to be any hope for humans, they must be defeated.

Thus also Luther's persistent use of the imagery of the devil as Leviathan who gets caught on the hook of the divinity. Luther recasts the image to fit his reversal. The tradition spoke of the humanity or the flesh as the bait that attracts the demon. Often the fishline was pictured as a chain of human beings from Adam down to Christ—to show Christ as "of the flesh" like us. Deceived by the flesh in seeking his ransom, the devil gets caught on the hook of the divinity. For Luther it is not simply the flesh or the humanity that is the bait; it is the *sinful* flesh that attracts Leviathan. The line is the chain of sinful beings for whom there is no hope: Adam who ate the apple, David the adulterer, Peter the denier, Paul the persecutor . . . and Jesus. The devil attacks with full right. There must be a battle, because only victory or defeat will settle the issue.[19] The point is that sin is the obstacle, not merely finitude or mortality. The devil can attack as accuser only through real powers: the curse of the law. The attack is serious because it is right and we have no defense. Only deliverance from the curse can save.

In Christ, in his own body, the issue is joined, not on the level of God or divinity as such. It is a power struggle in the one who is attacked. The victory comes only because in him is also the power of life which triumphs. The duel is a real one. Just so is it marvelous. It is not simply a foregone conclusion. Christ could and did die; he suffered the pangs of death and abandonment. Yet in the resurrection the divine power overcomes even death, and thus conquers, kills, devours, destroys, buries, and abolishes death, sin, the curse, the law, and all the tyrants.

Luther expresses both the reality of Jesus' death and the invincibility of life in Christ by using formulas that set both against each other in Christ's person—formulas that are the christological basis for subsequent anthropological formulas, such as *simul ius-tus et peccator*:

> He was at once damned and blessed, at once living and dead, at once in sorrow and joy, in order to absorb all evil in himself and to give out all goodness.[20]

> Those who crucified Christ believed he was totally abandoned by God and damned . . . , or they held him to be merely human and thus for entirely dead, whereas he was at the same time quite alive in his entire person (*tota persona*).[21]

To say that Christ has conquered death and sin is at the same time to say that he is divine, for such works belong only to the divine power—indeed, that is what the divine power is. To conceive divinity in this fashion is for Luther part and parcel of his great reversal.

> For it belongs *exclusively* to the divine power to destroy sin and abolish death, to create righteousness and grant life. This divine power [the scholastics] have attributed to our own works, saying: "If you do this or that work, you will conquer sin, death and the wrath of God. In this way they have made us true God, by nature!"[22]

This is Luther's argument for the exclusive character of atonement in Christ. God gives of himself to defeat death and sin. Only the divine power can accomplish that.

The resurrection, one must see, now becomes a full, functional part of the atonement. Since Christ has been raised, there is no more sin, death, or curse, for those in faith are grasped by the resurrection.

> To the extent that you believe this, to that extent you have it. If you believe that sin, death, and the curse have been abolished,

they have been abolished, because Christ conquered and overcame them in himself; and he wants us to believe that just as
in his person there is no longer the mask of the sinner or any
vestige of death, so this is no longer in our person, since he has
done everything for us.[23]

The believer has everything from Him who has triumphed
over death. But one must note well: The cross, the great reversal, must come home to us; it must be done "to us." We cannot
stand by as idle spectators speculating about things beyond,
wondering about how atonement works in heaven.[24] It works
as the thing it is here on earth: the death of the Son of God
for our sins. His death can work only as the death of the sinner who stands against him, for in the final analysis, to be a
sinner is to be one *who will not receive* from God. The obstacle
to reconciliation is unfaith: *sin*, not sins. Only when the sinner
dies and the believer is raised up in faith does the wrath of God
end, for only then is God, the boundless giver, placated. Then
God is satisfied. That is why Luther could make the amazing
statement that "the wrath of God is placated when sins are forgiven." God reaches the goal when he is allowed to be for us
who he is: the creator and giver of every good. Then atonement
is made.

Such a thought leads to the heart of the matter, the "for us."
If the wrath of God, the curse over us, is to end and atonement
be made, the cross must work on us and for us. We must be
saved and made new by it.

God's nature is that he makes something out of nothing.
Therefore whoever is not yet nothing cannot be made into
anything by God. Humans, however, always make something
out of something else. But that is vain, fruitless work. Thus
God raises up none but the rejected, makes none healthy but
the sick, gives sight to none but the blind, makes none alive
but the dead, none godly but the sinner, none wise but the

foolish, in short, has mercy on none but the miserable and gives grace to none but those without it. Therefore the proud, holy, wise, or righteous cannot be God's material and God's work and make rather synthetic, pretentious, false, painted saints out of themselves, that is: fakes.[25]

There is no direct way to God or salvation under the old heavenward scheme of the law. God cannot be a God of love, a God who gives, under such a scheme. Wrath will simply never end in actuality. At best, Jesus will be only the giver of "help"—call it "grace" or whatever—in our attempts to still the wrath, or at worst he will be just an example. Atonement in any actual sense is an impossibility; the wrath will continue. That is what Luther means by saying that Jesus must die to end the wrath of God; he must die to give himself to us, *so* to end God's wrath over us.

But if God cannot be a God of love under such a scheme, and we will not surrender the scheme, the way can only be indirect: it can only pass through the cross. The wrath of God cannot be brushed aside or toned down. Indeed, it must be magnified against us to turn us from our ways. The cross is not a method for appealing to our sympathy or good will. The happy exchange is not a bargain for the old Adam. Therefore Luther says of that exchange:

> We must look at this image and take hold of it with a firm faith. He who does this has the innocence and the victory of Christ, no matter how great a sinner he is. *But this cannot be grasped by loving will; it can be grasped only by reason illumined by faith.* Therefore we are justified by faith alone, because faith alone grasps this victory of Christ.[26]

The faith which simply receives the Christ hanging on the cross illumines reason to understand the way things actually are. Such reason sees precisely that we can be justified only by faith, that God's wrath eternally closes every other way. Indeed,

God must be a God of wrath to us before being for us a God of mercy. The horror of Golgotha is the only way to the kingdom.

> Grace seems externally to be pure wrath, so deeply does it lie hidden, covered with . . . thick furs or skins . . . and we . . . cannot feel otherwise in ourselves than Peter says (2 Pet. 1:19) rightly: The Word alone enlightens us as in a dark place. Yes indeed, a dark place. Thus God's faithfulness and truth must always first become a great lie before it can become the truth. Because before the world it is called a great heresy. So it seems also to us always that God will leave us and not keep his Word and become a liar in our hearts. In sum: God cannot be God unless he first becomes a devil, and we cannot get to heaven unless we have first been in hell, cannot be God's children unless we have first been the devil's children. . . .[27]

A reason illumined by faith in the Jesus on the cross must reckon with the *deus absconditus*. The wrath of God cannot be seen through. It is magnified to the point where to the world and the fallen creature, God and the devil are indistinguishable. This is so because the cross spells not only the death of Jesus but also the death of the sinner. Jesus' death is not a substitution for our death; it *is* our death. It is the death of the one who stands against God, the one who will not simply receive from God. A reason illumined by faith sees that there is no way around the cross; the only way is through it.

A reason illumined by such faith will also see—*a posteriori*—something of the necessity for the cross. It was necessary not because God needed it but because God wanted to rescue us from our bondage, our insistence on our own projects—our insistence on having a God of wrath. Luther put his finger squarely on the problem when he saw it as a question of who shall be God. When we refuse to recognize that it belongs exclusively to the divine power to destroy sin and death, and instead take it on ourselves and our works, we attribute divinity to ourselves. We then encounter the wrath of the God who wills solely to have mercy. Really to end the wrath, God gives the Son to die, thus to put us to death and make us new in him. From the point of view of a theologian of the cross there could be no other way. The theologian of glory might speculate that God could have done it otherwise, or say that the death was only concomitantly a part of Jesus' self-offering to God. But that is to look away from the horror of Golgotha and to avoid the way things actually are. If God could, in fact, have done it some other way, then there is *no* justification for doing it the way it was done. The horror of Golgotha, the terrible price, is too great. Thus Luther:

> Christ teaches . . . , that we are not lost, and sinners have eternal life, only because God had pity, indeed, that it cost him his own beloved child, whom he put into our misery, hell, and death. . . . Now if there were any other way to heaven, he would certainly have established it: Hence, there is no other.[28]

Therefore Luther's treatment points the way to overcome the old antitheses in atonement doctrine: satisfaction versus victory, objective versus subjective. The divine wrath against sin is satisfied when love wins the victory. When the divine self-giving in Jesus raises up the person of faith, the person who *receives*, God has reached his goal. Love conquers wrath for us and in us.

The reversal of direction in Luther's doctrine of atonement leads quite naturally therefore to an application—proclamation of the Word and giving of the sacraments—which does the deed to the hearers, to create faith. If the wrath of God is placated when sins are forgiven, when the body and blood of Christ are given "for us," atonement is done to us then. The reversal is carried to the end. "God was in Christ reconciling the world unto himself . . . and *he has entrusted us* with this ministry of reconciliation." Atonement is in the proclamation, in the giving of it. God's justification for being God, God's success at being God, if one can say that, consists precisely in God's ability to get through to us, to make reconciliation and still be God.

Luther's achievement points us in the proper direction. Its abiding merit is the great reversal: Atonement occurs when God succeeds, at the cost of the death of the Son, in getting through to us who live under wrath. God succeeds in giving himself to us in such a way as to bring a real end to existence under wrath, sin, and death. God's mercy wins the victory over wrath *for us.*

Particularly important is the manner in which Luther moves to strip the roses from the cross. Christ comes among us and dies a real death "wrapped in our sins." He is not paying God according to some celestial bookkeeping scheme. He is *dying*—suffering the punishment of being found "among thieves," because he willed it so. Nor is he a religious hero, demonstrating the potency of his God-consciousness or his faithfulness to his calling to the end, thus becoming the example for all our religious aspirations. He was dying: feeling in himself and in his conscience the agony of the ultimate separation. God is hidden in his death; indeed, God dies. What that means is that all the systems by which theology has sought to rescue Jesus from death, making a meaning of it which obscures the fact of it, are suddenly cut away. Our theological theories cannot save Jesus, just as they cannot save us. Only God, the God who creates *ex nihilo*, who is the power of life itself, can do that. The resurrection alone saves from death. A cross without roses brings something new: it puts to death and it raises up.

Critical Estimates

Did Luther succeed? Criticism usually comes from the point of view of the tradition, for the most part from Roman Catholic scholars.[29] The criticisms can be reduced to two major ones. First, the radical opposition of love and wrath seems to fracture the unity of God, especially when it is said or implied that God battles against himself. Dualism threatens. Second, the saving activity in the God-man Jesus seems to be carried out exclusively by the divinity; the humanity plays no part. Jesus, in the "happy exchange," *takes away* our sinful nature in order to give us his sinless nature. The human, the critics maintain, is not active, but only passive. Luther's view results in a dualism in God and monergism in salvation which cuts out the human nature of Jesus. The trinitarian continuity of the traditional view threatens to collapse. God fights against God; the God in Jesus Christ fights to overcome sinful human nature. It is his exclusive work.

A full discussion of such criticism would take us beyond the confines of this locus. Perhaps the most apt and direct reply would be to say that the criticisms come, for the most part, from a traditional scheme that fails to take account of the radical reversal of direction. The charge on the christological level, about the passivity or noncooperation of the human nature of Christ in salvation, is virtually an exact parallel of the charge made on the anthropological level: that human effort does not cooperate in the salvation of human beings. When the human task is understood as ascent toward heaven via the law, the charge is serious. If, however, the direction is reversed, if the ascent via the law is precisely the curse, if the inescapable trap of fallen humanity is to think of itself and of God in terms of that scheme so that one is always parceling out bits of human activity and bits of divine, hoping it will add up to salvation—if that is the problem, then something much more radical is necessary. The Christ of such a scheme would not *save* God's good creation. He would only attempt to assist us in our escape from it on our heavenward way, and in Luther's terms make only fakes and hypocrites. Luther's point is precisely that one must

die to all that in order to be saved. Christ is indeed opposed to
the cooperation of such sinful human nature. He is out to erad-
icate it in order that the true human nature, that which trusts
and loves God, may emerge from the tomb. Then one becomes
again the creature God intended. Then one can say that God
so loved the *world*, his own creation, that he gave his only Son.
Then God has reconciled the world to himself in Christ.

It is surely a drastic mistake to say that a Christ who enters
into the world under wrath and the curse "wrapped in our
sins" is not accomplishing anything according to his human
nature. He is suffering and dying! To be sure, he accomplishes
nothing by the world's standards. But what was there to "do"
before Pilate and the priests? The miracle, no doubt, was precisely that he did nothing. "Nevertheless, not my will but thine
be done!" If there had been anything to do, his Father would
have sent "legions of angels." But therein—precisely in the flesh,
according to the human nature—he "accomplished all things";
he "overcame the world." He fulfilled the Father's will in the
flesh. Luther no doubt saw this much more radically than
the tradition. There has really to be a death before there can
be life; and the death cannot simply be a sham. It cannot be
turned into support for the old scheme. Theological cries for
continuity can all too easily be attempts to escape death: "Let
this cup pass from me. . . ."

By the same token the dichotomy between wrath and love
cannot be avoided. There is no way to construct a theological
continuity between the two, because wrath will then simply
remain in force. Continuity here means that the old continues and wrath wins. Wrath can only be conquered; the scheme
of law under which we have placed ourselves is indeed real
and represents a terrible truth. If we insist on having God in
this way, God will oblige—and it will be real enough. God *is*
wrathful outside the promise. Wrath can be overcome only in a
concrete historical event, and the God of love manifest in that

event can only be *believed*, "from the heart." To be saved means precisely to be freed from wrath, freed from law, from having to do this or that. One can only believe that God is not divided, that God is one. God is not divided because in the actual revelation, the concrete event, God reveals himself as one whose sole aim is to be freely and truly trusted as a God of mercy. This God will not have it any other way. Luther's point is that we *can* be saved only by faith. Faith alone will give God's creation back to us together with our true human nature.

If Luther is to be criticized, it will have to be that he did not go, or perhaps was not able in his context to go, far enough. The weight of the tradition was still too heavy. The reversal of direction signaled by the idea of the "happy exchange" marks a great advance. Yet there are still vestiges of something quasi-physical about such an exchange. Natures and sins seem to be shifted around too much like quantities. Furthermore, the powers attacking the Christ "wrapped in our sins" seem still to have much too abstract and mythological a coloring for contemporary eyes. If anything, Luther's formulations still have too much of the traditional metaphysical and mythological freight. He has pointed us in the right direction, and often himself used formulations on which we can build. It remains the task of the final chapter to draw on this and to attempt some constructive proposals.

CHAPTER THREE

Reconciliation with God

Reconciliation with God can occur only through God's coming to us in Jesus to die and be raised. The necessity for the cross roots in God's decision to be a God of mercy in spite of our bondage and rejection. To be true to that decision, God must come to us and bear the rejection concretely and actually. God's wrath is the obverse side of God's mercy: God will not be known other than as a God of mercy. The cross is the price God, in mercy, pays to be concretely for us, to put to death the old and to raise up the new. When faith is created, God has reached the goal and is "satisfied."

Cur Deus Homo?

Why did God become a man—indeed, why did God do so in just the way he did? Why did God suffer and die a shameful and painful death on the cross?

Luther has pointed us in the right direction. Atonement theories have dealt too much with abstractions and have not paid enough careful attention to the way things are. It is time now to take the final step. The fact is that we simply cannot get on with God. We cannot reconcile ourselves to God. Why? Just because God is God. We cannot bear that. God is the almighty Creator of heaven and earth. God rules over all things, and God's will ultimately will be done. That is too much. Furthermore, according to the Scriptures, God is an electing God. God chooses. "I will have mercy on whom I will have mercy" is virtually God's name. The very thought of such a God is a threat to us.

Cur deus homo? Precisely because we cannot reconcile ourselves to God, precisely because God is an electing God, this God "for his own name's sake," must come to us to have mercy concretely, historically. The necessity for the atonement rests ultimately in the electing love of God in Jesus Christ.

Once again we may let Luther be our guide. The situation we have been describing and to which our discussion of atonement leads is exactly that described by Luther in *The Bondage of the Will*. When Luther says that we may use the term "free will"—if we must use it at all—to designate our disposal over "things below us" but not over "things above us,"[1] he was once again not laying out a theory but attempting to describe the way things actually are. We are, obviously, free in relation to those things "below" us. I can, relatively speaking, arrange my affairs as I see fit, administer my possessions, come and go as I please, do this or that. I can even decide to be pious and religious, go to church, and so on, if I so please. God, it seems, does not interfere with such affairs—except as occasional "accidents" or "interruptions" put obstacles in my way.

When, however, I come to the question of God, of that which is "above" me, I am faced with a different sort of problem. Why? Just because God is above me and because I can do nothing about that. In fact, I am bound to react in a certain way. The bondage of the will is the inescapable reaction of the alienated sinner to the very idea of God. It is not, as we might think, a deduction from the doctrine of God or God's immutability. Such abstract deductions do not *actually* enslave anyone; but bondage is real. Bondage has to do, for Luther, with our affections, with our love, with the real direction of the will. "Bondage of the will" is for Luther a description, finally indeed, a confession of our disaffection, our recoil from God's "god-ness," from God's being above us.

God is a threat and a terror to the alienated. Faced with the threat of God and especially with the mere idea of God's election, I can only say, "No." In defiance of God and all the logic of the case, I must simply assert my own freedom so as to have some say about my own destiny.

So, I must take over God's role. I must say to God, in effect, "God, I do not know what you plan to do; I cannot trust you. Therefore I must take my destiny into my own hands because I believe I can better decide such things."

So the assertion of "free will" is a faith. It is a faith in myself in defiance of the only God I know. The very reaction, the recoil, is the bondage. And I must do it. I simply am not free vis-à-vis that which is above me. I can only do one thing. The very assertion of freedom—the only thing I can do—*is* the bondage. The bondage is not something I am forced into. It is a bondage of *the will*. I do what I want. That is just the problem. I *can* do only what *I* want. I cannot do anything else—because *I do not want to*. It is not that I have no will. Indeed, I do. I am not a puppet. The question is of the way things are: of what in fact I do will.

We simply cannot be reconciled to one who is above us. The assertion of our freedom is simply a mark of our skepticism, of our defense against an almighty God. A theology based on such premises, however pious in appearance, can only be an attempt to tailor God to fit our aspirations. Atonement *theories* put God in the role of rescuing our sagging religious enterprises, our heavenward traffic. Jesus pays our debts, or becomes our inspirational hero.[2]

We picture ourselves as aspirants for heaven, straining to achieve the prize—our only problem being that we have occasional lapses or that we are too weak and need help to a greater or lesser degree, depending on how conservative or liberal we are. It is all a sham. The one thing we cannot stand about God

is that he is God. Luther was quite right: "The natural man cannot will God to be God. Rather he wants himself to be God, and
God not to be."[3]

Cur deus homo? Why the terror of Golgotha and the empty
tomb? Because God has *elected* to have mercy. God has decided
not to be for us the God of wrath whom we are bound to have.
God can be that God, and God's being so is quite real. But God
has decided not to be that God. If there is anything the Scriptures tell us, it is just that. God elects: "I will have mercy on
whom I will have mercy." The problem, however, is just that:
how to have mercy and how not to be a God of wrath for
a people who in their alienation are bound to have it so. To a
people unreconciled to God, a people who cannot trust God,
election is the most fearsome thing of all. "I will have mercy
on whom I will have mercy," in the abstract, is not comfort,
but terror. Thus, in order to be just who he has decided to be,
it is *God* who must come. There is nothing God can do about
wrath in the abstract. We cannot be saved by a better theology,
a better *idea* of God. God must *come* to save us. The cross and
the resurrection are the solution to God's problem: how to be
exactly who God wants to be for us; how to be an electing God
and still be a God of mercy for those who are bound; how to
release the captives. God, it is to be expected, knows that he is a
problem for us, and God has undertaken to solve the problem.
"His right hand and his holy arm have gotten him the victory."
Cur deus homo? To *be* merciful to us.

We must once and for all carry through the reversal of
direction in our thinking about and preaching of atonement.
God comes to us. God comes to break the bondage. There can
be no pandering to the so-called free will and its attempts to
go to God, for that is the mark of our disaffection, and under
it God remains the God of wrath for us. There must rather be
a case of battle in which God actually comes in Christ to break

into the "house of the strong man armed," to enter into real contention for the heart, mind, and soul of the disaffected.

That is the point of a theology of the cross. God cannot come directly to people bound to their own illusions. God can only die at the hands of such piety. God can only be rejected. So it must be if God is to unmask the bondage for what it is. Hence Luther maintained that in Christ, God comes "under the form of opposites," under the opposite of what an aspiring free will wants or expects. God comes not as the great and glorious ruler but as the humble, suffering, despised, and rejected outcast who is beaten, spit on, and executed, as one quite superfluous to the way we must run things. "He came to his own home, and his own people received him not" (John 1:11). So it had to be. There is no way to get through to the bound, disaffected will directly. Hence life comes only through death. To put it most bluntly, our so-called freedom cannot stop until it has done away with God altogether. Only when that happens, only when the blood is actually spilled, is there a chance that we might be saved.

Only if God comes—*actually*—will there be any help. Only the concrete and real historical lover can save those bound in the prison of their own loneliness. The historical event itself is the revelation; it is God's breaking through to say, "I love you." The historical event itself, the cross, the resurrection, and the preaching of it, *is* what God has elected, predestined, to do for us. God has elected to be a God of mercy, to come to us, to be for us. Nothing else can actually save us from God's wrath.

If one turns aside here to "work" on the doctrine of God so as to avoid offending "free will" one misses the entire point. One does not see that the concrete and actual coming itself alone is God's apology for being God, a God of mercy and thus of election. "God was in Christ reconciling the world unto himself." If one does not see that, one will turn the cross and the preaching of it into a general and trivial truth, the illustration of the fact that God is, in general, love. Instead of preaching, instead of saying God's concrete "I love you," one will lecture on the nature of God, on a God who supposedly loves everyone in general but never gets around to saying "I love you" to anyone at all.

The problem of the bound will, the disaffected lover, cannot be solved by lectures on the essence of God or by theories of atonement. Nothing, absolutely nothing, will save the alienated lover but the concrete word, the "I love you." The question of what God might or might not have willed in eternity can be answered only by what God does do in time, by God's coming and by the preaching of it and the doing of it in the sacraments. To say that God does not elect or predestine is simply to say that God does not come and that God does not do anything of any importance concretely in our time.

God, that is to say, has undertaken to solve the problem God poses for us by actually coming. God does not call off almightiness or election in so doing, but carries it *out* in such a manner as to save, to create believers.[4]

Cur deus homo? Because *we* are the enemy, we have sold out to the tyrants; because *Homo sapiens* is bound and cannot be reconciled by any other means. God has elected to be a God of mercy. To be a God of mercy to those who have sold out, God must come. Not only must God come, but God must die and be raised. The "must" here, of course, is not the abstract *a priori* "must" of a rational or legal scheme, but an *a posteriori* reflection of the mercy actually given. When one begins to glimpse the actual end of the wrath, one sees that it could not have been any other way: "There is no other name under heaven given among men by which we must be saved" (Acts 4:12).

The Necessity for Atonement

The necessity for atonement roots therefore in two things: our bondage and alienation, our unwillingness to be reconciled, and God's decision to be true to himself, to be a God of steadfast mercy nevertheless. The cross and the resurrection are God's own solution to the problem we have with God; they are the outcome of God's resolve. Here Emil Brunner's conclusion that, "rightly understood," atonement and special revelation are one receives its due. But one cannot divide the cross into an act of special revelation to us and a satisfaction offered to God at the same time, as Brunner tends to do. The cross is God's self-giving to us. Just so, it is revelation and atonement at once. It is the carrying out of God's election to be merciful.

Karl Barth is the most prominent recent theologian to have seen this. He made it the central tenet of his *Church Dogmatics*. The cross is not a juridically or ritually prescribed means for propitiating God, but the means whereby the grace of the electing God invades and manifests itself in our fallen world. God has determined first and foremost to be merciful to the world in Jesus Christ. The creation, the incarnation, the cross, and the resurrection are the carrying out of this decision to be merciful. The Son of God journeys into a far country to make the decision manifest. Accomplishing this against all opposition is precisely his victory. It brings restoration of communion with God. As such it is Christ's triumph over the powers of sin and death. There is thus a liberal use of "victory" language in Barth's doctrine. Jesus is victor over the powers of darkness, the "Redeemer from sin and death and the devil" (*Church Dogmatics*, 411:766).[5] Atonement can be spoken of as "God's triumph in antithesis, in the opposition of man to Himself" (ibid., 4/1:82). Jesus is the "victorious king" (ibid., 4/3a:165ff.).

As with Luther, however, the victory is not fundamentally different from a death for our sins, even a satisfaction of the divine righteousness. That is because Barth sees clearly that sin is first and foremost enmity against God's grace, the refusal to be one who receives from God. The Son of God in his journey suffers for our sin. He must suffer under the wrath of God. "In this place He has not only borne man's enmity against God's grace, revealing it in all its depth. He has borne the far greater burden, the righteous wrath of God against those who are enemies of his grace, the wrath which must fall on us" (ibid., 2/1:152). Since Christ comes into our place and suffers this wrath, Barth can say that it is now taken away from us. Christ has intervened for us. The "resolve in which man as such stands against grace" has been "expiated" (ibid., 2/1:152). Barth can speak of Christ as being "laden with our sin" and as one who "suffered punishment for our sin." All this, however, does not serve to change *God* as such. It serves to carry out God's resolve to be gracious. The enmity rejects everything not of grace. As the one in whom God has elected to be gracious to all creatures, Jesus must bear the rejection that must fall on all as enemies of grace. Jesus is the one in whom God elects to be gracious and just so must also bear the rejection that would frustrate that election. He is the elected and the rejected one. Only so, he can be *for us.* God's election would be a terror if God were not also the one who bears our rejection for us. Jesus "must" die to be truly *for* us.

Like Forsyth, Aulén, and others, Barth can thus say that atonement does not bring about a change in God, or simply a change of heart in the sinner, but rather a changed situation because of God's initiative. He can also speak in terms reminiscent of Luther's "happy exchange." God in Jesus condescends to the creature while the creature is taken up into the blessedness and unity of the life in Jesus. But Barth reverses the usual picture. Condescension and humiliation are associated with the divine nature of Christ, the exaltation with his human nature. In the self-giving of God we see the true divinity, and in the triumphant Jesus creatures are exalted to fellowship with God (ibid., 4:1–2). The exchange means that Barth, like Luther, sees that the vital aspect is God's self-giving, not God's receiving of payment. Jesus is not a substitute payment. His work is not something extraneous to us to which we then subsequently relate. He is the one through whom the work of God is done on us and in us. Since he is the one who in rejection and election carries out the decision of God, it is through him and in him that we die and are raised. The old person is destroyed and the new is raised up.[6] Only in this sense is Jesus our "substitute" or "representative." Barth uses the German term *Stellvertretung*, which is difficult to render directly in English. "Place-taker" would perhaps be most accurate if it were understood in an active and repletive sense: Jesus actively and fully takes up the place where we are and should be. We seek continually to escape that place. He stays to the end. Since Jesus dies for us, we suffer and die in him and with him.

Barth's view is similar to the view we have proposed. However, there is an aspect to Barth's thought which attempts to go further and thus reveals the peril of the line of thinking we have been developing. In his desire to overcome the anthropologism of the nineteenth century and its "subjective" atonement, Barth runs the risk of removing the atonement from the human sphere altogether. Following his own adaptation of Anselm's *fides quaerens intellectum*, Barth "reasons into" the event of revelation to find that the antinomies supposedly resolved by the life, death, and resurrection of Jesus have "already" or transcendently been posed and overcome in God. Everything is anticipated and established in God's decision to elect, to be known as a God of grace. Creation, fall, and redemption are simply the spelling out in time of that decision. The result is that one is never quite sure whether the historical event of the cross is the actual victory or just the revelation or manifestation of God's eternal victory.

Barth apparently would like to avoid this either-or and wants somehow to say both. If God's decision is to make himself known as a God of grace, then the victory is already assured by that prior decision, but at the same time can only be implemented by the historical doing of it, by making the decision known in the historical victory of Jesus. The decision was to *do* it. The result is a kind of oscillation in Barth's doctrine, where first one and then the other is said.[7] Can one have it both ways? The difficulty is somewhat the same as we have noted throughout the tradition. The eternal or transcendent victory would make the historical one a sham. It would put roses on the cross.

On the other hand, it has become apparent through the development of the tradition, and especially with Luther, that a strictly historical victory through a cross without any roses puts tremendous pressure on the doctrine of God: The *deus nudus*, the *deus absconditus*, the God of wrath, has virtually to be overcome by the "clothed," revealed God of mercy in Jesus Christ. A fearful dualism threatens between the *deus ipse* who, as Luther says, "neither deplores nor takes away death, but works life, and death, and all in all; nor has he set bounds to himself by his Word, but has kept himself free over all things"[8] and the God revealed in Jesus Christ. Barth expressly wants to banish the *deus ipse* and remove the threat of a deity so unbounded. That is a worthy objective. Everyone would like to do it. But how? Luther, again, was not spinning theological theory when he wrote those words. What he meant was that no mere theological assertion as such can bring God to heel. Theological theory cannot tear the mask from the face of the hidden God. One cannot see through God's wrath. Like virtually everyone else, Barth seems to want to try this—perhaps circumspectly, but to try it nevertheless. Thus he wants to reason solely on the basis of faith to arrive at the God who has elected to be merciful in Jesus Christ. He wants theologically to remove the threat of the *deus ipse.*

That Barth's attempt is valiant and brilliant goes without saying. But does it succeed? Perhaps the quickest answer is the reception of Barth's theology. It has not been perceived, finally or generally, as the lifting of the burden of "God" from human backs. Indeed, in its insistence on "revelation alone" it seemed to most to make the burden more oppressive. Luther's contention that one cannot penetrate the mask is only borne out. Instead of banishing the *deus ipse*, one succeeds only in mixing him with the *deus revelatus* and makes matters worse. Only the historical, concrete, suffering, and dying Jesus can save us from the wrath of the *deus ipse*. Only the revealed God can save us from the hidden God. Theology cannot do it. It cannot be the task of theology to assure us that there is no *deus ipse*, no wrath, no danger, and no antithesis really to be overcome in time.

Barth's attempt shows clearly that theology comes up against real limits vis-à-vis God. Its true task can only be to foster a preaching of Christ and the cross that creates faith, for only such faith saves us from wrath. The historical event *is* the victory. Anything which detracts from that—in theology or outside of it—must be resisted. For nothing can be done about the terror of the absent God, the "naked" abstraction, the "hidden" God; nothing but concrete presence for us can save.

God's coming to us to be for us in Jesus' death and resurrection is the overcoming, the end, the satisfaction of God's wrath. Proponents of the doctrine of vicarious satisfaction and/or punishment have rightly seen that the death of Jesus on the cross alone makes the reconciliation with God possible. God is not reconciled to us, nor we to God, without it. The mistake has been to claim that the event makes God merciful by vindicating God's honor, or providing payment to the demands of God's justice, or satisfying the bloodthirstiness of God's wrath, or some such construction. God is not changed in the sense of being *made* merciful by the historical event. The event takes place because God *is* merciful and desires to be so concretely *for us*, in spite of our opposition and bondage. God gives himself in Jesus because he will not be a God of wrath.

This points us toward a solution to the persistent dilemma of reflection on atonement: Is God merciful before the cross, or only after the cross? The dilemma can be solved if we can think in terms of "the way things are." The divine wrath cannot be theologized or talked away, especially not by platitudes about a God of love. By the same token, it cannot be theologized away by fictions about payment. Wrath is an actuality under which we live in our fallenness and bondage, our separation from God. Wrath cannot be ended unless the God of mercy comes in actuality. Even God can do nothing about his wrath except to give himself to us completely, in death and resurrection. Perhaps this is what those who have talked about the inviolable moral order and the holiness of the divine love have been pointing to. But they cheapened their insight by proposing that God could be bought off. Not even Jesus or God can do that. Wrath can be ended concretely only in God's self-giving to us. Something must indeed happen in our history. But it is not payment to God. It is a gift from God.

The wrath of God, perhaps we can say, is double-edged. On the one hand, it is the reality of God's absence from us, as the *deus absconditus*, the mask behind which we cannot see. But God cannot be absent in the sense of "not here" at all. Thus, on the other hand, the wrath of God is the inescapable reality of God's omnipresence as the God of law—God in nakedness (*deus nudus*), as Luther put it. The naked God is God as sheer timeless abstraction, as the bare idea of the almighty, the immutable judge of all things. In either case—as hiddenness or nakedness—it is the reality of alienation, of absence from us, that comes to expression. God is hidden to fallen creatures who will not have him as a God of mercy. By the same token, God is timeless and immutable abstraction, the *deus nudus*, to those who will not have God clothed in the concrete event—a sheer terrifying abstraction that merges indistinguishably into Satan, the accuser and destroyer. And one should make no mistake about it. That is the way God *is* outside of Jesus Christ. If one wants to have God so, he will oblige. Even God can do nothing about that.

Wrath, we can therefore say, is the obverse of God's mercy. It is God's refusal to be known finally as anything; other than a God of mercy. It is God's burning jealousy for his own. God hides from any who will not have him as the God of steadfast love. Because God will be a God of mercy, God's wrath forbids every other approach: "I will have mercy on whom I will have mercy!"

This points the way toward resolution of the problem of the relationship between the divine wrath and the divine mercy. One must again attempt to think in terms of the way things are. Since the problem is absence from us, there is no solution but presence for us. Since the problem is the naked abstraction, there is no solution but God clothed in the concrete event. That is why nothing can be done about the divine wrath in the abstract, in our systems as such. We may protest loudly that God is love, as liberal theology did; we may rail against God's timelessness and seek to remove it by erasing it from our textbooks. We will accomplish nothing if all that such protest and railing do is obscure the actual event of the cross. Not even God can do anything about divine wrath but conquer and end it *for us* by *coming*. Nothing can be done about hiddenness but revelation *pro nobis*. Nothing can be done about the naked abstraction except it be concretely eclipsed by the clothed God: in the manger; at his mother's breasts; on the cross; appearing beyond the grave. God present for us is the only solution to the absent God. Faith in the present God alone will save. There is no other way.

Once we attempt to think in terms of the way things are, we can see how subtle the problem is. Dogmatic expression can easily falsify accounts. On the one hand, God is not wrathful in the sense that God has to be paid off before becoming merciful. Because God is merciful and insists on being so, the Son is sent to die for us. On the other hand, there is a very real sense in which God is not what he aims to be for us, until God actually succeeds in accomplishing that aim. God is not, in actuality, merciful for us until the reality of wrathful absence has been overcome. Thus Luther could say: "As you believe, so is he." The God who dies on the cross for our sins, to put to death the sinner and raise up the new being, *is* the end of the absent God. In this sense it can be said with Luther that the death of Jesus satisfies God's wrath—the wrath of the God who will not be known other than as a God of mercy. Jesus fulfills the will of God; he realizes the promise. In him everything meant by the cipher "God" is actualized. The abstract becomes concrete; the hidden is revealed. God is placated because God's mercy accomplishes its aim. As Luther put it, God is placated when sins are forgiven—and we finally believe that.

> Since all have sinned and fall short of the glory of God, they are justified by his grace as a gift, through the redemption which is in Christ Jesus, whom God put forward as an expiation by his blood, to be received by faith. This was to show God's righteousness, because in his divine forbearance he had passed over former sins; it was to prove at the present time that he himself is righteous and that he justifies him who has faith in Jesus. (Rom. 3:23–26)

God vindicates God; God manifests his own righteousness in giving himself in Jesus to be received by faith.

We cannot conclude this section without underlining the fact that such atonement costs God. As Jürgen Moltmann has maintained, the ultimate mystery of atonement takes place between Jesus and God.[9] Even though God is not paid in order to become merciful, it costs God to carry out the resolve to *be* merciful for us in a fallen world. If the only way to overcome wrathful absence is concrete presence for us, then the suffering and the death on the cross is the cost to God. This is the kernel of truth in the old "objective" and "penal" theories. The cross is the price of mercy. It is not paid to God; however, it is paid *by* God.[10] God gave his divine Son, abandoned him to death for us. "God so loved the world that he gave his only Son . . ." (John 3:16). The cross is what it costs God to be who he will be for us, rather than the one we insist on.

One must even say that the cross changes God. God serves notice that he will not be any more the absent one, the hidden one, the naked God of wrath. In the cross God becomes "other," the God of mercy for us. God comes. God says no to being a God of wrath; God dies to that. One does not plumb the depths of the concrete historical event and its singular importance unless one sees it in that light—even driving it to the lengths of this apparent split in the doctrine of God. If the cross does not make just this actual separation between "God" and "God," between wrath and mercy for us, then it accomplishes nothing. Then it will be just another illustration of our immanent religious sensibilities. Theologians—especially more recently—often pay lip service to the idea of change in God, but usually blanch at real change and swallow it up in platitudes drawn from organic imagery. The hidden God, the naked God, the God who is just the counterpart of our religious aspirations—but for all that is real enough—that God dies. God becomes other. Something very real is at stake. If the cross is just another illustration of what we already knew, then God cannot be justified. If God does not become other for us, the price is too great.

That is also the kernel of truth in the doctrine that God is objectively changed by the cross. But it was wrongly put. The idea of a payment made to God's justice making mercy possible does not lead to any real change. God changes objectively only by dying to himself as a God of wrath, saying no to that forever for us. Only thus is there any change in the way things really are. Faith alone grasps the dying God, the concrete God, and *dies with that God* to be raised. Faith is a flight from God to God, from the God of wrath to the God of mercy.

Yet this faith believes that ultimately God remains the same, that God reveals his own innermost "heart" in the cross. The cross is what it costs God to remain true to himself, to remain a God of mercy. This God changes, one may say, to remain the same, to carry out the promise. In the cross this God becomes the God that is—who he is. He becomes reconciled.

Admittedly there is a discontinuity for thought: God changes; God remains the same; God dies; God comes alive in Jesus; God gets a new name in this event. The gap cannot be closed in thought. The reason is that the actual, historical event of the cross *is* the gap; it creates the fissure and stands forever in it. The cross cannot ever simply be woven into the seamless metaphysical or ideological tapestry of time. It is a tear in the fabric. There was darkness at noon, "the curtain of the temple was torn in two," and "the earth shook, and the rocks were split" (Matt. 27:45, 51). It is a wound that does not simply heal and leave no scar. The cry, "My God, my God, why have you forsaken me?" demands an answer, an historical answer, not metaphysical, theological, or exegetical anesthesia. The Scriptures tell us that Jesus refused the wine mixed with gall. Theologians must not attempt to give it again posthumously.

D. M. Mackinnon once remarked of current tendencies to exegete the cry of dereliction as an indication of the "growth of the influence of Psalm 22 on the passion narratives," and so on, in which one must not overlook the "happy ending" of the psalm, that modern scholars speak as though Jesus on the cross were meditating aloud, drawing on "the spiritual literature of his people" instead of crying out in agony and desolation. "One detects in certain quarters an eagerness to treat the words of

Christ in his passion almost as if they were the solemn liturgical utterances of the celebrant of a great service. After all, what is being described or represented is not a rite, but a murder and a defeat."[11]

It is an insult to the cross to make it another illustration of general and universally known truths. If the cross is an event of actual historical import, then it is just this permanent wound, this death, this scar in the body of historical humanity. The only answer to the cry of dereliction can be resurrection.

The gap cannot be closed for thought as such because thought will always turn the actual and the particular into the universal. It will turn the actual act of love into wrath. Faith alone takes flight from God to God. The gap arises because the shepherd leaves the ninety-nine and comes to get the one who is lost. It is a perilous journey, "and blessed is he who takes no offense." Faith is just to be grasped by the one who makes this journey from the hidden to the revealed, the abstraction to the concrete, wrath to love. Faith means precisely to be grasped by the almighty and immutable one in the despised and dying Jesus. Faith is to believe that it was *for me*. Faith is to be grasped by the actual decision of the electing God in the Word of Jesus preached *to me*.

Such faith is reconciliation with God. The faith created by the shepherd who actually comes to get the lost sheep can at last let God *be* God. The terror, the anxiety, the bondage created by the abstraction, by ignorance of what God may or may not have decided in heaven is erased by what God has in fact done on earth. Faith can then let God be precisely God. Faith has no need to remake or redo God. Indeed, its confidence is based precisely on the fact that it *is* God who has come in Jesus: actually the almighty God. A reason illumined by this faith will see that nothing can be done about God. Only God's coming saves. The "mystery hidden for ages in God who created all things" is now made known "through the church" (Eph. 3:9–10 and passim). God is satisfied when he is believed, trusted, as the one who has mercy.

Such faith is also our reconciliation with the world God created. Faith means to move from abstraction to the concrete, to become an historical being, a creature of God once again, of the God who creates *ex nihilo*. It is to trust the dying and rising Jesus, the one who cried, "My God, my God, why have you forsaken me?" It is to die with him and in him, to die to the law, to wrath, to all the abstractions, the tyrants, the accusers—to await the resurrection begun in Jesus. Faith is to wager that God is ultimately on the side of the man of sorrows, the one who came in the flesh, died, and rose: God was *in Christ* reconciling the world unto himself. Faith is to be reborn a creature of that God. To have faith is to become a part of the world—this world—God is reconciling unto himself. Then perhaps what Luther spoke of as the "happy exchange" will really occur: Jesus takes our place and gives us his. He becomes historical so that we too might become so and be saved by the God of history.

CHAPTER FOUR

Atonement as Actual Event

*The cross and resurrection of Christ must be under-
stood in more actual terms as his deed done to us. The
roses must finally be stripped away. Jesus came and died
because God is merciful, not to make God merciful. We
killed him because he forgave sins, not to make forgiveness
possible. Just so does he sacrifice himself for us. The universally rejected one is vindicated by God alone through
resurrection. Therefore we are judged and made new by
faith. Reconciliation is made between God, God's creatures, and God's creation when death and resurrection
are done to us in Christ.*

Toward a New Understanding of Sacrifice

Throughout the history of the tradition, the scriptural account
of Jesus' death and resurrection has been used largely as a
mine for texts to support this or that theory. The hermeneutic, whether ancient or modern, has with few exceptions been
allegory: The historical account is a code, a surface manifestation of a real meaning to be found on a different and transcendent level. The historical event must be translated into eternal
truth about the satisfaction of God's honor, or elevated to a
sublime example of dedication to whatever religious people are
supposed to be dedicated to, or transcribed into a story about
the deception of cosmic tyrants. None of that is evident from

the event itself. It comes from the moral, mythological, and metaphysical baggage we carry with us. The hermeneutic is basically gnostic: "Knowledge of the eternal logos" is the model.

Whatever the truth is in these views, the hermeneutic is mistaken. Argument about which theory Scripture supports in such cases is inconclusive and mostly beside the point. Above all, a new hermeneutical approach is needed. Luther has pointed in the proper direction with his movement away from allegory toward an understanding of the Word as active, as doing something to us. Only then will the "knowledge of the eternal" model finally be broken. The movement of the tradition has been toward understanding atonement as a concrete, actual event in our time. It cannot be a question of what the event or the words about it are supposed to signify on some transcendent level. If atonement is to be actual, it must be a question of what the event and the proclamation of it does to us, for us, in us, to save and reconcile to God. A dogmatic of and for the church today must recognize this and assist in the task: it must be so constructed as to foster the proper preaching of the Word of the cross. It is in this that the shepherd comes to get the one who is lost.

Dogmatic theology here faces a subtle and difficult task. This can be seen from the tradition. Dogmatics is itself a relatively abstract "second order" exercise and cannot deliver what it talks about. That can be done only in the preaching and the sacraments. But the theology must then be done in such a way that it fosters proper preaching. That means dogmatic theology must be aware of its own peculiar problem: that it can so construct itself as to inhibit or even become a substitute for preaching. Instead of fostering a preaching that actually does the deed in the present, it can offer an interpretation that allows the event to recede into the past. A theory about atonement becomes a substitute for and perhaps even protection against the one reason that matters: the cross occurred, so that it could happen to us in our present. A dogmatic theology that prevents the happening by providing its own reasons—however grand, impressive, and exegetically proper—has defeated its own purpose. The cross is obscured by the theological roses. The movement of the tradition shows that what is needed above all is to strip the petrified roses from the cross so as to foster a preaching that does atonement in the living present. Dogmatics must be so constructed as to point to atonement as an actual event.

How can this be done? We must learn to look at things as they are, to see what is before our very eyes. Jesus' death, the Scriptures and the tradition unanimously assert, was a sacrifice "for us." But in what sense? That is the point at which the argument usually starts. The disagreement has centered largely around the understanding of the sacrifice: its nature, its purpose, and its efficacy vis-à-vis God. The reason for the argument and disagreement, no doubt, is that this or that idea or theory of sacrifice has been used to interpret the death of Jesus in the attempt to give it universal meaning. Our investigation indicates that this surely must be the wrong way to proceed. One must start more concretely from the ways things are. The death of Jesus must interpret and fulfill the nature of sacrifice, not vice versa.

What actually happened? It is basically a simple story; Jesus came preaching the forgiveness of sins, doing signs and wonders, announcing the coming of the kingdom, and we killed him. We would not have it. "No one can forgive sins but God alone," we said (Mark 2:7 pars.). The fundamental charge was blasphemy. We are not above invoking even the name of God to protect our kingdom from invasion. Blasphemy against the fundamental order of things—religious, political, economic, social—that is the charge.

The issue is thus simple and straightforward: Either he represents God or we do, through our priests, scribes, lawyers, merchants, magistrates, and kings, all our protectors. It came to that in the end. Pilate, one of our "kings," asks Jesus, "Are you the King of the Jews?" He answers, "You have said so" (Mark 15:2). He is given kingly robes, crowned with thorns, and presented to his people. The fundamental decision is made: "Shall I crucify your King?" "We have no king but Caesar" (John 19:15). Some, it is said, wanted the charge altered to read, "This man *said*, I am King of the Jews," but Pilate insists: "What I have written I have written" (John 19:21–22). The drama plays itself to the bitter end: "Let the Christ, the King of Israel, come down now from the cross, that we may see and believe" (Mark 15:32). He dies hanging between two other offenders against the order of this age, crying out in agony and despair. But the tomb does not hold him. He appears to his followers beyond the grave.

What sort of sacrifice is this, and how is it "for us"? It is surely mistaken to say that his Father *needed* the sacrifice in order to be changed to a merciful God. The owner of the vineyard repeatedly sends his servants to claim what is his own, but the tenants kill them. At last they kill the son and heir, thinking to take all for themselves (Mark 12:1–12). Throughout the Gospels precisely the acts of mercy and compassion which Jesus performs in the name of his Father incite the keepers of the order of this age to kill him. Jesus has to die, precisely because God proposes to be merciful. God proposes to be merciful concretely and actually in Jesus. God proposes to come to us and say, "*Your* sins are forgiven." God proposes to open the eyes of the blind, to unstop the ears of the deaf, to make the lame walk, and to preach good news to the poor. We cannot let that happen here. Anyone who intends to carry out such a program must prepare to die. Where could anyone get the authority to do that? Forgiveness full and free with no strings attached is just as dangerous and criminal here as robbery and sedition. It cannot be allowed. It shatters all order. So he must die, just as the thief and the rebel. But he will not desist. "Jerusalem, Jerusalem, killing the prophets and stoning those who are sent to you! How often would I have gathered your children . . . , and you would not!" (Matt. 23:37). So comes about his sacrifice. He dies at our hand. Even in death he cries, "Father, forgive them; for they know not what they do" (Luke 23:34). And just so it is *for us*.

The liberals were right: God is love; God is merciful. They did not see, however, that God's decision to be so *concretely* in Jesus is just the problem, since it does not fit any of our immanent religious schemes. They did not see clearly enough that, because God is merciful, we had to kill God's Christ. They strained toward the truth, but failed because they were not radical enough. They did not see clearly enough that Jesus' death spells the end for us, not the final ratification of our highest religious ideals. P. T. Forsyth, too, approached the truth. But Jesus does not confess the moral holiness of God among us. This is not why he was crucified. He had the audacity to forgive sins. He "did" the *mercy* of God to us. He bore witness to that. Hence he had to be crucified. In that sense, as the liberals said, he was faithful to his calling—but not as the hero of a religious system. He stuck to the utterly wild and insane notion that he could forgive sins in the name of his Father.

Jesus dies for us and not for God. There is not just a little perversity in the tendency to say that the sacrifice was demanded by God to placate the divine wrath. We attempt to exonerate ourselves from the terrible nature of the deed by blaming it on God. The theology of sacrifice becomes part of our defense mechanism. This must now cease. Nothing in the Scriptures warrants it. Jesus' sacrifice for us cannot be explained in that fashion. A new understanding of the nature of that sacrifice is demanded. This new understanding must arise from the event itself and not impose previously constructed theories on it.

Current thinking about sacrifice has moved steadily away from narrow ideas of propitiation. F. C. N. Hicks's *The Fulness of Sacrifice* and Frances M. Young's *Sacrifice and the Death of Christ* provide examples. Hicks developed the idea that the blood of the sacrificial victim is or represents its life. Thus it is a mistake to focus narrowly on the death of the victim and identify it as propitiatory. Rather, in the sacrifice, the shed blood represents the surrendering of the life of the one making the offering. Sacrifice is fulfilled in Christ, therefore, not by a supposedly propitiatory death, for sacrifice does not mean the end of life. Rather Jesus' life is surrendered in order to be accepted, and in being accepted to be raised beyond earthly limitations to full communion with God. Thus his "body and blood" (e.g., in the Eucharist) give us a share in the divine life.

> He enters into our own self. It is Life given, broken, and surrendered; so transformed as to be universally accessible; that can enter into any life that has caught His spirit, has surrendered itself, allowed itself by dedication to be transformed, and so entering can become a part of each life and the common possession of all.[1]

Frances Young also insists that sacrifice must not be identified with ideas of penal substitution and propitiation. Sacrificial imagery is central to the thinking of the church, she claims, and covers a whole range of possible ideas. It can mean God's act of expiating sin as well as humankind's act of propitiating God. It could also be used in connection with the victory motif, implying aversion of the evil powers.[2] Thus sacrificial imagery relates to all the theories of atonement and should be reinstated in atonement thinking.

The picture is not complete, however, with an application to atonement theory. One must, for Young, press on to the "subjective" aspect of the sacrifice.

Evil in us is not met and conquered by an act external to us.

The objective act . . . must effect a transformation in the
believer.

The sacrifice of Christ was itself more than an atoning sacrifice; it was a sacrifice of worship and obedience. There were
two sides to his sacrificial act, the removal of evil and sin by
God, and the offering of perfect homage by man.[3]

The sacrifice of Christ must therefore be participated in through
sacrifice of the believer—especially in the context of the wor-
shiping community. "Sacrifice is properly treated as cult-
language, not the language of law-courts and judgments; in
this context, Christ's act is seen as a sacrifice in which Christians have to partake in order to receive its benefits."[4] This act of
self-sacrifice, one gets the definite impression, is really the apex
of the whole for Young. It corresponds to the heavy investment
she has made throughout the book in speaking of the "moralization" or "spiritualization" of sacrificial practice—that what
is demanded is not an empty act supposedly capable of buying-
off God but a real giving of self to God: "I desire mercy not
sacrifice," "The sacrifices of God are a broken spirit," and so on.

Both Hicks and Young demonstrate a movement away from
understanding sacrifice in narrowly propitiatory terms and an
attempt to reclaim a wider meaning for the life and worship
of the church. The objective is praiseworthy, but it is difficult
to avoid detecting a subtle but definite inclination toward the
more subjective understanding of sacrifice. The sacrifice of
Christ becomes the model to be reenacted by the cult community. Where "the blood is the life," the act of self-giving
is something that can "enter into" a life that "has caught his
Spirit," "surrendered itself, allowed itself by dedication to be
transformed," and so forth. Even when Young speaks with
great appreciation of the idea of sacrifice as a self-propitiation
on God's part, and tries to recover the objective aspect of it,

the attempt is vitiated by the tendency to swallow the whole in the sea of cultic imagery, pictures, and anthropomorphic and mythological language. She has not been able to penetrate to the actuality. As in most books on the sacrifice of Christ, there is very little about what actually happened back there in Jerusalem and on Golgotha, but a great deal about how sacrifice in general is supposed to work. This is then read back onto the events—which means that what happened actually has no particular significance.

The result, for both Hicks and Young, is that they are not able to reverse the direction. Sacrifice remains a means of Godward traffic. "Sacrifice," Young says, "properly understood, is integral to a religious response to the universe" (sic!).

> There is, of course, a considerable difference between a primitive tribe sacrificing to mysterious powers around it in nature and the Christian worship of God conceived as the Creator and sovereign of the universe. But there is one thing in common: sacrifice, material or spiritual, is a reaction to the unseen power believed to be hidden in the world about us, and the different types of sacrifice can be seen as expressions of different reactions to the environment.[5]

The sacrifice of Christ apparently does nothing to change any of that. Sacrifice is a means for somehow appeasing the "hidden powers" of the universe. Under these presuppositions it is a questionable thing to dismantle the notion of *propitiatory* sacrifice, for if Christ does not propitiate such hidden powers, then *we* shall have to do it by our sacrifice. Willy-nilly everything will fall back on us. No doubt that is the reason for the persistence of ideas about propitiation by penal substitution. If the direction is never reversed, propitiation is the only hope.

The great mystery surrounding all discussion of sacrifice is that no one seems to know exactly what it is, where it comes from, or what it is supposed to mean. The Scriptures themselves provide no real theological explanation of sacrifice and are even ambiguous about the propriety of doing it at all (see the many prophetic railings against it). There are directions about how to do it and when, but little indication of just *why* it is supposed to work. The result is that scholars and exegetes scratch around in religious phenomenology and ethnology for theories that are then imposed on the biblical material. Such practice may help to explain some cultic practices of the Old Testament, but it can be fatal when used to provide the "meaning" for the cross. It seems unlikely that Jesus' sacrifice could accurately be spoken of as his "religious response to the universe" or his "reaction to the unseen power believed to be hidden in the world about us."

To arrive at a new understanding of the sacrifice of Christ, one must above all pay close attention to what actually happened and what the Scriptures say about it. What happened was a murder. It was a cruel, bitter, excruciatingly painful, and utterly shameful execution. The apostle Paul must be our guide here. His writings are permeated by a sense for the utter folly, offense, and humiliation of the actual event. The "word of the cross" means just that—not some theory *about* it. Paul does not have many—if any—theories about the cross; he simply holds the actual cross in its horror before his hearers, hearers who are always, it seems, tempted to go off on this or that theoretical detour around the cross. "We preach Christ crucified," Paul says (1 Cor. 1:23), and crucified must, in the first instance at least, mean just that: hung on a cross to die the cursed and shameful death of a slave and criminal. One must not yet hurry on to say "sacrificed" so as to obscure and purify the utter folly of it with theological incense. How else could it be "a stumbling block to Jews and a folly to the Gentiles"? Martin Hengel is certainly right. One must no longer "dissociate talk of the atoning death of Jesus or the blood of Jesus from this 'word of the cross.'" "For the foolishness of God is wiser than men, and the weakness of God is stronger than men" (1 Cor. 1:25).

If we take the actuality of Paul's "word of the cross" as foundation, the Epistle to the Hebrews offers counsel as to how we might proceed. Not only is it the most sustained treatise on the sacrifice of Christ, it is also perhaps the most misunderstood—no doubt because we use it to reinforce our theories rather than let it speak. The epistle has two basic points: first, that Jesus was real; second, that his sacrifice was real in contrast to all others. Jesus was real. He was not a fake. He was not protected, not a Greek "divine man." He was made perfect through suffering (Heb. 2:10ff.); he had to go *through* death.

> Since therefore the children share in flesh and blood, he himself likewise partook of the same nature, that through death he might destroy him who has the power of death, that is, the devil, and deliver all those who through fear of death were subject to lifelong bondage. For surely it is not with angels that he is concerned but with the descendants of Abraham. Therefore he had to be made like his brethren in every respect, so that he might become a merciful and faithful high priest in the service of God, to make expiation for the sins of the people. For because he himself has suffered and been tempted, he is able to help those who are tempted. (2:14–18)

One should note that he has to be "made like his brethren" to *become* "a merciful and faithful high priest in the service of God, to make expiation . . ." and to be "able to help. . . ." The mercy must be an actual event, an "I love you."

Second, because Jesus was real, his sacrifice was real in contrast to all others. Previous sacrifices had only been pale, ineffective shadows of the real thing. They had been, so to speak, only a series of dry runs. With the cultic machinery and the endless repetition of sacrifices, we had only been practicing for the real event. Now, in the cross, the cruel and actual cross, it had happened. It happened, furthermore, not in the temple but out in the streets where everyone could see. He entered "once for all" (9:12) into the real holy place (heaven itself, 9:24) through the real curtain, his own flesh (10:20). He was killed not as part of a pious ritual in church but out in the streets, in a place of execution. Indeed, the writer concludes by saying that it all took place outside the gate, outside those holy places reeking of incense and creaking under the weight of inviolable traditions and reasons for everything.

In what surely must be one of the most offensive images in Scripture, the author likens Jesus' suffering "outside the gate" to the burning of the flesh and offal of the animals whose blood was taken into the sanctuary by the high priest. The real sacrifice takes place "out there" not "in the tent."

> We have an altar from which those who serve the tent have no right to eat. For the bodies of those animals whose blood is brought into the sanctuary by the high priest as a sacrifice for sin are burned outside the camp. So Jesus also suffered outside the gate in order to sanctify the people through his own blood. Therefore let us go forth to him outside the camp and bear the abuse he endured. For here we have no lasting city, but we seek the city which is to come. (13:10–14)

Such passages jolt attempts to construct a neat theory of sacrifice from the epistle. Jesus' death is compared not to the sacrifices in the temple and the ritual purification for sin but to the burning outside the camp of so much impure refuse. That ought to give us pause in a day when the phenomenology of religion and anthropology has supposedly unlocked for us the meaning of sacrifice and has looked to ritual and cultic practice from which to draw our meanings and theories.

The Epistle to the Hebrews, of course, presents no clear or consistent theory of sacrifice. The reason, surely, is that the writer does not start from some theory of sacrifice as such, but from the actuality of the death of Jesus on the cross, and by means of a contrapuntal comparison shows that the old practices have been completely eclipsed. The point is that the ritual was limited, bound up in itself, and never made it out into the real world where it could be universally for everyone, for all time. A change in the law (7:12) has come about in Jesus. His priesthood does not depend on tribal descent, but he is a priest "forever" "by the power of an indestructible life" (7:16). The blood sprinkled in the sanctuary may suffice for ritual purification for the priests, but not for the world. Jesus, however, suffered "outside the gate in order to sanctify the people through his own blood" (13:12). The sprinkling of defiled people with the blood of goats and bulls may suffice for ritual purification of the flesh, but "how much more shall the blood of Christ, who through the eternal Spirit offered himself without blemish to God, *purify your conscience from dead works to serve the living God*" (9:14). The contrast could hardly be more sharp. The sacrificial ritual was only "fleshly" and concerned itself with "dead works." The actual death of Jesus, however, the true sacrifice, penetrates through to the conscience to purify it from all that so one will serve the *living* God. Thus the author can conclude, "We have an altar from which those who serve the tent have no right to eat," and we are exhorted to "go forth to him outside the camp and bear the abuse he endured. For here we have no lasting city, but we seek the city which is to come" (13:10, 13, 14).

The Epistle to the Hebrews gives us a starting point. When atonement has slipped back into mere theological theory or pious ritual, it is time once again to go forth to him "outside the camp," to the real altar. The death of Jesus makes it clear that the cultic apparatus was only a rehearsal: We have been practicing for this one thing from time immemorial; now it has happened. We cannot go back to our rehearsals again.

The insistence on the reality of the sacrifice receives interesting confirmation from the work of René Girard, *Violence and the Sacred*.[6] Girard insists that we must look for a real origin for the practice of sacrifice, not just a psychological, cultic, or mythological one. Sacrifice, he maintains, performed the very real function of keeping violence outside the community. It has its origin in the actual murder of a surrogate victim. The estranged parties in the community, threatened by the destructive power of disorder, of unrestrained and unrevenged violence, descend on a surrogate victim who in some fashion or other is looked on as being responsible for the crisis. The surrogate victim is killed and the violence is averted. The sacrifice thus becomes the basis for a new order and harmony in the community. The surrogate victim "bears away the violence" in an actual sense. To say that the victim bears our sins is to say the same thing. Sacrifice as a real event averting violence is, according to Girard, the foundation of order and community. The surrogate victim is thus also the benefactor of the new order. The sacrifice as a real event both averts violence and unites the estranged parties possessed by its power.

Perhaps equally significant for our purposes is Girard's view of ritual or cultic sacrifice. Ritual sacrifice is an attempt to repeat and channel the benefit of the first and real sacrifice. It seeks to "extract from the original violence some technique of cathartic appeasement."[7] It seeks thus to reduce sacrifice to a formula, to remove all elements of chance. The aspects that were beyond human control—the time, the place, the selection of the victim, the procedure—are now premeditated and fixed by the ritual. Ritual sacrifice is founded on a double substitution: a ritually prescribed victim is now substituted for the original surrogate victim.[8] Most telling of all, however, is that such ritual sacrifice involves a certain obscuring of its own factual and real basis. That is because the ritual takes place within, subsequent to, the order already established by the original sacrifice and has as its aim the preservation of that order. It is preventive, not creative. The myths it tells about the sacrifice obscure the truth in attempting to point to it. Thus it is said, perhaps, that the sacrifice is necessary to appease "the gods" who are "wrathful." The cathartic violence is repeated on a substitute who will not evoke further revenge and prolong the violence. A lesser violence is "proffered as a bulwark against a far more virulent violence."[9] There is a transformation of the real into the unreal which is "part of the process by which man conceals from himself the human origin of his own violence, by attributing it to the gods."[10] "A delusion concerning its own factual basis—*not* the absence of that basis"—is, according to Girard, the trouble from which religion suffers.[11]

Girard's thesis provides significant background for the necessity of movement toward actuality and reality in speaking of atonement. One of our tasks must be removal of the delusion to arrive at the truth. The cross of Christ must be seen in that light.

The Accident

We need a new, perhaps even a noncultic and nonreligious idea of sacrifice. This is certainly what the writer of Hebrews was suggesting with his invitation to go forth "outside the camp." At the risk of committing the very sin constantly railed at here—multiplying images—we might try, as a kind of project in thought, a more common and everyday use of the term "sacrifice" and a different conceptuality, that of "accident." The idea suggests itself for several reasons. It picks up Lessing's challenge about "accidental truths of history." Perhaps it is the very accidental character that is of the essence. Accidents just happen, and there is nothing to do but rearrange everything according to what happened. Accidents are opaque. One cannot see through them. Yet they raise most directly and in the most crucial way the question of God for us. Sometimes we call them acts of God! In an accident, one does not even have time to ask whether what occurs is relevant to one's life or not. It just happens, and there it is. An accident is just that tear in the fabric of time we noted at the close of the last chapter.

No doubt the image could be developed in many different ways, but perhaps we can say it like this: A child is playing in the street. A truck is bearing down on the child. A man casts himself in the path of the truck, saves the child, but is himself killed in the process. It is an accident.

The development of such an image can help us see what is at stake. The accidental death of the man who saved the child could be called a sacrifice, indeed, even a vicarious sacrifice. He gave his life for another. And the point is that this is all one needs to say. It is not a ritual or cultic sacrifice—not a substitution—but a real sacrifice, an actual one.

When the sacrifice is actual, certain questions immediately become irrelevant or beside the point. One would hardly waste much time arguing about "to whom" the man sacrificed his life. Yet this is what theologians have done. The reason, no doubt, is that they have too often been thinking about a cultic rehearsal where nothing actually happens, and have attempted subsequently to endow the empty event with universal meaning via this or that theory. Since nothing is accomplished by the sacrifice, one must shore it up with much cultic and metaphysical underpinning.

The man in our story gave his life *for* someone. The question "To whom?" is unnecessary. To whom could he have given it? To the truck? Hardly. To the child? Not really. To God? At best only in the indirect sense that he was faithful to the divine mandate to love at whatever the cost, but certainly not to pay God. If the sacrifice is real, one says all there is to say when one says it was *for* the other.

So also the New Testament. Jesus died *for* us; on our behalf, he gave his life as a ransom for many. The New Testament shows no interest whatever in the question of *to* whom his sacrifice might have been made. One has said all there is to say when one has said "for us all."

But in what sense is the sacrifice for us? In terms of our story, it would be all too easy to identify ourselves with the more or less innocent child playing in the street and look on the sacrifice as that which averts death. Were we to do that, however, we would remain with something akin to a superficial victory motif and with a tendency to overlook human sin. To make the story work properly, we must say that we are not the child playing in the street, but the driver of the truck. If anything, the child is our neighbor, not us. Suddenly there is the someone who throws himself in our unheeding way and is splattered against the front of our machine. If atonement is to be seen as an actual event, the cross should have that kind of direct, shattering impact. The roses must be stripped away once and for all. The cross cannot be brought back "within the camp." It remains outside, a permanent offense.

When we say that we drive the truck, we add a dimension strangely and conspicuously missing in most theories of the atonement: *we* did it. The theories usually gloss over this lightly or tend to place the blame abstractly, as though Jesus were crucified in a vacuum and the judgment and crowd scenes in the passion narratives had no point. "His blood be on us and on our children!" (Matt. 27:25). "Do not weep for me, but weep for yourselves and for your children" (Luke 23:28). Looking at atonement theory, one would think such words had not been written. Perhaps René Girard is right: our theories tend to transform the real into the unreal in order to conceal from ourselves the human origin of our violence, attributing it to God. In a day when there is much debate about "who did it," we must not fail to give the right answer at last: we did.

Blaming the Jews for the crucifixion has been a terrible sin, a particular Christian attempt to conceal the truth which has had tragic results. Faced with the cross, we can only confess, "We have done it." If we cannot say that, he did not die for us. The hymnody of the church has recognized this even if dogmatics has not:

> Who was the guilty?
> Who brought this upon thee?
> Alas, my treason,
> Jesus, hath undone thee.
> 'Twas I, Lord Jesus,
> I it was denied thee.
> I crucified thee.
>
> —JOHANN CRÜGER

At this point we must do some demythologizing of the classic view and take what Luther said even further. The cosmic enemies in the classic view—sin, death, law, the devil—must be seen as operating *through us* in our bondage, however we may regard their objective existence. The cross is the place where the actual battle against us and thus ultimately for us is joined. Jesus throws himself in our path. As such, the cross is not in the first instance a revelation of the love or mercy of God. It is rather the climactic manifestation of God's wrath against sin, God's attack against a humanity that will believe neither in God nor in God's creation. It is the expression of God's jealousy against a world that will not have this God as a God of mercy. The cross makes it plain that "all have sinned and fall short of the glory of God" (Rom. 3:23). Jesus, the one bearing forgiveness from God, puts himself in our path. The demons recognize him and speak for us: "What have you to do with us, Jesus of Nazareth? Have you come to destroy us? I know who you are, the Holy One of God" (Mark 1:24). And in the end we kill him.

Just so does he "bear our sins in his body on the tree" (1 Pet. 2:21–24). We must remove the last abstraction from Luther's talk of the "happy exchange" and all the dogmatic language about

Jesus' bearing our sin. We cannot speak as though that were a matter of bearing some quantum or other, somehow equivalent to the sins of the whole world. That Jesus bears our sins in his body is no abstract affair, no strange metaphysical transference; it is actual and public fact. We beat him, spit on him, mock him as a "king," crown him with thorns, torture him, forsake him, kill him. He bears our sins in his body—actually. The real event occurs. It is not a rehearsal or a cultic substitution.

Here we must look, too, at the particular way in which Jesus died: on a cross. "He humbled himself and became obedient unto death, even death on a cross" (Phil. 2:8). He bore the curse: "Christ redeemed us from the curse of the law, having become a curse for us—for it is written, 'Cursed be every one who hangs on a tree'" (Gal. 3:13). Why that? It was the most degrading, shameful, despicable form of execution, the most terrible way to dispatch criminals and offenders against the established order, the most conspicuous and awesome manifestation of human justice. We cannot set up proofs or establish proof-texts for just why it had to be a cross, but we can see, perhaps, a certain inevitability in it all. He had to be executed as an offender against our order, under our justice. In that sense he had to bear the ultimate curse: the curse of the law. It had to be quite legal and proper. We must be clear about this. He was not crucified because of our peccadilloes against the order; he was crucified by the order itself, so to bring a new order. He was a sacrifice for original sin as well as actual sins. Just so does he bear our sin in his body—the sin of an order alienated from the God of mercy, and setting itself up against that God. Just so also is he "made to be sin for us" though he "knew no sin" (2 Cor. 5:17–21). He could be nothing other than a criminal, an offender, even though he is innocent. René Girard says that the system of justice has superseded sacrifice in modern society.[12] No doubt that is a reason for the shift to legal concepts in post-patristic atonement theory. The cross is the end of law.

Nowhere is God's utter rejection of our sin more apparent than at the cross. Nowhere is the truth of our sin more exposed to the light of God's judgment. God rejects it and judges it precisely by refusing to have anything to do with it. God will have nothing to do with our violence, our claim to be free, our drives to dominate. There is nothing God can or will do but die at our hands: bear our sins. If there had been anything else to do, Jesus' Father could have sent "legions of angels" (Matt. 26:53). But then the Scriptures would not be fulfilled, "that it must be so" (Matt. 26:54). God remains true to himself: "I will have mercy on whom I will have mercy."

But how could such an event have universal significance? If we reduce it to this actuality, is it not just an isolated historical event? Is it not just an accident? Driving our truck down the street, innocently going about our business, how could we be held guilty? Or could we not also say, "Someone else did it"— way back there? How can it be "once, for all"? The theories have attempted to answer the question by fitting atonement into cultic, juridical, and moral structures that are supposed to be universally valid. But that is to freeze it, to turn it into an idea, and so to transform it into just that wrath from which we need to be saved. It is to make the cross serve the status quo, take it captive to the already existing order. It becomes merely preventative, not curative or creative. When the writer of the Epistle to the Hebrews invites us to "go forth to meet him outside the camp," he bids us turn our back on all that. "For," he says, "here we have no lasting city, but we seek the city which is to come" (Heb. 13:14).

What must be recognized finally is that Jesus' death has universal significance "for us" because he was universally rejected and yet raised from the dead. "This Jesus God raised up, and of that we are all witnesses. . . . Let all the house of Israel therefore know assuredly that God has made him both Lord and Christ, this Jesus whom you crucified" (Acts 2:32, 36). When they heard this, we are told, "They were cut to the heart," and said, "What shall we do?" Having died once, Jesus dies no more. Jesus' death has universal significance for us because God raised him from the dead. He, the universally rejected one, is vindicated by *God*. He is not a hero for our systems. He is not vindicated by us. He is vindicated by God. The one splattered against the front of our truck comes back to say "Shalom." There is no strange transaction that takes place somewhere in celestial bookkeeping halls to make it universal. The one we killed, the one no one wanted, is raised from the dead. That is all. The stone the builders rejected has become the chief cornerstone.

Jesus had to die because God is forgiving and because God insists on being so. Jesus died precisely because he said, "I forgive you in God's name." He died because we would not have it. The resurrection is his vindication against us. Therefore, it is vindication against death, the power of death resident in our legalism (see 2 Cor. 3). It is the proof that he was right and we are wrong. God has made him Lord. God has now said what he has to say. God has at last "spoken to us by a Son" (Heb. 1:2).

This is precisely the difference between the Old and the New Testaments. The argument about whether there was grace or forgiveness in the Old Testament is beside the point. Everyone knows that God is gracious and forgiving. As Voltaire said, "C'est son métier" (that's his business). But left like that, forgiveness too is an abstract characteristic like any other. In Jesus, God actually comes to say "to you" what he was preparing to say all along. To say that it can be said to you means that it is now universal and must be said to all the yous in the world in the preaching of the church. If it can be said "to you," it can be said to all. It knows no bounds; it is unconditional. God, who is always gracious, was preparing, promising, to say it actually, concretely, in our time by first choosing a concrete people. This meant at first a restriction, a particularization. As such it means even a legalization, for a particular people must be shaped by law in this age. The peril of saying it precisely among his own is thus magnified to the utmost. "His own received him not" (John 1:11). To get it said precisely as forgiveness and not another law, Jesus must die and shatter all opposition even among his own. He must negate the law, the particularization, concretely, so that forgiveness can be said universally to all. Just so did he die for us. He died and was vindicated in the resurrection so that the "I forgive you" could actually be said. In that sense he won forgiveness for us. He won the right for it to be said. That is the New Testament. The testament or will that was prepared and promised is now actually given because the testator has actually died (Heb. 9:15ff.). Luther once put the matter succinctly: The sole difference between the Old and the New Testaments is that the Old said, "You must have Christ and his spirit," while the New says, "Here it is."[13] It is the "I now give it to you" that characterizes the *New* Testament. It can now be said to everyone. It is universal.

We should say something at this point about the question of universalism and its relative, cosmic salvation. Universalism, the idea that God must eventually save everyone, is an abstraction that like all such abstractions which try to prompt God does little real good and has no basis in Scripture. What Jesus won for us on the cross is precisely the right to say the saving word of forgiveness to all universally, and he commissioned his followers to *do* so. The will of God is revealed in the saying and doing. The task of dogmatics is to foster that concrete saying and doing in the confidence that it alone will save from all abstraction, law, and wrath. Universalism as an abstraction can add nothing to that, and it can harm the proclamation if it is taken to mean that there is no need to say the concrete word. If it functions to obviate the preaching, it is another abstraction that destroys the concrete and actual. Declaring people to be anonymous Christians or to be somehow universally saved can be like declaring the poor to be anonymous rich people. That is hardly a kindness. The abstraction is never completely kind or unambiguous. Only "he who comes" can save. Of course, the abstraction may serve other purposes. It may also function as a hope arising from having heard the concrete word—the hope that the God who has managed so to speak in Jesus will so speak to all, and use us to that end. In that sense it may function to remind us that we can have no vested interest in insisting that hell be populated. That is God's affair. It can also function to remind us that the authority we have is to preach the *good* news, to speak the word of forgiveness to all the yous concretely and that we do not have the authority to damn people—to say, "You are lost eternally." The universality given is the universality of the gospel. That cannot be withheld from anyone. It stops before no boundary. The eventual outcome of such speaking of the gospel is in God's hands. Theology cannot force God's hand.

The idea of a cosmic salvation also seems to have little basis in the Scripture, if taken to mean that through Jesus' death, resurrection, and exaltation the present empirical cosmos has undergone or is undergoing some mysterious change. The Scripture does not support a demythologizing that reduces salvation to a purely personal inwardness or existential self-understanding. There is indeed a cosmic dimension to the rule of the crucified and resurrected One. But for the time being that is hidden—the seed growing secretly. It will be manifest in the end-times, in the eschaton. Now Christ is "ruling from the tree." "The cosmos is penetrated by Christ, not because his exaltation has rendered redemption and existing reality one and the same, but rather because his Church, participant in the event of his cross and his instrument in its humiliation, its bodily dying, is extended and expanded over the earth."[14] The cosmic dimension is *eschatological*. The crucified and risen one must reign until he has put all enemies under his feet. Then the kingdom is handed over to God, who will be all in all (1 Cor. 15:28).

It must be recognized that unconditional and universal forgiveness is a dangerous and seditious thing in our world, in this age. It simply cannot be done. In this sense, too, the crucifixion had to be. Forgiveness is not safe unless it is creative, unless it actually brings a new world, a new age. So forgiveness can be given only in Jesus' name, in his name who was killed by us and was vindicated. In him forgiveness can be given because he ushers us through death to life in his kingdom. "Here we have no lasting city . . ." (Heb. 13:14).

> "Are you the King . . . ?" . . . Jesus answered, "My kingship is not of this world; if my kingship were of this world, my servants would fight. . . ." Pilate said to him, "So you are a king?" Jesus answered, "You say that I am a king. For this I was born, and for this I have come into the world, to bear witness to the truth. Every one who is of the truth hears my voice." (John 18:33–37)

The resurrection of the universally rejected one means that the accident both judges and saves us. It is a faith-creating and faith-demanding event. We are judged. If the one smashed against the front of our machine is raised, the entire enterprise in which we are engaged is judged. "It was an accident," we might say. "How can we be held guilty if someone just ran out in front of us? There was nothing we could do." Of course. Just as with Pilate, the priests, the people. "Of course, we didn't intend to kill the Son of God, but how were we to know? It was an accident." Indeed. But God vindicates him. The truth is revealed. Not the peccadilloes, not the little misdeeds or mistakes, but the entire enterprise is called into question. Not just the moment of the accident, but all that leads to our being there at all is called into question: the grim inertia of all our religious, economic, social, juridical, and political systems which will not and cannot swerve aside no matter who gets in the way. "Accidents will happen." "Sometimes the innocent, unfortunately, get crushed." But this innocent one is raised. Then we are judged in the sight of God, the God who raises the dead and cares about the innocent. The world, of course, goes on. The truck pauses only momentarily. The world will pronounce the death accidental, absolve the driver, and leave time to heal the wounds. But if the one killed is raised, something else happens: ultimate judgment, a full stop, and grace. "But to all who received him, who believed in his name, he gave power to become children of God; who were born, not of blood nor of the will of the flesh nor of the will of man, but of God" (John 1:12–13).

The resurrection of the rejected one judges and saves at once. Faith will grasp the accident as the revelation of God and believe that it was "no accident," that God placed him in our path. The cross and the resurrection are the specific way God wants to get through to us and reveal who God actually is. God's innermost being comes to expression here. God slips into our world just in the little crack of the accident, softly and lightly, but with the ultimate authority of absolute grace. God does not come in the palace of kings, the halls of justice, or the temples of the priests. Just an accident in time. There God can be truly for us. There is no room elsewhere.

But what does this add up to *for us?* Atonement as an actual event means that through the word of the cross and the resurrection something is done to us. Atonement is done to us. The resurrection of the crucified One means death and life for us. If the event, the accident, happens to us, breaks into our lives with the impact we have been trying to describe, then it will involve a full stop and a new beginning: a death of the old and the resurrection of the new in faith. The word of the cross must be a word that does the cross to us, not one that directs attention elsewhere so as to enable us to avoid it. That is the kind of hermeneutic needed today.

Dogmatic theology cannot take the path of Hegel and his followers in attempting to assimilate the death and resurrection of Jesus to an immanent rational scheme: infinite Spirit going out from itself and returning to itself, understood as the necessary unfolding of its own nature. As Bonhoeffer put it, this is the "ultimate deceit" and "final strength" of the human *logos* or reason. It forestalls the claim of the *logos* of the cross by "negating itself and at the same time asserts that this negation is a necessary unfolding of its own nature."[15] The death and resurrection of Jesus cannot thus be assimilated to an immanent rational scheme and turned into a "speculative Good Friday." If Jesus is the one who comes to us through just that accident of which we have been speaking, we are suddenly thrown out of all immanent rational schemes, all those projects, ideas, and ideals that are supposedly to carry us to our planned and preconceived destinations, and thrown entirely on him, the one whom we, in our plans, killed and who yet rose. We cannot take him into our schemes; he takes us into his concrete life. "For to me to live is Christ, and to die is gain," says Paul (Phil. 1:21).

Full discussion of the meaning of death and new life for us must await the later *locus* on the Christian life. Here we shall give only brief indication of its significance. The idea of death and new life takes us into the area which has, in the tradition, been termed the "subjective" dimension of atonement. Resisting all along as we have the idea of an objective change in God might open our treatment to the charge of subjectivism. It should be obvious, however, that such a charge cannot hold. The reason is precisely that the cross means death and new life. The old subject is not just given an example to follow, or inspiration to encourage its flagging religious ambitions. The old subject dies and a new one is called into being in Jesus by faith. When faith in the unconditional mercy of God is created, a new subject begins to emerge.

This means that atonement is intensely subjective, in the sense that it has a profound effect on the subject. But the subject-object dichotomy is not at all apt to designate what happens if actual "at-one-ment" is to occur. Since it is a matter of death and new life coming from the actual event, it is entirely objective in the sense that it comes totally from without. The subject has nothing to do with it. The subject is put to death. Indeed, one could argue that the so-called objectivity of theories positing a change in God is really only apparent. God changes, but I remain the same. God has to be "satisfied" to allow my system of legalistic thinking to remain intact. God is made to fit my picture. At bottom that is a very subjective stance. There is, ultimately, little to choose between so-called objective and subjective atonement theories. Both leave the subject more or less intact. The only argument between them is the degree of help needed.

If, however, atonement is the actual event, the accident that happens to us from without, it affects us profoundly subjectively. It ends the old life and begins a new one. It means death and resurrection. The old subjective views were partially right. They simply were not radical enough. They thought of a modification of the subject, not of its death and resurrection.

No doubt the claim that his death *is* our death is difficult for us to grasp. Again we are tricked by our tendency to get lost in abstraction. We think that something incredibly difficult or strange is being demanded of us. Living up to the law was difficult enough, but now we are told that we have to die. But the point is that his death is our death; he has died for us. Paul could put it quite simply: "We are convinced that one has died for all; therefore all have died" (2 Cor. 5:14). What is that death? It is simply the death administered through the word authorized by the cross and resurrection. When the word of forgiveness comes to a world bent on its own survival systems, that world is suddenly robbed of its whole reason for being. The death is suddenly having nothing to do. If Jesus lives after we have killed him, then we have died. To die means to be reduced to nothing, to be able to do nothing but wait. When the accident occurs, we are suddenly helpless. We can only wait for help. We are thrown out of the stream that usually protects us. If Jesus lives, then we as old beings are through.

We fear such talk of death and resurrection because we fear the loss of continuity. Is there not a continuity between the old and the new person? Is there not something to carry us across? It is a real and serious question. But it is of the same sort one should address to the cross. What was that death into which Jesus entered? Was he assured of continuity? The question is of the sort one must ask about forgiveness. Will I survive forgiveness? I may take it, perhaps, as old Adam and abuse it, use it as license, presume upon it, preserving myself, my continuity. Forgiveness will itself turn to poison if it does not bring that death and resurrection. It cannot be mixed with such continuity. Such talk of continuity may be used just to protect us from death. But we need have no fear. He has died for us. To believe that means to believe that my continuity is now entirely in him. We have already heard the author of the Epistle to the Hebrews say it: "He himself likewise partook of the same nature, that through death he might destroy him who has the power of death, that is, the devil, and deliver all those who *through fear of death* were subject to lifelong bondage" (2:14–15). Forth from the cross and the resurrection goes the absolutely unconditional word: it is all over; there is nothing to be done. Our death and resurrection are simply in the nothing. Faith is the death and resurrection. He has died for us in a double sense: died in the place we must die and died so as finally to get us, to claim us. To be finally grasped by the event itself, to have the accident happen, *is* to die and to be made new. It is to die to the old, to the abstractions, the universal truths of reason that are supposed to protect us from death, to the law, to sin, that is, to unbelief in God, in God's grace and creation. It is to die to all that so as to become oneself an historical being, not an abstraction. It is to be found in him who died accidentally so that one might be raised in him. It is to wait, to live by hope in the God who raised Jesus, the preacher of forgiveness, from the dead. To die thus and to await the resurrection is to be reconciled with the God who created this world.

Faith born of death and resurrection means that the believer counts on a new future, a new age, for the world God has created. Jesus' death for us must be taken also in that sense. He died to give us a new future, a new kingdom. If he is our death and resurrection, he is also our example. There is no difficulty in saying that when the event is actual. If his death for us opens a new future, then he is the pioneer, the one whom we follow. The kingdom he brought, the message of forgiveness, finds no room in this age. But we follow him. We may recall here the words from 1 Peter:

> For to this you have been called, because Christ also suffered for you, leaving you an example, that you should follow in his steps. He committed no sin; no guile was found on his lips. When he was reviled, he did not revile in return; when he suffered, he did not threaten; but he trusted to him who judges justly. He himself bore our sins in his body on the tree, that we might die to sin and live to righteousness. By his wounds you have been healed. (2:21–24)

Forgiveness does not work here, but we pray, "Forgive us our sins, as we forgive those who sin against us." For we look for the city to come. The significance of that must be spelled out at greater length in the *locus* on the Christian life.

Atonement understood as dying and rising in Christ in faith can also approach and be assimilated to the older patristic language of *theopoiesis*—of being "divinized" or "immortalized" through participation in the victorious and eternal divine life of Christ. There is always a danger that one may construe such divinization as an escape from death, as a detour around the actual death of Jesus. That would be the case if one maintained that because Jesus was divine he was protected from the death, and that one now participates in just that protection. One is not always certain whether the fathers avoid this danger successfully. If one is quite clear that the "divine life" we are participating in is that of the triune God who has gone through death in his Son, and that our participation means going through death, by faith, then one can indeed speak of and celebrate such *theopoiesis*. That would be the point and conclusion of Luther's language of the "happy exchange." He takes *our* life, our place, in order to give us *his*. The exchange must be an actual event, however. He must take our place, our death, if we are to have his life. In that sense, Luther can speak expressly in words akin to those of the fathers: "Therefore God becomes man in order that man may become God. Likewise strength becomes weak in order that weakness may become strength. He put on our form and figure, image and likeness, in order to clothe us in his image, form and likeness. . . ."[16]

Atonement conceived as an actual event thus does justice to the concerns of all the various theories. It is objective; it comes from without entirely. God's wrath is satisfied in the sense that God's resolve to have mercy breaks through the abstractions, the bondage in which we are implicated, to create faith. Just so, is it also intensely "subjective." When faith is created, a new subject emerges, the historical being who, as a member of the body of Christ, the crucified and resurrected one, has become an historical being who waits, follows, and hopes. What Schleiermacher and Ritschl wanted can be seen to come to fruition: The divine love establishes an actual historical community. But this is the body of believers who have died and

who look to the resurrection, who bear that stamp, who follow
Christ, not a community of religious or moral idealists. Actual
atonement is also the divine victory. The victory, however, is not
abstract or mythological. Sin, death, the law, the devil—all the
powers—are defeated in us. The new covenant is established.

> I will put my law within them, and I will write it upon their
> hearts; and I will be their God, and they shall be my people.
> And no longer shall each man teach his neighbor and each his
> brother saying, "Know the Lord," for they shall all know me,
> from the least of them to the greatest, says the Lord; for I will
> forgive their iniquity, and I will remember their sin no more.
> (Jer. 31:33–34)

> For God has done what the law, weakened by the flesh, could
> not do: sending his own Son in the likeness of sinful flesh and
> for sin, he condemned sin in the flesh, in order that the just
> requirement of the law might be fulfilled *in* us, who walk not
> according to the flesh but according to the Spirit. (Rom. 8:3–4)

Part II

The Christian Life

Introduction

A *locus* on the Christian life is potentially the most dangerous in dogmatics. It is concerned with giving an account of how the act of God in Christ impinges on, effects, and affects the lives we live. Such an account is potentially dangerous because, as the tradition shows all too patently, the rhetoric has a way of running away with itself and becoming inflated and oppressive. In the anxiety to demonstrate that the Christian life is different, vital, relevant, abundant, and obviously superior to every other kind of life, the encomiums pile up, often fired by enthusiasm and hubris rather than by reality.

The danger is at least threefold. In the first place, Christians are enticed into playing the world's game, into going everyone one better. The Christian life is measured by the world's yardstick. It is pictured as the unqualified fulfillment of all the old Adam's dreams, particularly the most pious and religious. Then the battle is lost. Christianity succumbs to moralism. Second, inflated rhetoric leads either to hypocrisy or to despair. One deludes oneself that one has succeeded (at least as well as the next person) in measuring up to it, or one despairs because one cannot. The former is perhaps most common. Third, the danger is that the rhetoric will float above reality, living a life of its own in dogmatic texts and sermons with little or no relation to what Christians or others actually think or do. It becomes a fiction that may entertain those who still have a taste for it on Sundays but has no vital function in their lives.

One of the first tasks of a dogmatic *locus* on the Christian life is to bring the rhetoric to heel so that it can perform its proper function. The rhetoric must be true to what the Christian life really is and should be. Dogmatics should attempt to foster a proper use of language so that the preaching of the Christian message actually is productive of a Christian life in the true sense and is not false or empty. We certainly want to claim that the Christian message fosters a life that is better, relevant, true, vital, and so on, but dogmatics must do this in a manner consonant with the Christian hope itself, not succumbing to the world's measurements.

We are concerned, that is to say, with the *Christian* life, the specific kind of life lived in the light of God's act in Jesus Christ, and not with just any kind of religious life or whatever the world may deem so or aspire to. The basic assumption is that if God has indeed acted to save us, without our aid or counsel, in Jesus Christ, then the *Christian* life will be quite other than those schemes where no such redemption is believed or hoped for—and other, moreover, in a manner consonant with the redemption itself, not with the world's conceptions of otherness.

It is important, therefore, to put the right question, lest we set off in the wrong direction at the outset. The basic question cannot be the direct one about what the Christian life is or what makes it different. The basic question must be one which arises from within, from the startling nature of the message of grace itself. The Christian life is one which results from grace already given; it is not a life somehow dedicated to achieving grace. In putting the question *about* the Christian life, one must be careful not so to call the Christian life into question as to kill it and put it back on the rhetorical treadmill. The Christian life should be good news, not law and drudgery. The question with which we deal must itself reflect the good news.

The apostle Paul set the basic question for us in just this fashion. "Are we to continue in sin that grace may abound?"

(Rom. 6:1). That is the basic question for the Christian life. It is the only question left to ask if one attends to the Christian message with any care and discernment. If God has done it all for us, then the real question is *whether and why there is anything left to do at all*. But are not the assumptions behind such a question and the question itself dangerous? Of course they are. But salvation by grace, proclaimed unconditionally, *is* a dangerous thing. Nevertheless, God has taken the risk and we must follow God in it. It cost God the cross. It cost a death. Paul says that for us too it is only through that death that we will find what the Christian life is: "We were buried therefore with him by baptism into death, so that as Christ was raised from the dead by the glory of the Father, we too might walk in newness of life" (Rom. 6:4). The Christian life is life from the dead. Therefore its basic question is one which must be put with a smile, with joy irrepressible: "*Is* there anything left to do?" Nothing must quench that joy.

A dogmatic chapter on the Christian life is dangerous because it has to do with death and life. We can see the danger in the question whether we should sin the more that grace may abound. If it is not properly answered, everything is lost. If we answer with a shocked No and piously turn our backs to return to our petty moralisms, as if it were not a serious question, we shall have to go our way to our own death. If on the other hand, in premature enthusiasm, we answer Yes and take the question as occasion for gratification of the flesh, it will turn to poison. Unless we catch something of the vision, we are in a precarious position. "To him who has will more be given; and from him who has not, even what he has will be taken away" (Mark 4:25). That is the ultimate danger.

Paul's answer is the only answer: "How can we who died to sin still live in it?" (Rom. 6:2). One must note the past tense: We *died*. We have to do with "the newness of life" out of death. Explicating that must be the concern of the *locus* on the Christian life.

Traditional Protestant dogmatics has done this by dealing
with the question of justification, the basic saving act, and its
relationship to sanctification, the fruit of the saving act in the
believer's life, and how this affects the believer's relationship to
church and world. In spite of protest that might be made against
narrowing the matter down to such ancient formulations, we
shall honor the tradition, believing it to be no random or time-
conditioned caprice that led to stating the problem of Christian
life in these terms. Justification by faith is, after all, *the* dogma
of the Protestant Reformation, and the only dogma about the
Christian life yet proposed. Dogmatics must discuss with
the tradition such things as justification, sanctification, law and
gospel, the "order" of salvation, the two kingdoms, the world,
and freedom, because only through such discussion with the
tradition can we arrive at responsible formulations today.

The question of the adequacy and relevance of the traditional conceptualizations will, of course, have to concern
us. Every interpretation is a reinterpretation, which at least
covertly addresses the question of relevance. No doubt that will
be equally true here. The question of relevance will concern us
more directly in our final section.

A dogmatic *locus* on the Christian life is not immediately
concerned with ethics as such, with specific counsel about
actions to be taken in concrete situations, or about how to live
amid the ambiguities, pressures, and boredoms of modern
industrial society. We are concerned rather with the foundation for ethics, with the tree and its roots rather than the fruit,
to use the biblical image. This too is apparent from our question
"Shall we sin the more that grace may abound?" The answer
to that question lays bare what the Scriptures call the "heart."
The way one answers it reveals one's "soul." This is difficult to
express in any one concept. It has to do with one's *vision*, with
what one ultimately sees and hopes for, with one's answer to
the question "Why go on?" It has to do with one's basic hold on

life itself, with one's faith. This does not mean that the question of the "fruit," the question of ethics, is at all unimportant. The good tree will bear good fruit. But we are concerned here with what makes the tree good so that it *can* bear fruit. The Christian life must be seen as a faith, a vision, a hope, a basic hold on life effected by God's act in Jesus Christ, which leads subsequently to attitudes and actions in the world for others.

On the deepest level the question of relevance has to do with this faith, vision, and hope. The question is whether this vision today has power to claim people in the face of alternative visions: Marxism, atheism, existentialist "absurdity," nihilism, tragic despair (tinged, perhaps, by religious or "Christian" ideas), or whatever. The question is not merely about the relevance of this or that particular formulation—whether, for instance, modern people still suffer from guilt or are afflicted with an "introspective conscience"—but whether the Christian vision can be presented with power to claim allegiance. The question is whether there is such power in the Christian view itself and whether it can be expressed without distortion. One might be tempted, of course, to make Christianity relevant by borrowing from or accommodating "the spirit of the times." That would be to sell one's soul to gain the world. This *locus* is written under the conviction that such strategy is neither honest nor wise. The power to claim people today must arise from the Christian message itself. Only thus can its relevance be established.

CHAPTER ONE

Justification

The death of the old and the resurrection of the new, by the word of justification in proclamation and sacrament, are the basis of the Christian life. Justification by faith in the divine word cannot readily be synthesized with thinking in terms of law, process, and progress, but must be seen as an eschatological event, as new life from death, in which the depth of human sin is unmasked at the same time as righteousness is granted. Law is ended as "the way," driven out of the conscience by Christ, and given its proper function in exposing sin, unbelief, and mistrust. To foster the Christian life, the proclamation of the church must do this, not just describe it.

Justification by Grace

"You, therefore, must be perfect, as your heavenly Father is perfect" (Matt. 5:48). "It is written, 'You shall be holy, for I am holy'" (1 Pet. 1:16). "A new commandment I give to you, that you love one another; even as I have loved you" (John 13:34). Such passages set in no uncertain terms the goal of the Christian life: perfection, holiness, and love. One could no doubt add others. But what do the exhortations mean?

The second part of each statement is the catch: "as your heavenly Father is perfect," "for I am holy," and "as I have loved you." We could find (and have found) it easy enough to set up schemes to realize in our own fashion the first part: the perfection, the holiness, the love. It is questionable, however, whether such schemes reach the goal set in the second part. Human schemes of perfection, holiness, and love are substituted for God's own perfection, holiness, and love. God's perfection, holiness, and love are *given* in God's action *for us* in Jesus Christ. To be perfect as God is perfect, holy as God is holy, to love as God loves, poses therefore a different problem than that to which our schemes are directed. God's perfection, holiness, and love pass ours by, going in the opposite direction. God and the sinner are truly and tragically like two ships that pass in the night. Therewith the problem of explicating the *Christian* life is exposed. Can these ships ever meet?

The problem comes sharply into focus around the idea of justification. The very term suggests a legal or moral process. It implies a standard, a law, according to which the justice in question is to be measured. The natural and inevitable human tendency is to think of the relationship to God in terms of such schemes and standards. There is a "way" to God: to perfection, to holiness, to righteousness and justice. If the way could be traversed successfully, we would arrive at the goal and be "saved." The sinner, though fallen, has a conscience, a *synteresis*, a voice or remnant of the moral law within that impels along the way. Perhaps the conscience is weak or damaged by the fall, but it is there and in need only of proper education and sensitizing. Law conceived as the way, as the eternal standard of justice, holiness, and righteousness, reinforced by the demands of the conscience, provides the basic logical and structural framework of the relationship to God.

Throughout this *locus* "law" is to be taken in a functional rather than a material sense. "The law" in this sense is demand, that voice which "accuses," as the reformers put it, arising from anywhere and everywhere, insisting that we do our duty and fulfill our being. Anything which does that exercises the function or "office" of the law. Law is not a specifiable set of propositions, but is one way communication functions when we are alienated, estranged, and bound. This understanding of law transcends the usual kind of argument, as when, for instance, it is maintained that "law" should be understood as "Torah," a gracious gift in the covenant rather than a harsh imposition, or when it is said that Paul misunderstood the law. Such exegetical considerations, important in their own right, are not decisive for the question at hand. It makes no difference at the outset, therefore, whether "the law" involved is biblical, the natural law, the law of being, the law of Christ, or the faces of starving children on the television screen. It is the way the communication functions, its "use," that matters. The assumption we fallen humans make is that the law is the way, that we can be saved by response to a demand, by "the works of the law." We assume we can end the voice by acceding to its demands.

The question about justification meets this universal human assumption head-on. No doubt that is one reason discussion of justification is central in the dogmatic treatment of Christian life. Here the issue is joined in the clearest fashion. How are we justified? How are we made just? How does the voice end? What does God's act in Christ have to do with it? Taken literally according to common meaning, the term "justification" would mean "make just" (*iustum facere*) according to the law or standard in question. The natural assumption is that justification is some sort of movement from the state of being unjust to the state of being just, from the state of sin or guilt to the state of righteousness. Taking the law as the way leads to interpreting justification as change, progress, process.

The New Testament, however, throws up insurmountable roadblocks along such a way. Taken as a whole, the New Testament is a sustained polemic against "the righteous." It is impossible to avoid that fact. It is not simply Paul who conducts the polemic, even if he brings it to its sharpest and most

penetrating focus. Everywhere the idea that we are justified
by our efforts under the law is attacked. The attack apparently
stems from Jesus himself. He came to call not the righteous but
sinners. The publican, not the Pharisee, was justified. Virtually
everything Jesus did was (rightly) interpreted by the "righteous" as polemic against them, who thought of the law as a
way to God. It is indeed true that only the righteous can enjoy
fellowship with God. But, according to the New Testament, the
righteousness available before God can never be reached by
the law, by responding to the demand. Paul was only bringing
into sharp focus the entire New Testament message when he
declared justification to be by faith in God's act in Christ. Justification is solely God's doing.

> But now the righteousness of God has been manifested apart
> from the law, although the law and the prophets bear witness
> to it, the righteousness of God through faith in Jesus Christ
> for all who believe. For there is no distinction; since all have
> sinned and fall short of the glory of God, they are justified by
> his grace as a gift, through the redemption which is in Christ
> Jesus, whom God put forward as an expiation by his blood,
> to be received by faith. This was to show God's righteousness,
> because in his divine forbearance he had passed over former
> sins; it was to prove at the present time that he himself is righ-
> teous and that he justifies him who has faith in Jesus. (Rom.
> 3:21–26)

Exegetes may argue that Paul's statements on the matter
are the most extreme and radical in the New Testament and
that one can find milder ones elsewhere. Such speculation may
be of exegetical interest but cannot be determinative for dogmatics. Dogmatics must be able to cope with the most sharply
focused and radical statements. If Paul is the most radical, then
dogmatics must cope with Paul and cannot search for milder
forms merely to soothe its tastes; the so-called plurality of the

New Testament message cannot be used dogmatically to escape the offense of its most radical formulations. Justification comes entirely apart from the law. Everyone is in exactly the same situation: *All* have sinned and fallen short of the glory of God. God shows *God's own* righteousness in justifying those who have faith in the crucified and risen Jesus. Justification is by such faith alone.

What does such justification mean, and what is its impact on our lives? It is immediately apparent that its proclamation is a severe challenge to our natural assumptions about justification as a "making just" according to our schemes of justice. It radically questions our ideas of progress and process. Paul was blunt about it. Justification by faith in Jesus means death and resurrection. It means death to the sinner, the old being "under the law," and life and freedom to the new. The being who thinks in terms of law dies in order that the believer might arise.

> For I through the law died to the law, that I might live to God. I have been crucified with Christ; it is no longer I who live, but Christ who lives in me; and the life I now live in the flesh I live by faith in the Son of God, who loved me and gave himself for me. I do not nullify the grace of God; for if justification were through the law, then Christ died to no purpose. (Gal. 2:19–21)

Such death and newness of life are Paul's answer also to the faint of heart who fear that radical leave-taking from law and its schemes will lead to immorality and license.

> Are we to continue in sin that grace may abound? By no means! How can we who died to sin still live in it? Do you not know that all of us who have been baptized into Christ Jesus were baptized into his death? We were buried therefore with him by baptism into death, so that as Christ was raised from the dead by the glory of the Father, we too might walk in newness of life. (Rom. 6:1–4)

The Christian life begins with baptism, with dying in Christ to the old life under law so that we might walk in newness of life, the life of faith. Paul knows that justification by faith raises the most radical questions. He puts the questions in the most radical form himself: Is the law bad? Shall we sin that grace may abound? Paul knows that unless the question is raised, we have not yet glimpsed what justification by faith is about and have not yet broken from the law. Paul also knows that one *cannot* answer the question by a return to the law. Shall we sin that grace may abound? One cannot say, "No, of course not, because there is still, after all, the law. . . ." One can only go straight ahead: You have died. How can you still manage to sin? Justification by faith means death and newness of life, a break with the past and a new beginning.

The history of the tradition shows that the church has had difficulty coping with the radicality of its own message at this point. It is fair to say, by way of generalization, that there were two attempts prior to the Reformation. One, found in the Greek fathers and in Eastern Christianity, works with the idea of divinization (*theōsis*): the elevation of the human into the sphere of the divine union with God. The other, characteristic of the Latin fathers and Western Christianity, works with ideas of law, satisfaction, and justice: becoming righteous with the aid of divine grace. In many ways the first, the idea of divinization bears the most promise and is closer to the views that eventually surfaced in the sixteenth-century Reformation. This is so because such a view stresses the radical newness that comes through participation in the divine, the creative "energies" unleashed for salvation in the resurrection of the crucified one. The human person is assumed into the internal life of God.[1] We are new beings in Christ by participation in the power of his life, apart from the law, and not so much by becoming good through our own efforts.

However, there are indications that even with such formulations the radicality of the New Testament message can be obscured and betrayed. It is not always clear in the Greek fathers whether the God in whom one participates is actually the *triune* God of the Scriptures rather than the God of, say, Plato or Plotinus. The human subject to be divinized seems to be a continuously existing substance who does not die to be raised in the incarnate, dying, and rising Son but is rather rescued *from* death to be gradually divinized. Thus divinization can all too easily come to be looked on as another process of gradual transformation, according to an ontological scheme not seriously interrupted by the *death* of Christ and the consequent *death* of the sinner, the Old Being. Where that is the case, the God in whom we participate is not the triune God but the God of the philosophers.

The manner in which the theology of divinization can then simply become another theology of works becomes evident when it is confronted with questions of morality and ethics—the perennial test case where bad conscience forces true colors into view. The following can suffice to say what happens:

> It is important to note that according to the Eastern Christian theology, the Incarnation means an ontological (i.e., physical and appropriate to human nature and being) superelevation, which, however, must also express itself ethically. Therefore good deeds of man are a *conditio sine qua non* of divinization. Thus a moral life and divinization are the two inseparable poles of Redemption. If one of them is given up, the whole structure necessarily collapses. Thus divinization entails very many existential, moral, ontological and inter-Personal implications, as well as inseparable unity of ontology and ethics.[2]

If such is the case, the theology of divinization is not decisively different from similar systems that developed in the West.

Where the incursion of the divine into the human does not mean the actual death of the old and the resurrection of the new, the tendency is to set up a way of salvation that is simply a synthesis with human religious ambition.

In the West, with its concern for law, righteousness, and justice, the problems of coping with the radicality of the New Testament message have been more overt only because the theology was less subtle. The basic presupposition has been that the law is the eternal standard according to which justice, righteousness, and salvation are measured and gained. Yet the task of squaring this presupposition with justification by faith, by grace alone, has caused continuous uneasiness. From the beginning, the tradition has wavered between rigorism and laxness, asceticism and indulgence. Unable to dislodge the law as the way, the Western tradition has attempted the impossible: to combine justification by faith with moral progress according to law. Instead of being a justification *apart* from the law, God's act is reinterpreted as a justification *according* to the law. God's act in Christ is looked on as providing "grace" to enable one to do the law and, at least in some respect, acquire merit toward salvation. Grace becomes a thing of some sort—even if of a very "spiritual" sort—a power or virtue or habit that is infused to enable those who avail themselves of it to go the way demanded in the law. Since this kind of combination of law and grace has been dominant in the West, we shall concern ourselves predominantly with it in the remainder of our treatment.

The movement toward combination reaches its finest expression in the great medieval syntheses like that of Thomas Aquinas. Justification is described as a *movement* from a *terminus a quo* (starting point) to a *terminus ad quem* (goal), that is, as a process. The movement is comprised of (a) the infusion of grace, (b) the movement of the free will toward God in faith, (c) a movement of the free will in recoil from sin, and (d) the remission of guilt.[3] The difficulty in defining justification as such a process is apparent from the scheme itself. Where does justification occur? With the infusion of grace or with the remission of sins? Aquinas tries to escape the difficulty by saying that the movement "could be called" justification because every movement takes its character from its end, the *terminus ad quem*. Furthermore, the movement is to be understood as instantaneous temporally. Nevertheless, it can be understood only as indeed a movement, a change in the moral subject from sin to righteousness, effected by the infusion of grace.[4]

The dogmatic distinctions only thinly veil the systematic problem involved in attempts to combine justification by grace with the idea of moral movement or process. In its simplest form the problem may be stated thus: If justification conceived as forgiveness comes at the beginning of the process, the process is superfluous (why undertake the process if one already has been given what is expected?); if, on the other hand, justification comes at the end of the process, justification is superfluous (why the need to be made or declared just if one has become so?). Both the divine act of justification and the human process of becoming just according to law cannot simultaneously be real. The attempt to put them together in the same scheme can only have the effect of rendering one of them superfluous or fictional. Given the entrenchment of law, conscience, and process, we need not waste time guessing which. History has relieved us of the necessity to speculate in any case. Law has remained the reality, the structural and determining factor for the Christian life; grace has become more or less fictional, a matter of pious talk whose relevance is eventually questionable.

The outcome of the attempted synthesis has been disastrous for the Christian life. Grace functions only as an anti-Pelagian codicil to make the scheme verbally Christian.[5] Our work and "cooperation" are the essential thing, even though we cover our tracks by *saying*, "Of course, it is all by grace." Every Christian dogmatic claims to hold justification by faith. Even Pelagius did so. It is, after all, a biblical doctrine, and one can hardly afford to deny it. But it is effectively reduced to a mere verbalism. Pelagius was more honest than the subsequent tradition when he denied the idea of a supernatural "substantial" grace altogether and equated grace with natural endowment and teaching.

Further, the attempt to synthesize justification by faith with the scheme of law and process can only mean that grace so conceived will tend to undercut and militate against works. Again, Pelagius was the one to see this clearly and to move against such grace. The church, of course, could not follow Pelagius since that would have meant the demise of grace altogether. The result is a Christian life suspended between grace *and* works, not knowing which way to turn. The church has vacillated between rigorism and laxness, legalism and liberty, asceticism and eudaemonism, self-denial and self-indulgence. The problem was apparent already in the early enthusiasts and gnostics. One could go either way. If law is the way, being Christian could mean that everything the law demanded was given—that the "resurrected life" or gnostic "spirituality" was already achieved—so that one could henceforth do as one pleased. Grace then makes works unnecessary. Indeed, one might further one's cause by a kind of negative asceticism: wearing out "the flesh" by profligate living, a kind of moral suicide practiced, apparently, by some gnostics. On the other hand, being Christian could mean just the opposite. Grace cannot displace the legal process. Grace is at best a help to fulfill the law; judgment is still outstanding. An ascetic life is the best insurance. One purges the flesh to rescue the spirit. One may attribute whatever success one has to "grace," but the works are primary. Grace becomes a verbalism, a fiction.

The vacillation has been apparent from the early schisms—Novatianism, Donatism, Montanism—to the present day.[6] The church knows it is commissioned to preach forgiveness and justification, but seems never able to have a clear conscience in doing so. Rigorist schismatics and "holiness" movements incarnate the bad conscience created when "too much" forgiveness or grace vitiates the resolve under law. So the church opts, willy-nilly, for a place in between. It pronounces forgiveness but demands penance. It forgives the eternal aspect of sin, but not the temporal. It places itself in the position of having to dole out grace in portions that it deems will not be harmful to the legalistic process. It becomes the administrator *over* grace, dispensing merits from its treasury to the deserving. The rhetoric about the Christian life piles up—often in innocent and well-meaning ways—to ensure the process against failure.

Justification by Faith

The attempt to synthesize justification and the legal process works only as long as it is not seriously questioned, that is, as long as the conscience it awakens is not too honest. The Christian life it fosters can be all too much like the emperor's new clothes in Hans Christian Andersen's tale. Its righteousness exists largely in the imagination of subjects afraid to question the authorities and risk exposing their own failure or inability to play the game. When someone naive or honest enough to speak the truth appears, the charade is over. This is what happens when reformation, most often under the influence of the radical New Testament gospel, occurs in the church. Reformation has happened and must happen again and again. Since the Reformation of the sixteenth century affords the classic example, we shall use that as the starting point for dismantling the synthesis between justification and law, suggesting "justification by faith" as an alternative basis for the Christian life.

Martin Luther experienced the failure of the synthesis in his own conscience. He applied himself to every resource to get the grace necessary to improve, but found in all honesty that nothing worked. The rhetoric just did not match the reality. When grace is a thing, a "virtue" supposedly available by prescribed channels, and when one is supposed to be justified (improved) by such grace, one is then simply excluded if one is honest enough to admit that the improvement has not, in fact, occurred. One can come to either of two conclusions, and perhaps to a bit of both. Either one has not turned the key to the channels of grace (one has not worked hard enough, applied oneself enough) or, more serious yet, God, the giver, the electing one, has simply decided not to give it. The "terrors of predestination" are the ultimate outcome of the attempt to synthesize God's act of justification with human progress under law. Unable to verify progress, one can only conclude that God has turned thumbs down.

The system turns against the seeker precisely at the point of greatest need. When justification means improvement and grace is the power to improve, "justification by grace" is potentially and finally very bad news for sinners. Regardless of the degree to which the rhetoric stresses the primacy of grace, one is thrown back on one's own resources. "Cooperation" and improvement under the system means that *everything* eventually depends on the human contribution. One can say that grace goes before, during, and after the action. One can say that grace provides 99.44 percent or even 100 percent of the power. It makes no difference. Everything will hinge on what the sinner is supposed to do. The synthesis is useless when it is needed most. A grace rendered fictional cannot help. That is what Luther discovered.

The assertion of "justification *by faith*" in the sixteenth-century Reformation can be understood only if it is clearly seen as a complete break with "justification *by grace*" viewed according to the synthesis we have been describing, as a complete break with the attempt to view justification as a movement according to a given standard or law, either natural or revealed. For the reformers, justification is "solely" a divine act. It is a divine judgment. It is an imputation. It is unconditional. All legal and moral schemes are shattered. Such justification comes neither at the beginning nor at the end of a movement; rather, it establishes an entirely new situation. Since righteousness comes by imputation only, it is absolutely not a movement on our part, either with or without the aid of what was previously termed "grace." The judgment can be heard and grasped only by faith. Indeed, the judgment creates and calls forth the faith that hears and grasps it. One will mistake the reformation point if one does not see that justification "by faith" is in the first instance precisely a polemic *against* justification "*by grace*" according to the medieval scheme. Grace would have to be completely redefined before the word could be safely used in a reformation sense.[7]

Justification by divine imputation is grace for sinners. Indeed, we can be candidates for such righteousness only if we are sinners—and completely so. For Luther that meant that in place of all human schemes of movement from sin to righteousness we must put the absolute simultaneity of sin and righteousness. Imputed righteousness as a divine act brings with it the *simul iustus et peccator* (simultaneously justified and a sinner) as a simultaneity of total states. We must take care in grasping what is being said here. The *simul iustus et peccator* is not a conclusion drawn from a bad conscience under the legal system; it is not resignation to the fact that no matter how hard we try we never quite make it. That would put us back in the same scheme as before. The confession that we are sinners at the same time as we are justified is a conclusion drawn from the divine action, the divine imputation and forgiveness. The simultaneity of sin and righteousness as total states is the *actual* situation revealed by the divine act of justification. The divine act itself shatters all human presumption about progress and process. God has something else in mind.

This is readily apparent from a look at Luther's lectures on Romans, where the *simul iustus et peccator* is first set forth. Commenting on Rom. 4:1–7, Luther maintains that imputation of righteousness to Abraham and its equation with forgiveness of sins can be understood only in terms of the simultaneity of sin and righteousness.[8] If God *imputes* righteousness, if God simply *forgives* sin, then we *must* be sinners. It would make no sense for God to impute righteousness if we were partially or wholly righteous already. God would be wasting breath. Thus in order for *God* to be "justified when he speaks and true when he judges" we must be sinners *at the same time* as God's speaking makes us righteous. One is justified by hearing and believing God's judgment, and such hearing and believing lead to the realization and confession that we *are* sinners. We are unmasked by the overpowering divine judgment. The love given reveals, at the same time, how unlovely we are. Only on the strength of the love given could we see and face the truth simultaneously.

Luther's understanding of the *simul* is a radical attack on human ideas of progress according to the law. At the outset in the commentary on Romans he suggests a major revision of the fundamental scheme. "The exodus of the people of Israel has for a long time been interpreted to signify the transition from vice to virtue. But one should, rather, interpret it as the way from virtue to the grace of Christ." The Christian life is not an exodus from vice *to* virtue, but *from* virtue, to the grace of Christ! "Because," Luther continues, "virtues are often the greater and worse faults the less they are regarded as such and the more powerfully they subject to themselves all human affections beyond all other goods."[9] The more the pursuit of virtue succeeds in absorbing all desires and affections, the more dangerous it becomes.

Thus, for Luther the most vital enemy of the righteousness of God is not so much the "godless sinner" as the "righteous" who are absorbed in their own ideas of law and moral progress. Such theologians think, Luther says, "*ad modum Aristotelis*" (after the fashion of Aristotle), where the gaining of righteousness means acquiring virtue and removing sin.[10] For such thinking, imputation could only be a kind of legal fiction or manner of speaking, due to the incompleteness of the process or "in view of its end." Imputation is a kind of temporary loan until righteousness is *really* earned. Against this pattern, Luther sets an entirely different sort of thinking: a thinking "*ad modum scripturae*" (in the scriptural mode), in which the divine imputation is the creative reality which by the very fact of imputation unmasks its opposition, the reality and totality of sin, *at the same time*. If God is to be justified when he speaks, all thinking, speaking, and judging *ad modum Aristotelis* must be banished from theology. Before the divine tribunal no saints, only sinners, appear.[11] Justification by divine imputation creating faith is a complete break with the exodus from vice to virtue because the divine imputation is fully as opposed to human righteousness as it is to unrighteousness.

The divine imputation *makes* us sinners at the same time as it declares us righteous. Luther was insistent that at the outset these be understood as total states. This requires a radical reorientation in thinking about the Christian life. It destroys our usual notions of moral progress. The point is that we *can* be saved *only* by listening to and believing God and God's judgment. We can be saved only by faith in what God says about us and our final destiny. Viewed *coram deo* (before God), our virtues are no better than our vices. The difference is only a matter of taste. Some like vice and some like virtue; both do what *they* like. And virtue may be the more dangerous precisely because it gains everyone's approval. Sin is revealed by the absolutely unconditional nature of the divine action. Sin is revealed as a totality, not a partiality: of our virtues as well as our vices. We begin to see that the attempt to gain virtue was fully as reprehensible as the pursuit of vice. One attempt is no more inspired by the love of God than the other. When we begin to believe God and God's judgment, sin is unmasked simultaneously. When God says, "I forgive you. I declare you just for Jesus' sake," sin is unmasked and attacked at once. To be justified by faith is to believe *God's* word, God's judgment, and to begin to realize that only that word will save. The divine judgment, the divine word, is a totality, complete, unconditional, creative in and of itself. It unmasks and attacks its opposite. When one recognizes by the power of the divine judgment that one is *simul iustus et peccator*, the real battle for the Christian life can begin. Sin as a total state can be fought only by faith in total imputed righteousness. Anything less would lead to hypocrisy or despair.

Justification by faith always appears dangerous, because of our incurable tendency to think in terms of law, virtue, and moral progress. Church people, religious people and their teachers, are especially inclined to think that way. Hence justification by faith generally has most difficulty precisely in the church. It is more apparent there than elsewhere, perhaps, that we live "under" the law. Hence the church always seems to stumble when it comes to this doctrine. It fails to realize that this incurable disease is precisely what we have to be saved *from*.

Nevertheless, the sentiment that justification by faith is dangerous is, in a way other than expected, quite right. That is because justification by divine unconditional decree spells death to the old being. Like the demons who recognized Jesus, the "old Adam" rightly senses that in justification the end breaks in—the end to the pursuit either of vice or virtue. That is precisely why it is so feared. Resistance takes all sorts of guises. Justification by faith is said to be "too cheap," to lead to moral laxity and ethical quietism, to erode human responsibility. Justification is only for people with morbid and introspective consciences, not for the healthy and robust. The ruses are all quite true, of course, as long as one accepts the old Adam's premises and tries to subordinate grace to law. But in essence they are nothing but attempts to stave off the death of the old. They are defense mechanisms against the grace of the One who died and rose for us, defense mechanisms against justification for his sake. Justification is dangerous indeed. It spells death to the old. But only then will there be newness of life.

Somehow the church has rarely realized the radical nature and power of this message of justification. It has trembled on the brink of freedom and then turned back. The reason must lie in our incurable tendency to think in terms of "something to do." If "doing the law" is hard enough, how can we die? Language about death and new life is *terra incognita* left largely to ascetics and mystics. Death of the old comes to be looked on as a particularly strenuous exercise in "self-denial" and "purgation of the flesh," the ultimate in spiritual exercises, preparatory to final "mystical vision." But that is simply to turn death into another law. Spirituality becomes the art of getting as close to suicide as one dares.

The failure has been to realize that the divine pronouncement of justification for Jesus' sake *is* the death and the new life. To believe the message of justification *is* to die and be raised to newness of life. Justification as imputation for Jesus' sake declares precisely that there is nothing to do. It is unconditional. To die is to be put in the situation of being able to do nothing, to be absolutely passive, to wait for the word: "Awake, O sleeper, and arise from the dead, and Christ shall give you light" (Eph. 5:14). The word of justification is precisely that kind of word. It kills the old exactly because it pronounces that there is nothing to do. Faith is to believe that and to be raised from the destruction of all our schemes, to something new. Faith is to be delivered, to participate in the exodus from virtue to the grace of God.

Therefore faith that believes the justifying act of God *is* death and resurrection. It is to be delivered from life under the law to something utterly new. Paul does not present death as one more thing to do. He simply announces the accomplished fact:

> We are convinced that one has died for all; therefore all have died. (2 Cor. 5:14)
> We were buried therefore with him by baptism into death, so that as Christ was raised from the dead by the glory of the Father, we too might walk in newness of life. (Rom. 6:4)
> I through the law died to the law, that I might live to God. I have been crucified with Christ; it is no longer I who live, but Christ who lives in me; and the life I now live in the flesh I live by faith in the Son of God, who loved me and gave himself for me. (Gal. 2:19–20)

The divine judgment flowing from the death and resurrection of Jesus, the word of forgiveness and justification pronounced for his sake, *is* the doing of death and resurrection to us. The faith created by that word *is* the death and resurrection. Luther knew it too:

> "I am crucified with Christ." Paul adds this word because he wants to explain how the law is devoured by the law [Christ]. If Christ is crucified to the law, so also am I. How? *Through faith.* I am crucified to the law; I have nothing more to do with it, because I am crucified to it and vice versa, because I have died with Christ *through grace itself and faith (per ipsam gratiam et fidem). . . . If you believe in Christ then you are co-crucified through faith spiritually,* just as he is dead to the law, to death,

etc. Paul is not speaking here of the *imitatio*, which means to *become* co-crucified. That happens in the flesh, as Peter (1 Pet. 2:21) says: "Christ suffered for you and left you an example that you should follow in his steps." Here Paul does not speak of that crucifixion, but of the primary co-crucifixion by which the devil and death are crucified. Where? In Christ, not in me. That crucifixion by which I die to the law is resurrection, because Christ has killed my death and bound up my law. *And I believe that.*[12]

To believe in Christ *is* precisely to die to the old and be raised to the new. It is not an action, an "imitating" (though that comes later "in the flesh"), but simply an "undergoing," a being slain and raised up by the word. It must not be looked on, however, as figurative or symbolic. The death inflicted by the word of justification which reduces us to nothing is the real death, the true spiritual death. It is so because it is the death of sin, the death of all defiance against the God who will have mercy. It is the death of death, because the believer survives in Christ. "It is no longer I who live, but Christ who lives in me." Indeed, Luther can say that the only thing to which the word "death" really and truly applies is sin. Because of Christ, sin will die and never return. Only of sin can that be said.[13] The other death, the physical death we must die, Luther calls *das Todlein* (the little death).[14] The spiritual death encountered in the word of justification is the real death. To survive that is to be raised to newness of life. Rejection of it, refusal of the totality and the reality of it, is to allow the old Adam to continue his own way to whatever death awaits him. We *can* be justified only by faith.

If justification thus conceived brings death and newness of life, it is basically an eschatological act. The breakup of the legal scheme and accompanying ideas of human progress means that a new reality is introduced: the eschatological kingdom, the new being in Christ.

That realm of judgment in which the situation of our being as sinner is so totally depotentiated is nothing other than the kingdom of the last things. In the final analysis it is this and the coming aeon that stand opposed to each other in the *simul iustus et peccator*. The person in Christ is the person of the new age. The judgment of God which proclaims this person as established over against the opposing earthly situation is likewise the anticipatory proclamation of the new world. The faith which receives and grasps that new status in Christ is an eschatological event; it is ever and anew the step out of this world of the visible, tangible, given reality, the world in which the *totus peccator* is the reality, into the eschaton.[15]

Justification as death and resurrection, as an eschatological event, means that the question about the Christian life must be posed anew, from a radically different vantage point. If we are robbed of our plans and ideals under the law, we seem suddenly to have lost our reason for being. The ground has been cut out from under our feet. If justification means suddenly being told there is nothing we have to do, if we come up against just that death, what are we to do? We must see that this is a real question. It is possible that we might not survive such an act of justification. It could ruin us. It is from this vantage point that Paul's question, *the* question about the Christian life, is launched: Shall we sin the more that grace may abound? What shall we then do? What is the way forward from here? We shall have to take up these questions in our subsequent chapters. Before we do, we must begin to ask about the place of law in the light of this gospel of justification.

Law, Gospel, and Conscience

Justification by faith "apart from the works of the law" is a radical questioning of the place of law in the dogmatic system. Law is disenfranchised as a way of salvation.

> The righteousness of God has been manifested apart from law, although the law and the prophets bear witness to it, the righteousness of God through faith in Jesus Christ for all who believe. (Rom. 3:21–22)
>
> For Christ is the end of the law, that every one who has faith may be justified. (Rom. 10:4)
>
> If a law had been given which could make alive, then righteousness would indeed be by the law. (Gal. 3:21)
>
> Now before faith came, we were confined under law, kept under restraint until faith should be revealed. . . . But now that faith has come, we are no longer under a custodian; for in Christ Jesus you are all sons of God, through faith. (Gal. 3:23, 25)[16]

Grasped by the gospel, one sees immediately that the law is not the way and that no synthesis is possible. There is an end and a new beginning. The slave has become a son and heir (Gal. 4:1–7). A death has occurred, so that the wife is no longer bound by law to the husband but is free to remarry without being charged with adultery. "Likewise, my brethren, you have died to the law through the body of Christ so that you may belong to another, to him who has been raised from the dead. . . . We are discharged from the law, dead to that which held us captive" (Rom. 7:1–6).

Such an eschatological gospel raises shattering questions about law, about the basic structures and presuppositions of life "in this age." It is important to see that it is the unconditional, eschatological nature of the gospel itself that does this. The particular makeup and problems of individuals and their conscience—of a Paul, an Augustine, a Luther, or whomever—have nothing to do with the matter. The new marks the end of the old. One cannot put new wine in old skins. Anyone grasped by the gospel will have to put the questions. Paul put them himself with a radicality and seriousness hardly surpassable. "What then shall we say? That the law is sin?" (Rom.

7:7). "Is the law then against the promises of God?" (Gal. 3:21). "Do we then overthrow the law by this faith?" (Rom. 3:31).

Paul answers his own questions in each instance with a resounding negative: "By no means!" "On the contrary, we uphold the law" (Rom. 3:31). Paul can answer with that resounding negative, however, only because in the light of the gospel the place and function of the law are fundamentally redefined and because in the redefinition the law is actually strengthened and established. The law was "added because of transgressions, till the offspring should come to whom the promise had been made" (Gal. 3:19). It is not the way itself; that is precisely why it is not against the promises. The promises are the way; they alone "make alive"; they alone are intended to do so. "If a law had been given which could make alive, then righteousness would indeed be by the law" (Gal. 3:21). Then indeed the law and the promises would be diametrically opposed, and the promise would destroy law or vice versa. "If justification were through the law, then Christ died to no purpose" (Gal. 2:21).

The law has a function quite other than the promise. The law was given to make apparent the trespass, to reveal and convict of sin, to expose the fundamental lostness and incompleteness of life without promise, life without God, without future. "Before faith came, we were confined under the law, kept under restraint until faith should be revealed. So that the law was our custodian until Christ came, that we might be justified by faith" (Gal. 3:23–24). The law makes apparent our incompleteness; it "confines," shuts in, does the work of the custodian, making plain that the goal has not been reached. The law makes sin apparent. "If it had not been for the law, I should not have known sin" (Rom. 7:7).

This functional description of the law must not be understood in a psychologizing sense, as though it were merely a matter of an overly sensitive "introspective conscience" being afflicted and convicted by the law so that one is convinced that one needs salvation. That would mean only that the system based on law and conscience remained intact: One is convicted of one's vices and misdeeds under the law and driven to despair over the inability to be virtuous so that one cries for the help of grace in one's *own* quest. In all that the old Adam remains quite intact—shaken, perhaps even "despairing," but still intact. The cry of the conscience-stricken old Adam is still just the last grasp at the self and its quest for virtue. If one cannot make it on one's own, perhaps one can commandeer "help" by being sorry enough. Repentance is looked on as an act—the last attempt of the old Adam to rescue itself from shipwreck. Consequently, such repentance may well be only for the morbid and overly sensitive failures of the system, not for the robust.

Such psychologizing does not get at the question of *sin*. It may reveal a few sins; but they are mostly peccadilloes, the little vices or hindrances that frustrate our quests for virtue. Righteousness is still by the law, and Christ still died to no purpose. When Paul, and all serious reformers in the church, said that without the law sin would be unknown, something much more radical was meant. The claim must be seen *theologically* precisely within the context of the argument about justification by faith. When Paul, for instance, in Rom. 7:7ff., uses the law "You shall not covet" as an example, claiming that the very law awakened "all kinds of covetousness" in him, that is not to be understood merely in the psychological sense that prohibition feeds the fires of lust and desire for forbidden fruit. That hardly explains Paul's meaning when he goes on to say that sin, "finding opportunity in the commandment, wrought in me all kinds of covetousness" and that "apart from the law sin lies dead." Paul can hardly mean that without the law he would not lust after this or that and that such sin comes into being only when the law forbids it. The point rather is that the law, the prohibition of vice, even when heeded, leads only to the pursuit of virtue *apart from the promise*, in defiance of the gift of mercy. I am not cured of covetousness by the law at all. Now I covet virtue; I embark on the path of self-righteousness, self-salvation. Sin as refusal of God's mercy, of God's justification for Jesus' sake, is awakened precisely by the law. The law tempts me to go it by myself.

The law, therefore, exposes *sin*, not just sins. Not just our little failures over which we might despair in our covetousness of virtue are uncovered, but sin itself: the quest of self-salvation and whatever success we may think we have achieved. What is revealed is that sin dwells in us, that we are "sold" to it, and cannot escape. Our failures as well as our successes are only different kinds of covetousness. That is why Paul can say, "Apart from the law sin lies dead" and "I was once alive apart from the law, but when the commandment came, *sin* revived and I died; the very commandment which promised life proved to be death to me. For *sin*, finding opportunity in the commandment, deceived me and by it killed me" (Rom. 7:8–11). The law, given the fact of sin, could, even though it is holy, just, and good, do nothing but awaken more sin. And this is the function of the law, "in order that sin might be shown to be sin, and through the commandment might become sinful beyond measure." What is revealed thereby is not that the law is sin but precisely that the law is good and "spiritual" and that "I am carnal, sold under sin." I can will what is right and good, perhaps, but I simply cannot do it. For "under the law" I cannot escape being a covetous being. Sin dwells in me. Encounter with the law makes that plain. I can hear and approve, thus acknowledging the goodness of the law; but I can in no way do it. Thus, I do what I do not want, so "it is no longer I that do it, but sin which dwells within me"—the point being not that I am thereby exonerated, but that I am condemned because I see that the law is good while I am sold under sin.

Precisely in this manner the law is upheld and established. Once its function is seen in the light of the message of justification by faith, it stands forth in pristine clarity and beauty. Only when one tries to mix law and gospel, only when one thinks that righteousness comes by the law, will the law be disestablished. Then the law will have to be reduced to manageable proportions. One will have to indulge in casuistry to make it applicable to this or that case. One cannot let it sound. Instead of letting it function to reveal sin, it is used to mask sin. Thus it is watered down, tamed, neutralized.

The Reformation's insistence on justification by faith as an eschatological event brought with it a reassertion of the functional understanding of law. Luther especially insisted that law must be clearly distinguished from gospel and the proper "uses" of the law carefully explained. The distinction between law and gospel and the doctrine of the uses of law are of primary importance because they contain the key to virtually everything we want to say subsequently about the Christian life.

The basic distinction between law and gospel should be clear, since we have been talking about it all along. The law is not the way of salvation, and the gospel is something quite other than law. What good then is the law? Paul has provided an answer: The law functions to unmask sin. The sixteenth-century reformers started from this and extended it to a more formal doctrine of the "uses of the law." Since the first formulations, there has been debate about whether there are two or three uses of the law. Luther, it seems, generally spoke explicitly only of two,[17] whereas Melanchthon and later reformers spoke of three. They are, in chronological order rather than order of importance, (1) the political use (to restrain evil and preserve order), (2) the theological use (to expose and convict of sin), and (3) the use in the life of the reborn (to guide Christian living). Here we shall treat only the theological use (the most important for the Lutheran reformers), since that follows directly from our argument, reserving discussion of the others for subsequent chapters of our *locus*.

For Luther, as for Paul, justification by faith means complete reassessment of the place of the law. If law and gospel were both ways of salvation, one or the other of them would have to give way. Since, however, gospel is the way, law must be seen in an entirely different light. Only thus will it be truly established. Its use is not to provide a way of salvation. It is not an eternal ontological structure providing a way to final reward, ratified and legitimated in the individual conscience. Its use is to reveal, unmask, and convict of sin. It says, "No exit!" It makes absolutely final the fact that we can be saved only by faith in the justifying word which comes quite apart from the law. *Lex semper accusat* (the law always accuses).[18]

Once again, this is not to be understood in a psychologizing way. Perhaps the most convenient way to get at the issue is to approach it in terms of the question of conscience. Invariably, in a world turned in on itself, talk about the accusing function of the law is psychologized in terms of the modern understanding of the introspective conscience. Karl Holl, the father of much modern Luther research, added to the difficulty by characterizing Luther's religion as a *Gewissensreligion* (religion of conscience).[19] Talk about the accusing function of the law was thereby drawn into the Kantian and Freudian trap. The picture is that conscience sets up a certain order, a "categorical imperative" perhaps, an unimpeachable "ought" under which we stand. This "ought" is then taken as the voice of God—or at least as an echo, however faint, thereof. When this voice awakens feelings of guilt, one is supposed to turn to Christ for relief. The accusing function of the law ostensibly fits this scheme. It produces the guilt by appealing to the conscience, so that one will turn to Christ. If Christ does not salve the conscience, one will then have to turn elsewhere: to the psychiatrist's couch, or to some other stratagem, to Nietzsche's posit of the "superman," to denial of "god" altogether, to nihilism, or whatever. Holl was wrong, however, as is every tendency to treat the issues involved here in this internalizing way. Christ becomes a mere "help" to make the system work. But then we only become further mired in the quicksands of conscience. That is the sad tale of the modern world.

The accusing function of law vis-à-vis the conscience must be seen in the light of what we have discovered about the gospel of justification by faith. The sin which the law reveals and convicts of is precisely the sin of the system proposed by "conscience": the idea that there *is* a way of virtue by which the accusing voice could be stilled. That such virtue is to be gotten with the aid of Christ makes little difference. The scheme is simply another variation of the attempt to synthesize law and gospel. A Christ who is supposed to help the system of virtue set up by conscience will never cease to accuse. Such a Christ will soon have to be brushed aside. This too the modern world knows well. The law which accuses in the true sense is a reflection of justification by faith. What it reveals is that there is no way, no system of virtue by which the voice of conscience can be stilled. Not even Christ or "grace" can help one acquire enough virtue to do that. The law reveals that not only our vices but also the very quest for virtue condemn us; for also the quest is a denial of the God who justifies by faith. The law accuses *finally*, so that there can be an end and a new beginning.

Conscience must be seen in the light of faith. As Luther put it, *Christ* must reign in the conscience. Law does not belong there at all. We can be saved only by simply believing the promise of God. One must just be still and listen. "Conscience" and the "stern voice of duty" will insist that this is "too cheap," "too easy," and a thousand other things, and summon us back to the battle for virtue. But that is just the problem. To succumb to that voice is precisely to lose: to lose Christ and return to the self. The law returns to the conscience. Sin finds its opportunity in the very goodness of the commandment, as Paul put it. One can be saved from sin for good works, *only* by faith. Christ and his unconditional grace must reign in the conscience. There *is* no other way. Everything must begin and end by simply trusting that word which says, "*You* are mine and I will never let you go."

The point, therefore, is that the law must be expelled from the conscience by Christ and kept out in faith. The law may have its legitimate place in ruling "the flesh"—that will be the subject of a later chapter—but only Christ belongs in the conscience. The person God intends is the person of faith who is one person, "one cake," with Christ.[20] One is delivered over to conscience in the moment one desires to be a personality in and of oneself. The helplessness of the sinner over against conscience is grounded in this insistence on being-for-oneself, in the modern conception of the personality as that which stands on and lives out of itself and its own internality. Left to oneself, one is at the mercy of conscience and its fickleness and unpredictability. Who knows when and in what form, however preposterous, it will attack? Conscience is in that sense indeed a reality, but a reality to which one is delivered only in separation from God. It is like the thirst of the alcoholic or the desire of the addict. It was meant for good, but since it has lost its good, it is arbitrary and insatiable and drives only to death.[21]

Conscience is not therefore just an "introspective" affair in which one is convicted by the inviolable voice of the law within and its eternal order. Conscience does not reflect order and constancy. It is insatiable, fickle, and arbitrary. It does not represent God's presence within us, it represents his absence, that we are left to ourselves. Conscience can unpredictably make mockery of any presumed freedom and emancipation. Who knows when some long-forgotten past indiscretion will return to haunt? When tragedy strikes or death draws near, what preposterous associations will not conscience make to answer our agonized and tormented "Why?" One may take steps to still the voice, usually by "works." But the voice is insatiable, especially in the face of death. "The world," Luther says, "becomes too small"[22] because of the conscience. It is not just moral law within that afflicts because of conscience. The world, all of nature without, can close in on us. A favorite of Luther's which crops up again and again is the "rustling leaf" of Lev. 26:36.

> There is nothing smaller and more ignored than a dry leaf lying on the ground crawled on by worms and unable to protect itself from the dust. . . . But when the *moment* comes, horse, rider, lance, armor, king, princes, all the strength of the army and all power is frightened by its rustling. Are we not fine people? We have no fear of God's wrath and stand proudly, but yet are terrified and flee before the wrath of an impotent dry leaf. And such rustling of the leaf makes the world too small and becomes our wrathful God, whom we otherwise poo-poo and defy in heaven and on earth.[23]

Modern Protestantism and psychologism have denaturalized and moralized conscience so that it has nothing to do with the external world. That was not the case in Paul or the reformers. For Paul, to be under the law means to be trapped by "the elemental spirits of the universe" (Gal. 4:3). For Luther the rustling leaf strikes terror, because being cut off from God we do not have life in ourselves and something out there can take it from us. Cut off from God and delivered into the grip of conscience, we cannot dispose over our lives. The conscience thus reveals to us our "being-in" the world, a world which becomes too narrow for us. Conscience makes us refugees and exiles with no place to rest. Cut off from God, conscience drives us ultimately to wish that there were no God. Apart from Christ, atheism is finally the only hope.

It is in this light that one must see the accusing function of law. To recognize that law always accuses is precisely to assign it its proper use, to fix its limit and establish it. The law must not be admitted into unholy alliance with the conscience. It must not be confused with gospel. To do so is absolutely fatal. Between the work of the law and the promise of the gospel stand the cross and the resurrection, as the absolute dividing line. The law kills the old so that the new can be raised up. One is not cajoled by law and conscience into being a better person. One is put to death as the seeker after virtue, so that one may be raised to newness of life.

This eschatological vision marks the ultimate distinction between law and gospel. Law and its function are limited to the old age. Gospel is the coming of the new. Christ takes up his place in the conscience. Law is driven out to perform its proper work elsewhere.[24]

The functional understanding of law arises therefore from the eschatological nature of the gospel. Justification by faith apart from the works of the law means a fundamentally new view of reality. For the fallen world, the law represents reality, possibility, and opportunity, the only future the world knows or can conceive of, the only known scheme that works. That is why the world clings to it so desperately. Justification by faith, however, proposes something else: the power of the in-breaking of God's kingdom in the midst of our time. The gospel, the sheer goodness and favor of God in Christ, God's complete unconditional mercy, gives possibility, not the law. The law was added "because of the trespass," the failure to see. The law accuses and kills. It reminds the world that it has fallen from its true destiny.

The law is not just "laws"; it is the voice arising from any-where and everywhere, the whole creation "groaning in tra-vail" waiting for the sons and daughters of God to appear (Rom. 8:19ff.). It is the "letter," the empty shell of a world that has lost the Spirit. It is like having to command someone to make love who has forgotten or never knew how. It is the darkness of a world that can no longer see and must have rules instead. It is the rustling of a leaf on a dark night which strikes terror and cries, "Where are you, Adam?" The very existence of law means that what it demands, what it points to, is gone; and no amount of law-preaching will bring it back. Insofar as law brings knowledge, it does not bring knowledge of the good, but knowledge of sin:

> . . . not knowledge of that which should happen, but knowledge of that which has already happened; not knowledge of open, but of excluded and lost possibilities. . . . Whether one is a Jew, or a sinner, or heathen; whether pious or godless; every mode of existence is like others in spite of all difference in that it is existence under the law. Every religion or world view, even the atheistic—also a Christianity which has been perverted from faith to an ideology—has the common structure of law. They are all against faith. For "lex est negatio Christi" (law is the negation of Christ).[25]

The understanding of law ultimately has its roots deep in the hermeneutical problem of "letter and spirit," as it is reflected in the 2 Cor. 3:6 passage: "[God] has made us competent to be ministers of a new covenant, not in a written code [letter] but in the Spirit; for the written code [letter] kills, but the Spirit gives life." Previous tradition took this passage in a Platonizing sense, to mean that the letter was only an inadequate sign, an allegory of a deeper spiritual truth. To pass from letter to spirit was the way because to remain on the level of the letter would be to die in the land of mere "appearances," where all is decay and death.

Allegorical exegesis is built on this presupposition. The mere "literal" history must be translated into "spiritual truth," into eternal verities, doctrines, and laws (above all, laws). That "the letter kills" means that the letter is inadequate, partial, a secret code to a deeper meaning. To be saved one must find the "spiritual truth." The spiritual truth, however, is only whatever form of law the spirit of the times suggests. It is the quicksands of conscience. With few exceptions the hermeneutic has remained the same to modern times. The characters may change, but the plot remains the same. Law is taken in a material and ontological sense as providing the way of salvation. That is the "secret" of the allegory, the moral of the story.

The functional understanding of law roots in a fundamentally different hermeneutic, which takes the 2 Corinthians passage at face value. The letter, the written code, the literal account kills; and the Spirit alone gives life. The letter is no secret code for the old Adam to solve, so as to find the way to life. The letter, the whole history of God with his people, leads to the cross and spells one thing for the old Adam: *death*. Only then will it mean new life in the Spirit, new life in the Second Adam. The whole text of Scripture, indeed the whole of history and creation, which becomes "too small," works in the first instance as the letter, the *opera literalia dei* (literal works of God), the "masks" of God which accuse and destroy the old Adam. The letter kills. It makes apparent that there is no way out.[26]

"Do we then overthrow the law by this faith? By no means! On the contrary, we uphold the law" (Rom. 3:31). To uphold the law means first to let it sound in its unrelenting, pristine majesty, without any "veil" (2 Cor. 3), to allow it to do its work as letter which kills. This upholding is possible, however, only because there is something else: The Spirit gives life—the *Holy* Spirit of God, not the spirit of the times. Indeed, the letter kills *so that* the Spirit can give life. In this way the exodus from virtue to the grace of God occurs. We pass through the waters of baptism, through death to life by the grace of God.

Justification by faith gives possibility; law does not. God's eschatological kingdom is humanity's tomorrow. The law must function first and foremost to cut off every other possibility. Only thus will we be reborn into the world God creates. The "letter," the story of God's struggle with his people, our story under law, must work to end every attempt to escape, every form of self-justification according to our own schemes and projects, in order to place us before the God of time to wait and to hope. The killing function of the law makes us historical beings. It cuts off every form of escape: metaphysical, religious, or psychological. That is its chief "use." Only when that happens will other uses open up as well, for only when the law kills in that fashion will we receive this world back as a gift. Only when we cease to use law as an escape for the self will we begin to see what law is for here as well. The possibility of a *Christian* life opens up.

We cannot conclude this already lengthy chapter without at least some preliminary words about the relevance and primacy of the doctrine of justification by faith in the discussion of the Christian life. It has become virtually a platitude today that justification language is hardly appealing to "contemporary" religious sentiment, and that biblically speaking and otherwise there is a host of other "images" (e.g., life, light, love, meaning, truth, overcoming alienation, liberation) that might serve better. No doubt such considerations must be taken into account when one is concerned with the task of communication and preaching. Dogmatically speaking, however, one cannot avoid dealing with the relationship to God and God's work toward us in terms of the doctrine of justification. This is true for several reasons. The first is the historical reason: The dogma was formulated in those terms, and dogmatics can no more avoid discussion of them than it can avoid discussion of "substance," "essence," "nature," and so on in dealing with the Trinity and christology. One may want to go on and redefine, but one must start with the dogma and attempt to understand it in its own terms.

Second, discussion of justification is necessary because it deals directly with the basic structural components of the

biblical and dogmatic systems: the concepts of law and justice. These are not simply a Pauline obsession, nor the preoccupation of those with afflicted consciences. Throughout the
Scriptures, it is a fact of prime importance that God is the final
judge. Justification deals directly with the ultimate judgment of
God. Furthermore, justification by faith deals directly with the
root human sin under the law: the sin of the self-made person,
the sin of self-righteousness. Justification by faith is not a sop
for those of afflicted conscience; it is an attack as well on the
secure. No other image makes the point as directly and clearly
as the doctrine of justification. It is no coincidence that Paul
uses the doctrine precisely in such instances: against the "Judaizers" and against the "enthusiasts" who think already to have
made it. One could well argue that the doctrine of justification
by faith is most needed precisely when people sense the least
need for it!

Finally, justification language is crucial precisely *because* of
the communication problem. The basic question is what we are
supposed to do in communicating the word of God to others.
Justification language tells us straight out: We are to *justify*, to
pronounce just, and *deliver* the judgment. The reason for the
primacy of justification and related concepts of imputation,
reckoning, forgiveness of sins, and so on is that speech shaped
by and around these concepts is a quite particular use of language: It does what it says. Justification decides the issue it talks
about. It does not merely talk about or describe what salvation
might be like, it actually gives it. It simply says: "I pronounce
you just for Jesus' sake." The deed is done.

Justification and forgiveness of sins are dogmatically primary precisely because they stipulate directly what sort of
communication is supposed to take place in the church. There
are indeed other images in Scripture and elsewhere. They tend,
however, to remain just that: images. They describe and illu-
mine the relationship to God in enlightening, helpful, and

often inspiring ways. But they do not establish it. Description in the indicative mood, no matter how enticing, can all too easily lapse back into law. I am left wondering what is the matter with me, that I do not experience such marvelous things.

When it was said that the article on justification is the "article by which the church stands or falls," it was this kind of communication that was at stake. Here is the point of the "proper distinction between law and gospel." The church is to pronounce, to *do* the imputation, unconditionally. Particular preoccupation with or dependence on the legal metaphor or the problems of conscience is not the reason, dogmatically speaking, for the primacy of the doctrine of justification. The reason is to show clearly and unmistakably the kind of communication that must go on in the church. If the church forgets to speak the kind of language demanded by justification, a language that actually does what it talks about, then the church will "fall" and lose its reason for being. The sixteenth-century reformers saw the whole of Scripture agreeing on justification, and insisted that all doctrine be judged in the light of justification precisely for this reason. The point is to deliver the goods.

Robert Jenson and Eric Gritsch have made this point by characterizing justification by faith as a dogmatic proposal to the church catholic which is "metalinguistic," that is "not a particular proposed *content* of the church's proclamation, along with other contents" but "stipulation of what kind of talking—about whatever contents—can properly be proclamation and word of the church." It is "an attempt to state minimal identifying characteristics of the language activity we call 'gospel.'"[27] Justification means being addressed by an absolutely unconditional affirmation and promise, an end and a new beginning, a death and resurrection. If this is in any way compromised and flattened out into a mere description, it becomes a report *about* Christianity instead of the deed which *makes* Christians. Then it is no longer the gospel.

CHAPTER TWO

Justification and Sanctification

Justification and sanctification must be grasped as a dynamic unity in the light of God's eschatological act that brings new life from death. "Progress" in sanctification is not immanent moral progress but the coming of the kingdom of God among us through the power of unconditional justification. Growth is growth in grace. Sanctification cannot be separated from, or more than, justification. Sanctification occurs when unconditional justification begins to take the person away from sin, not just to take sin away from the person. There is death to the old, and rebirth to the new in heart, mind, and soul. Justification sola gratia sets free from works and just so inspires spontaneity and naturalness in doing truly good works.

The Separation of Sanctification from Justification

"Are we to continue to sin that grace may abound?" The question obviously makes people nervous. To that degree also the answer is likely not to be grasped: "By no means! How can we who died to sin still live in it?" (Rom. 6:1–2). Justification means the end of law and of thinking according to law. It means the death of the old and the resurrection of the new in faith.

We know that our old self was crucified with him so that the sinful body might be destroyed, and we might no longer be enslaved to sin. For he who has died is freed from sin. But if we have died with Christ, we believe that we shall also live with him. For we know that Christ being raised from the dead will never die again; death no longer has dominion over him. The death he died he died to sin, once for all, but the life he lives he lives to God. So you also must consider yourselves dead to sin and alive to God in Christ Jesus. . . .

But thanks be to God, that you who were once slaves of sin have become obedient from the heart to the standard of teaching to which you were committed, and, having been set free from sin, have become slaves of righteousness. I am speaking in human terms, because of your natural limitations. For just as you once yielded your members to impurity and to greater and greater iniquity, so now yield your members to righteousness for sanctification. (Rom. 6:6–11, 17–19)

If we are unable fully to grasp the identification of justification by faith with death and resurrection, we will encounter nothing but difficulty in relating justification and sanctification. We will always be struggling and tinkering with the system of law, trying to make it work by all sorts of theological fine tuning.

Something of that sort seems to have occurred after the Reformation. Justification by faith as imputed righteousness was accepted and became the talisman of the new movement, but death and resurrection, the end of the law, was not. We need not tarry here to ask why.[1] Broadly, what happened was that after the Reformation, Protestants again attempted just what could not be done: to synthesize justification by faith with thinking "after the fashion of Aristotle," with thinking according to the scheme of progress under the law. What resulted was a theology which carries within itself a profound inner contradiction.[2] Again, either one or the other (the righteousness which comes by faith or thinking "after the fashion of Aristotle") has to give way. Again, history shows the former to be most often the loser. The law once again takes its place as the structural backbone of the dogmatic system.[3]

Once that occurs, two things immediately follow for dogmatics which try nevertheless to be Protestant and evangelical. First, justification must be defined as an absolutely forensic
declaration. Second, it must be antiseptically removed from all
contamination by the subsequently necessary idea of progress
in sanctification on the other. Justification must be understood
as absolutely forensic, that is, as a sheer decree acquitting the
guilty party. Thus the following:

> "Justification denotes that act by which the sinner, who is
> responsible for guilt and liable to punishment . . . , but who
> believes in Christ, is pronounced just by God the judge." This
> act occurs at the instant in which the merit of Christ is appro-
> priated by faith, and can properly be designated a *forensic* or
> *judicial* act, since God in it, as if in a civil court, pronounces
> a judgment upon man, which assigns to him an entirely differ-
> ent position, and entirely different rights. By justification we
> are, therefore, by no means to understand a moral condition
> existing in man, or a moral change which he has experienced,
> but only a judgment pronounced upon man, by which his rela-
> tion to God is reversed, and indeed in such a manner, that a
> man can now consider himself one whose sins are blotted out,
> who is no longer responsible for them before God, who, on the
> other hand, appears before God as accepted and righteous, in
> whom God finds nothing more to punish, with whom He has
> no longer any occasion to be displeased.[4]

From this summary by Heinrich Schmid, one can sense
something of the beauty and objectivity of Lutheran orthodoxy, but also something of the anxiety involved in holding
the position. Justification is stated boldly. It is a forensic act, a
purely legal judgment, made by God for Christ's sake, as distinguished from a physical act, a judgment made on the basis
of or entailing some empirically verifiable characteristic or
action in the person judged. And indeed, the forensic nature
of the judgment, taken just as such, is not the problem. That is

orthodoxy's finest achievement. The problem lies rather in the presupposition of the system: that the law is the eternal standard according to which the judgment is made. Thus arises the anxiety. In order to keep the forensic judgment pure, one has absolutely to separate justification from a "moral condition" or "moral change." Given the presuppositions, one can maintain the comfort of justification only by separating it absolutely from its effect.

But then it becomes difficult to say exactly why sanctification and good works must (may? will?) follow. One lands willy-nilly back in the same systematic problem encountered all along. Either forensic justification makes the process unnecessary, or the process makes justification as a forensic act unnecessary and fictitious, again a mere "anti-Pelagian codicil." It is not strange, therefore, that dispute should have broken out over the necessity of "good works." If forensic justification fully saves, how necessary are good works? Shall we not sin the more that grace may abound? When the eschatological nature of the justifying event is lost, when it is no longer a matter of death and new life, when the old subject simply remains under the law, justification threatens to become mere justification of the status quo. Then one must come down hard on the necessity of good works in order to forestall moral laxity. But then the dynamic, the spontaneity and *hilaritas*, of faith is lost. One answers the question "Shall we sin the more that grace may abound?" by saying, "By no means! Because good works are necessary too, for salvation, you know!"[5] Then the battle is lost.

The increasing isolation of forensic justification as an "objective" sheer judgment could mean only that Protestant divines were faced with the question of mediation all over again. How does the subject appropriate something so objective and pure without contaminating it? How can this be conceived without confusing it with a subjective process? The question, of course, masks the real problem: How can the subject appropriate such justification without dying and being made new, that is, how can the subject survive intact? The answer, of course, for anyone who takes the New Testament seriously, is that the subject cannot. Justification involves death of the old and rebirth of the new. Given the presuppositions of the orthodox Protestant scheme, however, a way must be found to avoid such death. A way must be found to make the subjective appropriation of the objective fact conceivable as an order, a process. One has to provide a theological shuttle service between the objective and the subjective. The Reformation's *propter Christum et per fidem* (because of Christ through faith) becomes a succession, a progress, in which the *propter Christum* is the objective truth and the *per fidem* the subjective appropriation. Wilhelm Dantine states the point:

> The merit of Christ waits before the closed door of the heart like an immovable object, even though it carries in it the entire salvation of mankind. Only some action from within the heart can open the door and permit the salvation treasure to enter the existence of man. Even if one seriously takes into account the fact that faith was correctly evaluated as a gift of the Holy Spirit, did it not nevertheless lead to an understanding of faith as an independent means, and, finally, as the merit of pious inwardness? . . . One can also diminish the merit of Christ by appealing to the Holy Spirit, especially if one reduces this merit to a dead, heavenly "thing" no longer capable of action as Lutheran Orthodoxy has already done. . . .
>
> The so-called objective fact of salvation thus really forms only something like a common foundation. It represents a basis on which the so-called subjective fact is only then able to begin the really decisive action. It almost seems as if God had to be reconciled anew through faith.[6]

The split between the subjective and the objective could only mean that the theologians would have to busy themselves with the question of order once again. The result was the so-called *ordo salutis* (order of salvation). The first steps were taken already by Melanchthon in speaking of three steps of *notitia, assensus,* and *fiducia* (knowledge, assent, and trust), by which one moves from knowledge of the objective fact to assent under the weight of certain "proofs" and finally to trust under the influence of the Holy Spirit.[7] Such an initial analysis cannot but invite further refinement, especially at the last step of trust. How does such trust come about? Later dogmaticians developed the *ordo salutis* to deal with the problem, involving such steps as the call (*vocatio*), illumination, conversion, regeneration, mystical union, and renovation. In doing this, according to Heinrich Schmid, they "seek to collect under one general topic, all that is to be said concerning what God or more accurately the Holy Ghost, does, in order to induce fallen man to accept of salvation through Christ, and what takes place in order to bring about the designed change in man."[8] No doubt such a collection could be helpful, were it looked on simply as an attempt to spell out with fullness what justification by faith means. The attempt to set it forth as an "order," however, is disastrous. Even Schmid, whose love for the orthodox fathers is evident, is constrained to remark, "The introduction of an independent development of these conceptions led to an arrangement of the entire doctrine which we cannot call a happy one."[9] Among other things, it led to a fundamental distinction between the means of salvation on the part of God (word and sacraments) and the means of salvation on the part of man (faith and good works). Faith becomes the subjective condition for salvation.

The attempt analytically to describe the *ordo salutis* was a tricky task, and the dogmaticians could not agree on the correct order. Justification, forensic or otherwise, tended to get lost in the dogmatic woods. Dantine observes:

> Its limitation to the territory of applied grace took increasing effect . . . and perhaps one will even have to conclude that here

the old truth has again proved itself, according to which the greatest radiance is always followed by the deepest misery. . . .

A contributing factor to this decline was, without a doubt, the particular development of the *ordo salutis* . . . , into the scheme of which justification was squeezed as into a bed of Procrustes, there to lose its essential center and strength. . . . The Spirit, in Himself free and sovereign, was transformed into a front-rank man at attention, as it were, and the only consolation about this iron chain of interlinked divine operations was now that almost every dogmatician had a different notion of which order of march the living God should follow. At least a little freedom was left for the Holy Ghost, albeit only through the disunity of the dogmaticians! Later, a more and more penetrating interest in the proceedings and occurrences in the human realm was all that was needed to make a chain of religious occurrences in the human soul out of acts of a Spirit squeezed into a human scheme. Finally the whole order of salvation was transformed into a human process of development.[10]

The attempt to spell out the order only leads back to where it all began. Of course, one could say that discerning the order was a purely analytical task for dogmatic purposes and that such "order" was to be conceived as "instantaneous" and not a temporal succession. But Thomas Aquinas had said the same about his doctrine. And once the step is taken it seems inevitably to return to a temporal scheme.

The separation of justification from sanctification in this manner thus leads only in one direction: The process of sanctification becomes the primary reality; justification fades into the background as something everyone presupposes or takes for granted, but which possesses no real dynamic. Justification becomes a kind of frozen idea. Once that happens the way is open to further temporalizing and psychologizing of the "order." This is what happens in at least some forms of pietism. A "dead" orthodoxy could be vitalized only in the same way as an "arid" scholasticism (by mysticism, for instance): turn it into a "way" with a certain series of "steps" (awakening, conversion, etc.) in the religious progress of the individual subject.

Therewith the fate of justification as an objective truth, as an eschatological act from without, is sealed. The subject and its religion occupy the center of the stage. A psychologized *ordo salutis* can readily be recast as the "pure practical religion" of the subject, shorn of all "objective" and "theoretical" elements (Kant), or as a religion of "pious feelings" (Schleiermacher), or even stretched out into a "history-of-salvation" (von Hofmann and others) and finally universalized into a "history of spirit" (the Hegelians). History as such becomes the process in which the divine realizes itself in time in the subject. Time itself becomes a process of "sanctification." Justification as an eschatological act is lost altogether. Eschatology is absorbed into immanent teleology.

The Unity of Justification and Sanctification

Justification cannot be synthesized with the idea of progress according to law. We saw that in our chapter on justification by faith. Now we have also seen that justification cannot be separated as a purely forensic act and hermetically sealed from sanctification conceived as progress according to the law. Justification then becomes irrelevant. Only one way remains open: to grasp justification and sanctification as a dynamic unity in the light of the eschatological nature of the divine action. Justification by faith means the death of the old and the resurrection of the new. Sanctification is what results when that is done to us. "How can you who have died to sin still live in it?" That is the only way our question can be answered. If there is progress or growth involved—and no doubt there is—it must be conceived quite differently from the progress according to law, from the quest to become a virtuous person. The aim of this section is to grasp the unity of justification and sanctification, and the kind of growth involved.

Since later developments in Protestantism precluded proper grasp of the relation between justification and sanctification, it is necessary to return *ad fontes* (to the sources) for help. We have to discover whether the Reformation is of moment dogmatically at all, for if what developed out of the Reformation is to be taken as its entirely legitimate offspring, there is not a great deal to choose between it and previous dogmatics. At best the Reformations dogma would be a minor adjustment or complementary truth to the older systems, in which the issues were stated usually in more comprehensive terms. We must return to the original sources to discover whether this is the best Protestant dogmatics can do.

We can best attack the problem by asking whether in Luther, for instance, who posits the *simul iustus et peccator* with such vigor, it is possible to discover any distinctive ideas about sanctification or Christian growth. The *simul*, it is to be recalled, was posited precisely to counter the idea that justification is to be synthesized with ideas of progress according to law. The justifying act unmasks and exposes all our pretense about becoming virtuous persons, by the very fact that it is an unconditional divine imputation to be received only by faith. To be justified by God's act means to become a sinner at the same time. The totality of justification unmasks the totality of being a sinner. Thus the *simul iustus et peccator* as total states would seem to militate against any talk of progress in sanctification.

There are many utterances of Luther's which reject all ideas of progress.[11] Sanctification must simply be included in justification because the latter is a *total* state. Sanctification is simply to believe the divine imputation and with it the *totus peccator*. Where can there be more sanctification than where God is revered as the only Holy One? God is revered as such only where the sinner, the real and total sinner, stands still at the place where God enters the scene. Like Moses before the burning bush, or Isaiah in the temple, or Saul on the Damascus road. That place is the place where the sinner must realize that his or her own way is at an end. Only those who stand still and hear, who know that they are sinners and that Christ alone is their hope, only they give God the glory. Only they are then sanctified—by God and God's holiness. All human holiness is simply consumed by the divine fire.

From this point of view the way of the sinner in sanctification, if it is a movement at all, is a movement from nothing to all, from that which one has and is in oneself to that which one has and is in Christ. Such a movement can never be completed this side of the grave. Nor could it be a continuous movement through increasing degrees of approximation. Rather each moment, each encounter with the shock of divine holiness, could only be at once both beginning and end, start and finish. The Christian could never presume to have reached a certain stage in sanctification, which then is to form the basis for the next stage. Anyone who has ever been overwhelmed by the magnitude of the divine imputation knows that it is always a matter of beginning again. Thus Luther would say: "To achieve is always to begin again."[12] Encounter with the divine holiness soon disabuses one of all idle dreams of progress.

By the same token, however, the light of the gospel begins to shine through the mists of our dreams. The imputation means that the Christian never has an endless process of sanctification ahead which must be traversed in order to arrive at holiness. Those who have the imputed righteousness may know that they have arrived. The ultimate goal has been given. Such people would know, of course, that this is not a goal one has attained but one always granted anew for the sake of Christ.

According to this initial reading of the imputation and the *simul*, the movement of the Christian life is not a continuous or steady progress, but rather something more like an oscillation or resonance, in which beginning and end are always equally near. In attempting a diagram (admittedly a risky venture!) Wilfried Joest suggests the following:[13]

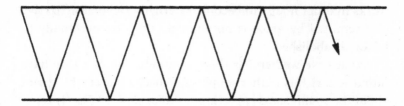

The bottom line represents the person as total sinner in and of himself or herself, while the top line represents the person as totally just in Christ. The zigzag line represents the oscillation, the *transitus* of the Christian life.

While this view of the Christian life resulting from the divine act of justification is foundational, it does not give the whole picture. In many instances Luther himself does speak of a kind of progress or growth. He can even speak in surprising fashion of the Christian as one who is *"partly* just, *partly* a sinner" (*partim iustus, partim peccator*). In this vein he can speak of faith as a beginning, but not yet the whole. Faith is not a perfect fulfillment of the law but only the beginning of fulfillment. Indeed, what is still lacking will not be imputed for Christ's sake. The imperfection of our actual attempts to fulfill the law stands under the protective mantle of nonimputation. In such instances, Luther speaks of faith in the imputed righteousness as the "first fruits of the Spirit" (*primitias spiritus*) which is not yet the whole. Such faith is the beginning because it is the beginning of the actual hatred of sin and its expulsion and the doing of good works. In faith the law is fulfilled *imputatively*, but thereafter it is to be fulfilled *expurgatively* (by driving out sin), for when the Spirit is given one begins *ex animo*, from heart and soul, to hate all those things that offend the Spirit.

Indeed, one begins not only to hate the things but also to hate one's very *self* as sinner (the *odium sui* so odious to more fragile theologies) and to hope and long for the day when such will no longer be the case. Luther can even say we are to do good works in order finally to become externally righteous. To have sins remitted by grace is not enough; they are eventually to be totally abolished.[14]

What have we here? Is this a contradiction of all we have found so far? Has Luther simply gone back on everything said about the *simul iustus et peccator* as total states? What is especially remarkable is that the champion of justification by faith can speak of the expurgation and abolition of sin in terms which even the most enthusiastic exponent of moral progress would find shocking. How is this possible? Some say that in the heat of later battles and in disappointment with the moral laxity of the young Reformation, Luther like Melanchthon had to change his tune somewhat. But statements of the sort in question are present from the very beginning. They are to be found, for instance, precisely in the same context where the *simul iustus et peccator* was first formulated: in the lectures on Romans, to chapter 4:1–7. Not knowing what to make of this, some scholars think that Luther had not yet rid himself of remnants of the medieval tradition or Augustinian humility-piety. When this kind of material is found, Luther is suspected either of not ridding himself completely of medieval piety or of compromising his principles in the face of practical exigencies. Since it is found both early and late, however, it is more reasonable to assume that it belongs to the substance of Luther's Reformation theology, and to suspect that once again he has simply not been understood very well.

It is necessary, therefore, to look more carefully to discover what is meant. Here we can perhaps do no better than to look at the section in the lectures on Romans, since that is the place where the *simul* was first propounded and has also been the object of much of the controversy. After setting forth the *simul iustus et peccator* as the result of the divine imputation, Luther moves immediately to a discussion about concupiscence. He castigates the scholastic theologians for thinking "after the fashion of Aristotle" that the sinfulness of concupiscence is actually removed by what they call "grace," and that what remains is only the "seeds" of sin. He says that he was entirely led astray by this, "because I did not know that though forgiveness is indeed real, sin is not taken away *except in hope*, that is *in the process of being taken away* by the gift of grace which starts this removal, so that it is only not reckoned as sin." And a bit later he expands this:

> Yet this concupiscence is always in us; therefore, the love of God is never in us, except insofar as grace has given us a beginning of it. We have the love of God only insofar as the rest of concupiscence, which still must be cured and by virtue of which we do not yet "love God with our whole heart" (Luke 10:27), is by mercy not reckoned as sin. We shall love God only at the end, when it will all be taken away and the perfect love of God will be given to those who believe and who with perseverance always yearn for it and seek it.[15]

Thinking "in the fashion of Aristotle" according to human notions of progress leads to an entirely false notion of sanctification. The human notion of progress it presupposes always remains intact. The question then is how much one can accomplish according to the scheme either with or without what was called "infused grace": how far up the ladder of progress one could get. When, in order to exalt the supposed power of such grace, it was simply *asserted* that concupiscence is removed in some fashion or other, the discourse tended to lapse into fiction and lose touch with the way things are. In this scheme, grace becomes a theological abstraction added only to make the scheme "Christian," merely an added help in the scheme of what human powers properly should accomplish. But that is just pious sublimation of natural desire, the sanctified self-centeredness which Luther knew all too well did not lead to actual love of God. The scheme leads only to hypocrisy or despair. One either deceives oneself into thinking concupiscence is actually gone or despairs if one is honest enough to admit it is not.

Faith, however, born of the imputation of total righteousness, begets the beginnings of honesty as well. Such faith sees the truth of the human condition, the reality and totality of human sin, and has no need to indulge in fictions. It will see that concupiscence indeed remains and that it is *sin* but that God nevertheless does business with sinners. Such faith will see the fantastic magnitude of the divine act and thereby *begin* to hope that one day concupiscence will be gone. Such faith will begin, at least, to love the God who comes all the way to die for sinners. Such faith will begin to hate sin and to hope for that righteousness it knows it can never attain by any human power with or without "infused grace." Only imputed righteousness grasped by faith leads to such beginnings. Faith which in the light of imputed righteousness sees the truth about sin, will cry to God "out of the depths": "Wretched man that I am, who will deliver me . . . ," and actually begin to "hunger and thirst after righteousness."

When Luther speaks in this vein, he speaks of *actual affections* (love, hope, hatred of sin, etc.) and not about theological abstractions. The unconditional nature of the divine imputation which sets the *totus iustus* over against the *totus peccator* kindles the first beginnings of actual hope and love for God and God's righteousness; whereas before there had been only hypocrisy or despair. There is no contradiction for Luther

between the *simul* and the *partim*, once the divine imputation
has destroyed all thinking "after the fashion of Aristotle." If
justification is unconditional and total, it explodes into love
and good works. If not, it simply leaves the self to contend with
its own righteousness and despair.

What sort of progress or growth is here envisaged? Is the
transitus in the life of the Christian no longer simply an oscillation between two wholes? Under the impulse of the imputed
righteousness, does one gradually improve, so that "nonimputation" covers what is left? Does one not, after all, return to point
zero every time one begins again? Could one perhaps apply
the popular slogan "Become what you already are" and see the
Christian life as a gradual process of catching up to the *totus
iustus*? Does one set of accomplishments form the basis for the
next—as with the steps of the mystical way? Does one attain a
certain approximation of the goal?

Such a scheme might suggest itself on first glance. But many
go wrong here. If there were growth of that sort, progressive
sanctification would mean progressive emancipation from
the divine imputation. The more one progresses, the less grace
one would need. Such thinking would lead to Karl Holl's idea
that justification is an "analytical" rather than a "synthetic"
judgment, that is, a judgment made by God on the basis of
God's analysis of the whole process and its successful completion (one is declared just because God knows one will *become*
so), rather than a judgment which by its sheer unconditionality and liberality makes (synthesizes) what it declares.[16] If there
were such a process and justification were an analytical judgment, we would be back at square one. Imputed righteousness
would be a temporary loan given to cover lack of capital until
one earned enough oneself. The more one acquired, the more
the imputation could recede into the background. The picture
would be something like this:

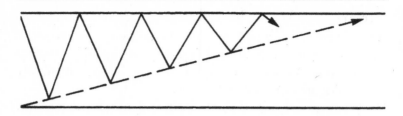

One gradually leaves the line of the *totus peccator* and by the power of grace ascends to the line of the *totus iustus*.[17]

But this would be a serious misunderstanding of Luther's point. Imputed righteousness is not a mere starting point, a temporary loan, and it cannot be allowed to recede into the background. It is the perpetual fountain and constant power of whatever we may accomplish. To look on it as something we gradually need less of would be to deny it altogether. Imputed righteousness, precisely because it is synthetic, unconditional, pure, makes its own way and creates its own justice.

We cannot understand what Luther means by growth or progress in sanctification unless all ordinary human perceptions of progress are reversed, are stood on their heads.[18] The progress Luther has in mind is not our movement toward the goal but the goal's movement in on us. Imputed righteousness is *eschatological* in character; a battle is joined in which the *totus iustus* moves against the *totus peccator*. The "progress" is the coming of the kingdom of God among us. That is why complete sanctification is always the same as justification and cannot be something more added to it or separated from it. Complete sanctification is not the goal but the source of all good works. The way is not from the partial to the whole, but from the whole to the partial. Good works do not make a person good, but a good person does good works—as the famous maxim has it. Imputed righteousness is not a legal fiction but the "power of God unto salvation" which attacks sin as a total state and will eventually reduce it to nothing. It is always as a *whole* that it attacks, as unconditional, freely given, absolute gift. It attacks its opposite in the form of both hypocrisy and despair. The good works that result are not building blocks in the progress of the Christian; they are the fruit of the whole, the "good tree."

Expulsion of sin is therefore quite the opposite of a morally conceivable process of sanctification. In the latter process the person remains more or less constant, and only the properties are changed. The person is the "substance" in scholastic terms, whose "accidents" are altered. One supposedly "puts off sin" as though one were peeling paint from a wall or taking heat from water.[19] The entire picture must be reversed: The person is taken away from sin. The heart, mind, soul, affections—that which constitutes the person in the biblical sense—are taken away from the lust either for vice or for becoming a virtuous self. Imputed righteousness, precisely because it is unconditional, does not offer a new paint job. It does not merely "take sin away" and leave the moral person intact. It begins to take the person away from sin. There is a death and new life involved, which proceeds according to no immanent moral scheme.

> Human righteousness . . . seeks first of all to remove and to change the sins and to keep man intact; this is why it is not righteousness but hypocrisy. Hence as long as there is life in man and as long as he is not taken by renewing grace to be changed, no efforts of his can prevent him from being subject to sin and the law.[20]

Sanctification always comes from the whole, from the penetration of the eschaton into time, and thus involves the death of the old and rebirth of the new. One never does leave the "always beginning anew" behind, for the beginning is the first fruits of the resurrection.

The movement, the growth, envisaged by Luther is thus a reversal of this-worldly conceptions.

Where he is concerned to describe sanctification, he very often grasps at formulations which stand the natural-rational picture exactly on its head. For our question the following is the result: The progress of the sanctified Christian life for Luther is unconditionally a procedure *sui generis*. It can be compared to no immanent moral movement, with no continuous psychological development in the realm of the identity of the ethical subject with itself. Furthermore: Wherever that progress takes place—whether in the beginning or farther on—it always happens as a whole. If it takes place extensively only in little steps, or in isolated actions against particular sins, intensively the whole is always there; the total crisis, the entire transformation of the person, dying and becoming new, is wholly present.[21]

Joest suggests the following diagram (again in spite of the risk involved in such attempts):[22]

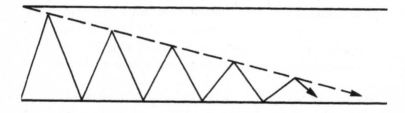

The way does not lead from below, the *totus peccator*, upward; rather, the totality of righteousness imputed to faith descends toward the lower reality. The difference and opposition between the two is not increasingly overcome from below by the ascent of the sinner, but rather from above, by the descent of the totality of grace. The movement does drive toward fulfillment, however, when by the power of the coming reality the *totus peccator* shall finally die completely and by grace alone be turned totally to love the God who gives it. *Then* we shall love as we are loved. In the end we shall realize that if we are to be saved, it will have to be by such grace "only." The growth envisaged is growth in grace and just so is it growth in truth about ourselves vis-à-vis God and God's righteousness.

In this view, justification and sanctification are a dynamic unity. Sanctification is what happens when the unconditional and eschatological event of justification breaks into one's life. Sanctification is what happens when one acts out of faith in the gift of total and complete righteousness, when one simply takes God at God's word. Faith issues in good works—that is, neither in laxity and vice, nor in rigorism and the lust to be a virtuous person—done for the sake of the other.

This opens up a new view of the Christian life. The movement is always from faith to works. One cannot measure Christian existence by works, concluding back from the works to one's status before God. Every attempt to do that is a mistake. Not only does it lead to hypocrisy or despair for the individual, it also destroys all possibility of seeing the goodness of our works. It is the devil's art, Luther says, to spoil precisely the goodness of our works. This happens when one puts works *before* faith, or concludes from works to the status of the Christian. For then "under the law" we will only come to the conclusion that we have not done much, that absolutes are too hard to reach, and that everything is in vain. Trying to base one's life on works, one will lose even them.

Being Christian means to find one's being in faith, in simply hearing the unconditional proclamation of the righteousness that is not in works. Such a position will be attacked by both the vicious and the virtuous, by the sub-Christian and the super-Christian. But if one is going to be saved from both vice and virtue, there is no other way. Hearing the divine declaration alone will set free over against works. And we must be free. The movement from faith to works must be a movement of freedom. If not, we become prisoners of our works. We look at *them* to find our being, our status. We are walled in by our deeds like prisoners in a dungeon. "When you look to what you have done you have already lost the name of Christian. It is indeed true that one should do good works, help others, advise, and give, but no one is called a Christian for that and is not a Christian for that."[23] The quest to be a virtuous or pious person is *not* a Christian quest.

> Making pious people is not the business of the gospel but only making Christians. It is more a matter of being Christian than being pious. Someone may well be pious but not a Christian. A Christian does not know how to say anything about his piety, he doesn't find anything good or pious in it; should he desire to become pious he will have to look to some other and foreign piousness.[24]

A proper dogmatic view of the Christian life does not, therefore, identify with the old ideals of piety and the quest to be a virtuous person. Being holy or saintly in that sense cannot be identified with being Christian. The Reformation means a complete break with such thinking.

> Here it finally dawns on one why Reformation comes about, because here it is not merely mistakes and shortcomings that are repaired, but here the *ideal* that shaped the entire life of the Middle Ages is rejected: "Therefore one is not called a Christian because one accomplishes much; something higher is here. Rather it is because one takes something from, draws from, Christ, and simply lets oneself be given to. When one no longer takes from Christ, then one is no longer a Christian. The name Christian stays only in the taking and not in the giving or the doing, and that one takes from no one except from Christ. When you begin to regard what you have done then you have already lost the name of Christian."[25]

Such a view is preposterous for the world and the old Adam, but this is exactly what it means to die to the old and be born again to the new. One must simply be still and listen where God enters the scene—and believe, for only such faith will save.

This rejection of the ancient ideal of piety and sanctity is what lies behind Luther's shocking advice to Melanchthon: "Be a sinner and sin boldly, but believe even more boldly and rejoice in Christ, who is victor over sin, death, and the world."[26] The point is that when one begins to be grasped by the overwhelming gift of grace, when one is beginning to die to the old, the temptation (*Anfechtung*) will always sound: "Is it not dangerous?" "Are you not going too far?" "Is not the grace too cheap?" "If you lose your 'virtue,' what will protect you then?" Luther's advice in such situations was: "Be a sinner and sin boldly, but believe even more boldly." The point is not to go out and find some sins to commit. The point is rather not to be deceived by the glitter of ideals, of sanctity and piety, by the quest for the Holy Grail. Christ and Christ alone has dealt with sin and saves sinners. It is impossible for there to be any sin which is not removed by him and by him alone. "Be a sinner and sin boldly, but believe more boldly" is simply the stance of a faith which knows that Christ alone saves sinners.

Out of such faith *good* works come. Sanctification happens. The good works come out of the spontaneity, the freedom, the "*hilaritas*" of faith. They come out of the love and the hope that begin to dawn when one realizes the unconditionality of grace, when the old self dies. The good works come out of the beginning of the "always beginning again." They come from the *good* tree. They come from faith.

> Faith is a divine work in us which changes us and births us anew out of God (John 1:13), and kills the old Adam, makes us into entirely different people from the heart, soul, mind, and all powers, and brings the Holy Spirit with it. Oh, it is a living, busy, active, mighty thing, this faith, so it is impossible that it should not do good. It does not ask if good works should be done, but before one asks, has done them and is always active. Whoever, though, does not do such work is a faithless person, peeking and poking about for faith and good

works not knowing what either faith or good works are, who putters and patters many words about faith and good works.[27]

Luther spoke of "*quellende Liebe*" to designate the spontaneity and freedom with which works flow forth from faith.[28] The phrase is difficult to translate into English; it means a love "bubbling over," "springing forth" as from a spring. The point is that the love bubbles forth from itself because of faith and is not dependent on the attraction of its object.

But here again caution must be exercised. There is a long tradition in modern Protestant ethics which attaches itself to this kind of statement and uses it to maintain that Protestant ethics, in distinction from Roman Catholic ethics, is "spontaneous" rather than legalistically forced. This became the basis for what was called an "ethics of disposition" or "motivation" (*Gesinnungsethik*). Inspired mostly by nineteenth-century idealism, the idea is that genuine ethical action must flow spontaneously from within rather than be forced from without. The problem, however, is what this "within" is. For most of modern Protestantism, this "within" is "the voice of conscience," the "moral law within," or the "human moral autonomy" of Kantianism. It is a mistake to identify what is being said by Luther and the other reformers with this *Gesinnungsethik* of modern Protestantism. The "spring" of the "bubbling-over love" is not "the moral law within" or the supposed "autonomy" it fosters. The "spring" is the word of God, the justification given for Jesus' sake. That "spring" alone purifies the heart from the lust for either vice or virtue so that good works will flow forth.

The word is spoken; faith hears. From that good works flow. We hear every day anew. We begin again. Sanctification comes to us from God's eschatological word and kingdom. It is the spontaneity of life in the Spirit. Surely such a view at least more nearly approaches what we find in the New Testament than do more traditional views. Synthesizing justification with sanctification under the aegis of a legal scheme has as little to do with the New Testament message as does a stringent separation of the two; because the New Testament does not see the two as different enough either to synthesize or to separate. The reason is the eschatological vision. The entire question of one's being as Christian is bound up with one's stance vis-à-vis the eschatological kingdom breaking in Jesus. All distinctions, sinner/righteous, Jew/gentile, slave/free, male/female, and so on, are simply wiped out insofar as they are supposed to be determinative for one's being before God. What matters is one's *faith*, *love*, and *hope*.

This is what stands behind the sayings, teachings, and parables of Jesus as well as the injunctions of the Epistles. The kingdom of heaven is like treasure hidden in a field which, when a man found it, he went and sold all he had to possess (Matt. 13:44 and par.). The joy at stumbling onto something entirely unexpected changes everything—like a precious pearl so long sought and finally discovered, or a lost coin, or a lost sheep. Nothing really matters but that. Not to see that is to be blind, according to the Gospels.

Two types of people are set over against each other: the type whose being is determined by works, and the type whose being is determined by faith and hope, who have caught the vision. When the Gospels must decide between the two, always that which gives praise to and lives in the light of God's grace is commended and chosen, regardless of status or achievement. The publican is justified rather than the Pharisee (Luke 18:9ff.). The prodigal who wastes his life but yet returns gladdens the Father's heart, while the son who remains in the house does not see (Luke 15:11ff.). Simon the Pharisee simply cannot understand Jesus' acceptance of the "woman of the city" who washes his feet with her hair. Only faith can grasp that scene. The woman is the truly sanctified one. That is the shocking thing. She acts out of faith and hope and therefore knows what to do. Her sins are forgiven "for she loved much; but he who is forgiven little, loves little" (Luke 7:36ff.). From the usual human perspective the logic of that statement is hopelessly garbled. From the eschatological perspective the statement makes perfect sense. The forgiveness and the love are part of the same package.

The teachings of Jesus and the injunctions in the Epistles must be viewed in the same light. They are posed from the eschatological perspective. They have to do with what one who is slain and made alive by the eschatological word does and is to do. One cannot expect that such teachings will be generally understood or approved by the children "of this age." That is not because Christians are so much the paragons of virtue that the world scoffs at their strictness and rigor—that Christians try to be perfect examples of that virtue which the world generally approves but does not want to be "too serious" about. It is rather because the Christian life will be *hidden* from this world and inexplicable to it. Sometimes—perhaps most of the time—the Christian life will appear to follow quite ordinary, unspectacular courses no doubt *too* ordinary for the world. But sometimes it will appear to go quite contrary to what the world would deem wise, prudent, or even ethical. Why should costly ointment be wasted on Jesus? Would it not be better to sell it and give to the poor? Should not Jesus' disciples fast like everyone else? Why should one prefer the company of whores and sinners to polite and virtuous society? Why should a Christian participate in an assassination plot? The Christian life is tuned to the eschatological vision, not to the virtues and heroics of this world.

It has become something of a platitude among religious people that the Sermon on the Mount sets forth the sort of ideal life the world might aspire to and admire. On the contrary, the Sermon on the Mount is one of the most antireligious documents ever written, because of its eschatological perspective.

The people it calls "blessed" would hardly qualify as members of virtuous and religious society: the poor in spirit, the mourners, the meek, those who hunger and thirst for righteousness (not those who *have* it!), the merciful, the pure in heart, the peacemakers, the persecuted for righteousness sake, the reviled. The religious and the virtuous are not on the list and in all likelihood would not wish to be. Indeed, the attempt to break the hiddenness is precisely the dangerous thing: "Beware of practicing your piety before men in order to be seen by them; for then you will have no reward from your Father who is in heaven" (Matt. 6:1). Those who wish to be vindicated in their piety before this world, who wish to be praised by other people, *have* their reward: "Thus, when you give alms, sound no trumpet before you, as the hypocrites do in the synagogues and in the streets, that they may be praised by men. Truly, I say to you, they have received their reward" (Matt. 6:2). The goodness or the Christianness of one's life should be hidden even from oneself: "But when you give alms, do not let your left hand know what your right hand is doing, so that your alms may be in secret; and your Father who sees in secret will reward you" (Matt. 6:3).

Good works, that is, come as spontaneously and unspectacularly and naturally as fruit from the good tree. Good works should be as natural, say, as running to pick up and comfort a hurt child. No one would think to call that a good work. It is just natural. But that is exactly the point. One would not, attending to the child, bother to let the left hand know what the right hand is doing. One would not be practicing one's piety before others to be seen by them. One would be caught up in concern for the child. And when it was over, it would be forgotten. The truly good works, no doubt, are all those we and the world have forgotten. But the Father sees "in secret." His eschatological kingdom will come. The hidden will be revealed.

But how is that possible—such naturalness, such spontaneity? Do not these descriptions remove the Christian life from
the realm of the humanly possible? Of course. That is just what
it means to say that the eschatological word as law, as letter,
reveals sin—reveals just how lost we are at the same time as
the Spirit gives life. That is what it means to say that we can be
saved only by God's grace in Jesus. We can be saved only by
listening to his word of justification and believing it. That alone
will begin the cure, even if it is a matter of always beginning
again. The world may perhaps suggest a thousand better ways
that appeal to our ambition and pride or self-reliance. But they
will not work. They will lead neither to sanctification nor to
good works. "No one who puts his hand to the plow and looks
back is fit for the kingdom of God" (Luke 9:62). One who is
justified by faith is sanctified by being drawn into its eschatological vision and hope. One who catches that vision will be
sanctified by it; one who does not is blind. "For to him who has
will more be given; and from him who has not, even what he
has will be taken away" (Mark 4:25).

CHAPTER THREE

Justification and This World

Justification as an unconditional act does not abolish the law, but upholds it in all its stringency, obviating both antinomianism and the "third use of the law." Justification by faith fosters a new understanding of the life of the Christian "under the law" in this age. Because the end and goal are given to faith, the law is now to be incarnated "in the flesh." To be "saved" means to be "reborn" into this world. God's commandments take the Christian into this world, not on a quest for another or for one's own holiness. A distinction between the "two kingdoms" (this age and the next) must indeed be maintained for the sake of the unconditional gospel, but this must not mean either synthesis or separation. The unconditionality of the eschatological kingdom prevents synthesis at the same time as it prohibits separation or premature escape from this world to the next. Thus this world is given back to the believer as God's good creation for the time being as a place for service.

Justification and the Law

Justification as an unconditional eschatological act apart from law and its works demands reassessment of our ideas about the law. Paul put the question for us: "Do we then overthrow the law by this faith?" Does justification make us antinomians, enemies of the law? So it might seem at first glance, and especially in light of the persistent polemic against thinking in terms of

law, moral progress, the quest for virtue, found in the earlier
pages of this *locus*. The answer Paul gives is therefore likely to
be puzzling: "By no means! On the contrary, we uphold the law"
(Rom. 3:31). How is the law upheld precisely by maintaining we
are justified entirely apart from it? Attempting an answer to
that question is the task of this section. It is important because
it is one of the building blocks in constructing an understanding of the relationship between eschatological justification and
life in this world. Living under the law is a determinative factor for life in this world, this "age." If a positive relationship to
it is not established, eschatology will lead only to abandoning
this world—a temptation all too prevalent in Christian circles.

How does justification by faith uphold the law? We have
already seen the beginning of the answer in the treatment of
the functional understanding of law. In the light of the unconditional nature of justification, the law functions first and
foremost to reveal sin, to reveal that apart from justification
by faith there is no hope for us. Precisely justification as an
unconditional gift, therefore, insists that law be established
in its absolute clarity, stringency, and strength. Precisely justification will insist that there be no loopholes in the law, no water-
ing down, no casuistic amelioration. "I testify again to every man
who receives circumcision that he is bound to keep the whole
law" (Gal. 5:3). To break one commandment is to break them all.
One cannot comfort oneself with the platitude that one is at least
as good as the next person, or congratulate oneself on being a
champion of the law even if one does not exactly keep it.

> But if you call yourself a Jew and rely upon the law and boast
> of your relation to God and know his will and approve what
> is excellent, because you are instructed in the law, and if you
> are sure that you are a guide to the blind, a light to those
> who are in darkness, a corrector of the foolish, a teacher of
> children, having in the law the embodiment of knowledge and

truth—you then who teach others, will you not teach yourself?
(Rom. 2:17–21)

Precisely from the point of view of the eschatological breaking in of the kingdom in Jesus, no relaxation of the law is envisaged. Indeed, the law is restated in all its vigor.

> Think not that I have come to abolish the law and the prophets;
> I have come not to abolish them but to fulfill them. For truly, I
> say to you, till heaven and earth pass away, not an iota, not
> a dot, will pass from the law until all is accomplished. Who-
> ever then relaxes one of the least of these commandments and
> teaches men so, shall be called least in the kingdom of heaven;
> but he who does them and teaches them shall be called great
> in the kingdom of heaven. For I tell you, unless your righ-
> teousness exceeds that of the scribes and Pharisees, you
> will never enter the kingdom of heaven. (Matt. 5:17–20)

Only one who knows about the end and telos of the law will
be able to accept that. Indeed, only from the point of view of
unconditional justification will one be able to put Matthew
together with Paul. Precisely because imputed righteousness
is an absolute gift, which is the end and the telos of the law
given to faith, it upholds the absolute demand of the law as its
counterpart. When the end and the goal are not *given*, the law
becomes endless, insatiable, and threatens to devour everything
and destroy everyone. It becomes the irresistible weapon in the
hand of the accuser, Satan, the attorney for the prosecution.
Then *we* must take steps to end it: We must water it down, apply
it casuistically, comfort ourselves moralistically with whatever
"dole of vanity can serve the human soul for daily bread," or
call our analyst to cure us of our hang-ups. That is the secret
of antinomianism of every sort, overt and covert—and most
antinomianism, as we shall see, is covert, parading in the guise
of championing the law. "Christ is the end of the law, that every

one who has faith may be justified" (Rom. 10:4). Wherever that is not realized, there is trouble and people are, quite literally, destroyed.

Unable to rhyme Matt. 5:17–18 with Rom. 10:4, the dogmatic tradition has experienced nothing but trouble over the law. When one does not see that "heaven and earth" *do* "pass away" in the eschatological fulfillment anticipated and grasped by faith, and that just such fulfillment *is* the end and the goal, Paul and Matthew are at irreconcilable odds. Unable to grasp this fulfillment as end, the tradition for the most part had to indulge in what was strictly forbidden by both Matthew and Paul: tampering with the content of the law to arrive at a compromise. The result was the idea that in Christ the ceremonial laws of the Old Testament were abrogated (thus throwing a sop to Paul's claim that Christ was the "end" of the law) while the "moral" law was not (thus supposedly satisfying Matthew's claim that not one iota or dot would pass away until "the end"). But that is patent nonsense which only confuses the issue further and completely obscures the eschatology involved. Neither Testament makes that kind of distinction between ceremonial and moral law. Indeed, it seems that in most instances, ruptures of the ceremonial law are more serious than those of the moral law. Furthermore, the tradition was left with the problem of deciding just what was moral and what was ceremonial. Are the first three commandments, for instance, moral or ceremonial? One might, of course, as happened most generally, try to settle on the decalogue as the moral law. But there is a good deal in the Old Testament and the New outside the decalogue which might also qualify as moral and ethical material of the highest quality. Who is to decide?

The outcome of such confusion was, in general, that natural law became the arbiter. Natural law decides what is moral and what is not. But therewith the fate of the church's understanding of law was sealed, as well as of its eschatological outlook.

Natural law became the structural backbone of the theological system, displacing eschatology. Without eschatology, however, the church had to take over administration of the law and reduce it to manageable proportions, distinguishing "mortal" and "venial" transgressions of law, applying it casuistically to this or that case, separating what ought to be done by everyone from what might be done by the more serious and dedicated. In short, under the guise of being for the law the church tended to become covertly antinomian. As a result, the question of law never ceased to bother, and outbreaks of reformation in the name of the gospel became the recurring fate of the church.[1]

Where the gospel of justification by faith is not comprehended in its full eschatological sense, as bringing end and new beginning, death and new life, there will be trouble with the law. Where the gospel is not grasped, the law will not be grasped either. The important point is faith: that Christ is the end of the law so that everyone who has *faith* may be justified—faith experienced as new life from death.

Where Christ is not the end of the law—its goal and fulfillment—then we with our theology must take steps to bring it to heel. That is the root cause of all antinomianism in the church. Antinomianism is a curious and interesting phenomenon dogmatically because it is the attempt to remedy one mistake by another. It is the attempt to remedy the mistake of nomism by the mistake of antinomism. Once the eschatological outlook has been displaced by an eternal order of law, antinomianism is the attempt to remedy the situation with a false and realized eschatology. It is the attempt to end the law by a theological *tour de force*. Antinomianism wants to solve the problem of law by removing it or relaxing or changing it.

This is demonstrated by the antinomian controversies following the Reformation. Once justification by faith had again been reasserted in radical fashion, it was natural that heavy pressure would be brought to bear on the received understanding of law. John Agricola rightly sensed that justification by faith could not simply be combined with the older idea of law as an eternal order, still evident in some of Philip Melanchthon's theological constructions.[2] Agricola tried to solve the matter by positing a temporal (and perhaps spatial) end to the law. Since Christ is the end of the law, the law must be banished from the church. The law belongs in city hall; only the gospel is to be preached in the church. True repentance comes from the preaching of the New Testament message about Christ, not (as Melanchthon is supposed to have held) from the Old Testament and the law. The nomism that results from loss of eschatology is countered by an antinomism, by false eschatology.

Nomism is ill-equipped to counter antinomianism with evangelical weapons, because it has already compromised the eschatological gospel. Hence it can fight only from the position of law and charge its opponent with the sin and heresy of antinomianism. The victory of nomism over antinomianism in the church is therefore hardly cause for celebration. True opposition can be launched only from the position of a faith which has been grasped by the eschatological justification. If justification exposes sin and upholds the law against sin at the same time as it grants fulfillment, one cannot speak of a temporal or spatial end to law in *this* age. The end is eschatological: anticipated in faith and given in full only at the parousia. The remedy for antinomianism is not nomistic but eschatological. From the perspective of one who knows that Christ is the end of the law *to faith*, antinomianism is not so much a heresy as an impossibility. One cannot get rid of law by theological erasure. The end does not come because theological textbooks say it has. The law must and will remain "on account of sin," until the final end of the sinner and the complete appearance of the new being. Law cannot be banished by theologians. Any attempt to do so will lead only to its return in worse form. Agricola, for instance, wished to banish the Old Testament law, but turned right around and made a law of the New Testament. Only Christ is the end of the law. The end is an eschatological event. Faith is grasped by that and thus, *knowing the end*, upholds the law. One who is grasped by the eschatological vision waits for the day when law will be no more because what it demands and points to will be given in full.

The debate about the "third use" of the law shifts the argument to the other pole of the eschatological dialectic. If the former controversy was about the use of law *before* faith, this latter is about use of the law *after* the eschatological event. The question is whether one can or should speak of a "third" use of the law in addition to the political use (to restrain evil) and the theological use (to convict of sin): a use of the law by the reborn Christian *as* Christian, in which law functions as a "guide to the Christian life." One can see immediately that the issue is still the eschatological one: What difference does the eschatological event make vis-à-vis the law? Does "the Christian" still need the law after believing the word of justification? Some say yes, some say no. The Protestant tradition has had, and continues to have, representatives on both sides of the issue.

The confusion results, once again, from failure to argue consistently from an eschatological perspective. Thus there is most often a good deal of terminological ambiguity. What does one mean by "the reborn Christian" who now, supposedly, "uses" the law in a "third" way? Is it because one is a Christian that one now uses the law in a third way? Or is it because one is not yet completely a Christian that one still needs the law as a guide? The classical definition would seem to be that it is the former. Because one is a "reborn Christian," one may now use the law in a way different from others: not to convict of sin or to restrain evil but simply as a guide to what one should do as a Christian.

If that is what is meant by the "third use," it is clear that anyone grasped by the eschatological perspective must resist it, for the sake of the radical newness of eschatological hope. Law cannot be reintroduced *after* the end, for the end means perfect fulfillment. A perfect lover would not need laws about what to do. A perfect Christian would not need to be told what was right or wrong. One must hold out for that vision lest law conquer all. The day when all will be "written on our hearts" is the center of the biblical promise. To surrender that is to surrender biblical eschatology. Luther, it seems, argued consistently from this point of view and is thus generally regarded as opposing a "third use" of the law.[3]

From the eschatological perspective the legitimate concerns badly expressed in the idea of a third use of the law can be sorted out. First, one who has been grasped by the eschatological vision looks on law differently from one who has not. But that is not to say that one sees a "third" use. What one sees is precisely the difference between law and gospel, so that law can be established in its *first* two uses this side of the eschaton. Before that vision or when it fades, law is misused as a way of salvation, a means of escape. One does not know the difference between law and gospel.

Second, one grasped by the eschatological vision will recognize the continuing need for the law. But this too does not mean a third use. Rather, just because of "rebirth" in faith, one will see how much one is a sinner and will be until the end. One will see that one is not yet a "Christian." One will see precisely that one has no particular advantages over those who are not yet reborn. One will see one's solidarity with the rest of the human race and wait in hope until the end, leaving the heroics and pretensions to spiritual athletes.

The idea of a third use of the law after rebirth thus obscures the eschatological nature of that event and consequently mistakes our relationship to this world. "Rebirth" does not mean premature translation in time into a state different from that of the rest of humankind, in which one is now privileged to use the law differently. That would be a false eschatology. Rebirth, since it leads to the understanding of self as *simul iustus et peccator*, simply cannot share such an idea of conversion. One is never converted in that sense, because one must be converted anew each day. Until the end, therefore, one grasped by the eschatological vision will know that he or she needs the law in precisely the same way that the rest of humankind needs it: to restrain evil and convict of sin.

The idea of a third use furthermore contains a certain amount of hubris. It seems to assume that humans are the users of the law, so that one can now speak of the Christian as "using" the law in a third way. But that cannot ultimately be the case. God is the author of the law; God, not we, is the user of the law. We cannot preside over the law's use in order to speak of a third use which neither restrains evil nor convicts of sin.

Ultimately it must be asked whether the idea of the third use does not entail a covert antinomianism. Antinomianism, we have said, roots in the fact that when the eschatological end of law is missed, theology must step in to alter and tame that law. What are we to say of a law that has become a more or less harmless guide? What is actually proposed is an alteration in the view of law to fit the view of the Christian life as immanent moral progress. Because one does not want to die, one disarms the law and makes it relatively harmless. Law is changed to accommodate sin.

The eschatological perspective cannot abide such a view of law. "Whoever then relaxes one of the least of these commandments and teaches men so, shall be called least in the kingdom of heaven." If one is seriously to maintain imputed righteousness as the eschatological power of new life out of death, one can speak neither of a temporal end to the law nor of its transformation into a third thing, a more or less neutral guide. The law is not to be changed; the *sinner* is to be changed. For Luther the sinner as the *totus peccator* is attacked by law unto death, until the new being arises who actually begins to love that law, that will of God. There are only two possibilities vis-à-vis law as the expression of the will of God. It is either an enemy or a friend, but never a neutral guide. It impinges on us either as the letter which kills or as the Spirit which gives life, but never as something in between.[4]

Exegetes who think they are doing the Old Testament a favor by making its view of law akin to the "third use" may therefore simply be covertly antinomian. Thinking to construct an apology for the Old Testament and its law, they succeed only in robbing it of its majesty and power—what the reformers called its "office." For the reformers there was nothing pejorative in speaking of the Old Testament as *law*, in majestic and even terrifying glory. Just so, the Old Testament gained a status and "office" worthy of and pointing to its counterpart in the New. Only tender antinomians have to find ways to apologize for it.

The same kind of interpretation would apply to the New Testament paraenetic materials. It can hardly be maintained that the exhortations of the New Testament, taken literally, in any degree attenuate the will of God or God's law. If anything, the stakes are raised precisely because of the gospel. We are even exhorted to arise from the dead. How shall we do that? The exhortations are either bad news or good news—between which our actual life as *simul iustus et peccator* resonates until the day when Christ shall be all in all. But they are *not* something in between.

To be true to a view of the Christian life rooted in justification by faith, one must arrive at a different understanding of the relationship between life and law. We cannot look on life as ascent into the ratified air of what the world calls spiritual. That is always the world's substitute for eschatology. Rather, life is a descent, an "incarnation" in the world in service and love. Luther tried to get at that with his formula "*conscientia in evangelio, caro in lege*" (the conscience in the gospel, the flesh in the law).[5] The conscience is ruled and captivated by the gospel, by the eschatological vision. The "flesh" however, the empirical life I live in this age, remains "in the law," and in a double sense: The law attacks "the flesh," which is inimical to the will of God, and under the impulse of the spontaneity and joy fostered by the gospel this empirical life is to become the fulfillment of the will of God. Because of the gospel in the conscience, the Christian is free so that the true battle can be joined in the flesh.

The greatest danger for the eschatological view that speaks of the death of the old and the resurrection of the new is that the idea of the "new person" can all too easily become a mystical theologoumenon without substance, something the theologian calls on to solve all dogmatic problems. That, no doubt, is what those who insisted on the "third use" of the law were most afraid of: the "reborn" Christian who does not know what to do and is cast on his or her own feelings or autonomy. The new being, however, is to be incarnated in down-to-earth fashion in the concrete calling of the Christian in this world. In that battle—in the calling in this world, in the flesh—the law of God is ultimately not an enemy or an emasculated guide but a true and loved friend. For one should make no mistake about it: *The law of God is to be and will be fulfilled.* It will not be fulfilled, however, by our powers, but only by the power of the righteousness of God given to faith.

The Self as God's Creature

When justification by faith is grasped as an eschatological event that puts the old to death and raises up the new, we receive ourselves and the world back again as God's good creation. If Christ is the end and goal of the law, he is also the end, goal, and existential limit of our lives in this age. "For to me to live is Christ, and to die is gain" (Phil. 1:21). Where that is not the case, we shall have to depend on our efforts under the law to carry us to whatever "beyond" awaits. The law then becomes endless and we its eternal slaves. Furthermore, the law is then "used" by us (not by God, its author) as a preparation for eternity, an escape hatchway from this world. It is not used *for* this world as was intended; it is used for the next. It is a preparation for eternity, a means by which I supposedly can shape my own destiny—which is to say, extend my selfishness into eternity, if I can manage it.

Where the eschatological nature of justification is not grasped, self and world as God's good creation are also lost. Being a creature of God is not good enough. We are always on our way somewhere else, using the law as our instrument and even piously attempting to enlist the aid of Christ and his grace in our quest. We then have no time for this world or for others. We are preparing for eternity. "God, I thank thee that I am not like other men, extortioners, unjust, adulterers, or even like this tax collector. I fast twice a week, I give tithes of all that I get" (Luke 18:11–12).

But here once again the "eschato-logic" proves itself: "From him who has not, even what he has will be taken away" (Mark 4:25) and "Whoever would save his life will lose it" (Mark 8:35). The attempt to combine justification with such self-understanding under the law leads only to loss of the goodness of creation. If we think to exalt grace as the source of strength to make our escape, this can be done only by denigrating our created, natural strength. To give glory to grace we have to take it away from creation. Thus we end by turning grace into a blasphemy against creation. "Total depravity" in this context means a total annihilation of natural goodness. We lose the very life we had thought to save. Once again, the impossibility of combining salvation by works with grace demonstrates itself.

We can receive the self back as God's good creation only when we begin to view our lives from the perspective of eschatological faith. Christ is the end of the law to faith. The eschatological kingdom is God's unconditional gift. It comes by God's grace and power alone, in God's good time. That is the end and goal of our lives, our personal existential limit. When this is grasped in faith, we begin to see at last that our corruption and depravity consist not in falling from some moral and spiritual height, but precisely in aspiring to such heights on our own strength and virtue. We succumb to the temptation "You shall not die, you shall be as gods, knowing good from evil." Our depravity consists not in what we have lost of our created goodness, but in what we have added to it: precisely the attempt to "be as gods," to escape from creation. The totality of our depravity consists in the blindness: We do not even see that our virtues are as sinful as our vices. Both under the guise of being virtuous and religious and in addiction to self-serving vices, we are bent on escaping from creature-hood and creation. Creation is not good enough for us.

Justification as an eschatological event gives unconditionally the end and goal of life, to faith "for the time being." They are given to faith, not to sight. It must be done so, for justification must create freedom. It must truly heal and save the disaffected heart, soul, and mind. This can be done only if all is done in complete freedom and spontaneity. The goal of life cannot be forced on us. Therefore it comes in hidden form, *sub contrario*, given to *faith*. By such faith the end and goal are given, and we can begin to believe in the goodness of being a creature, to wait "for the time being" for the coming of the kingdom in its fullness. We are given back the self as a good creation; we are given time for this world, for this creation.

That is what being saved means. To be reborn means to be born again into the world God created, to become a member of the truly human race. To die to the old means to die to both the viciousness and the heaven-storming pretentions of the religious old Adam and to walk in the newness of *created* life.

What was lost in the fall was *faith*, in God and God's creation. To be saved, healed, is to receive creation back again as God's gift, to again receive time for it, to get room to live, to rejoice and give praise to the Creator. It is to have one's lips unsealed so that the mouth will "show forth his praise." This happens when the end and the goal are given in Christ.

What then does one do when one is saved? One lives in this world as God's creature "for the time being." What does that mean? It means that—as Luther's catechism has it—we should "fear, love, and trust in God above all things," and do what God has commanded us to do—in "the flesh." With the conscience claimed by the eschatological promise, the "flesh" lives in this world in the law of God. The point in saying that is not, now, to reinstate what was called the third use of the law. The "flesh" in *this* world "for the time being" is to do the commandments of God not in some third way but as its entry into this world where the rest of humankind lives.

One can best see what the Reformation originally meant by this by looking at a writing like "The Judgment of Martin Luther on Monastic Vows" (1521).[6] The point is simply that following God's commandments will take us into the world of the neighbor in service and love, not into the world of self-chosen and self-serving "religious" works. The point is not that Luther sought to relax the ideals or to polemicize against communal life as a possible base for service to the world, or to reduce everything to the lowest common denominator of what is attainable in daily life. The point is rather that in the context of the penitential system the monastic vows lead to self-chosen holiness which is not commanded by God. God, for instance, does not command poverty as some sort of ideal for everyone who wishes to be truly holy. Such vows do proceed not from faith or from the commandment of God but rather from one's own lust for holiness. And whoever has this lust for holiness will never be satisfied with the commandments of God, because the commandments of God take one away from self into the world of the other.

Living by the commandments of God "in the flesh" is the opposite of one's own quest for holiness. It means incarnating what God has commanded in and for the world. The law is to be used in that way, as its author intended. The rejection of monastic vows, and with them the quest for one's own holiness, meant for Luther a new understanding of and love for God's commandments. What God commands takes us into the natural, created world. Here the proper place of "natural law" is to be found. By natural law most seem to mean "supernatural" law, a law built into the universe which, if followed, leads to eternal bliss, a kind of built-in permanent escape mechanism. Revealed law is then something like the completion, the clarification of what has been dimmed by the fall, the final extension of the escape ladder. That is not what Luther meant by it, even when he compared and often identified the commandments of God with "natural law." He meant precisely *natural* and not supernatural law. The commandments of God do not command anything contrary to life, anything supernatural or superhuman, but rather what anyone who properly consults his or her reason would have to acknowledge as good and right—exemplified, say, by the golden rule. Following the commandments of God and the natural law will hardly serve one's inflated and grandiose quests for holiness, but it might lead to good works in this world. It will not lead to the isolation of pole-sitting "holy men," but it might make Christians who are involved in giving themselves to this world. When the conscience is captivated by the gospel, "the flesh" living in the law does *good* works: It does what God wants.

Once again it is seen that such obedience is not spectacular in the world's eyes. It is quite ordinary most of the time. God's commandments do not lead to spiritual heroics: just honor your parents, do not kill, steal, commit adultery, covet, and so on. But this is just the sort of life about which one might say, "Yes, we all ought to live naturally and peacefully like that." At bottom the good work to which God's command leads is something so self-evident, so unspectacular, so plain, that it speaks a language everyone should understand.[7] The eschatological end given to faith gives us back the gift of life, of created life in this world. It *saves* us. It makes us human beings again.

This World as God's Creation

The relationship between justification and the world as we know it brings us to the much discussed and disputed doctrine of the two "kingdoms" or "realms." So much ink has been spilled over this matter that it is not possible for us here to follow all the arguments. Perhaps, however, in light of what we have already said, the issues can briefly be sorted out. If justification is an eschatological event that creates the faith we have spoken of, then through such an event faith receives the world back again as God's good creation. The understanding of the world as God's good creation is the result of eschatological faith, not of speculation about how it all began. When the world's end and goal are given to faith, it begins to appear, to faith alone, as the world God intends.

Since the eschatological kingdom is promised only to faith and not yet to sight, there is for the time being a duality; there are two "ages," two sorts of "rule" or sovereignty. This is the basis for any doctrine of "two kingdoms," and it must be maintained in spite of the distortions and ill use the doctrine has suffered through the centuries. The distinction between this age with its kind of rule and the coming age with its rule must be made for the sake of the eschatological and unconditional nature of the gospel. Where the distinction is blurred or lost, the gospel will be drawn into various compromises with the workings of this age, made conditional, and eventually be lost.

"My kingship," Jesus said before Pilate, "is not of this world; if my kingship were of this world, my servants would fight, that I might not be handed over to the Jews; but my kingship is not from the world" (John 18:36). Nothing one can do with the resources of this world can avail to bring in or establish Jesus' kingship. The distinction at that point is absolute, and must be so, or there is no gospel.[8]

Problems with the doctrine of the two kingdoms arise not because two such sorts of rule are distinguished but because the doctrine comes into a world that already possesses its own doctrines of two kingdoms. The doctrine comes into a world which in its fallen state is already split: material versus spiritual, sensible versus intelligible, real versus ideal, secular versus sacred, and so on endlessly.[9] Since the territory is already occupied by various "two kingdoms" doctrines, the eschatological doctrine is usually mixed with one or the other of them. The world already has its laws, its ways to heaven; and the inevitable tendency is always to enlist the gospel in one cause or another and so lose it.

The question therefore is not whether "two kingdoms" or types of rule or kingship should be distinguished (that cannot be avoided), but how they can and should be related. The question of the relationship of the two kingdoms is really the macrocosm of what we have already seen in the microcosm of the relationships between law and gospel, and between justification and sanctification. The attempt to synthesize law with gospel is disastrous. Likewise the attempt to synthesize the rule or kingship of Christ with that of this age and its ambitions will be disastrous and ultimately destructive. In the microcosm of individual piety it produces either despair or presumption. It drives to self-destruction: either despair over self and failure or pride in the ability of the self to deny itself and come as close as possible to suicide without actually committing it. In the macrocosm it produces tyranny, oppression, imperialism, genocide, and murder. One or another of the world's false eschatologies is enforced and sanctified with the name of Christ and the gospel. Like the "flesh" which in the microcosm is to be shucked off for the sake of the "spirit," in the macrocosm the "masses," the "non-Aryans," the "unbelievers," the "minorities," all who do not fit the plan, become expendable.

Faced with such attempts at synthesis, a "two kingdoms" doctrine inspired by the gospel will always say no. The gospel of Jesus Christ simply cannot be synthesized with the causes of this age, however grand or just. The eschatological kingdom comes as an unconditional gift. God puts to death the old and raises up the new *in Christ.* Where that is not held absolutely, humans take up stones, cudgels, and arms to kill, supposedly to complete the job left unfinished by Christ. The result is self-destruction in the microcosm and destruction of others in the macrocosm. God gave the Son to save the world, *this* world. He has died for us. One cannot bring in the kingdom by discipline, tyranny, or by exterminating its enemies. By such means, one only realizes the kingdom of the adversary.

The second error would be separation of the two kingdoms. In the microcosm of individual piety, this occurs in the absolute separation of justification from sanctification. One tries to combat the premature synthesis of justification and sanctification by leaving the scheme of law intact, by making justification a forensic sheer declaration and separating sanctification as a subsequent process under the "third use" of the law. The result is a false eschatology. One prematurely escapes from the world into an isolated realm—perhaps the church—where one is separated from the rest of the world with one's own special use of the law. The rule or kingdom of Christ has been identified or confused with one of the world's idealisms.

In the macrocosm, this error identifies the eschatological kingdom of Christ with the church; and the church, understood as a species of ideal religious community according to the world's models, is separated from the mundane and pro-fane affairs of this world. Religion is separated from the state, and from politics, economics, and so on. But the result of such separation is again that the world is abandoned to the adver-sary. Where vestigial remains of humanistic tradition persist, justice will prevail to some extent, but probably not for long. A world that has forgotten what law is for will easily find ways to justify human avarice and malice, most often under the form of high-sounding ideals and the promises of false eschatologies.

Both the synthesis of the two kingdoms and their separa-tion result from false eschatology. Synthesis thinks it possible to combine Christ's kingdom with this-worldly projects; sepa-ration thinks it possible prematurely to escape into an eschato-logical vestibule apart from the world. Neither is possible for a faith born of unconditional justification. Justification is the end and goal; it is death and resurrection. As such it is the believ-er's absolute personal and existential limit, which makes pos-sible a turning to this world, a receiving back of this world as God's creation. We shall receive the world, this world, as God's good creation, as the place to which we turn to serve, only to the extent that we believe unconditional justification as our true eschatological limit and goal. The gift of the eschatological kingdom is the only thing which opens up for us *this* world as also God's kingdom. The creaturehood of this world is a belief and hope, granted to faith.

To faith, neither synthesis nor separation is possible. The distinction is absolute: God's eschatological kingdom comes solely and unconditionally by God's power, inaugurated by the death and resurrection of Christ, carried to faith by the proc-lamation, and empowered by the Spirit. And precisely because the distinction is absolute, we are given back this world as God's creation in which to serve and carry out God's will in anticipa-tion of God's ultimate triumph. Thus we pray: "Thy kingdom come, thy will be done, on earth as it is in heaven." Because

the distinction is absolute, there is only one place, one kingdom for the time being, in which we can live, work, and serve:
this world. No escape is possible. We must wait, serve, and
hope, until the kingdom of this world is become the kingdom
of our God and of Christ. It is perhaps curious: Only where
the kingdoms are thus distinguished will there be functionally
one kingdom. Whenever the distinction is not absolute, the
eschatological kingdom will be confused with one of the world's
religious kingdoms, and all will be lost. The world's doctrines,
no matter how much they *claim* to be "one kingdom" doctrines, always *function* as two; this world, the present world, is
always sacrificed for the sake of some other ideal world.

The world is given back to us as a place in which to serve—
indeed, as the only place in which we can serve. To die and to be
raised to newness of life by faith is to die to all escapism—either
of the "fleshly" sort or the "spiritual," and to be reborn a creature in God's creation. To die and be raised to newness of life is
to die to all individualism and to become a member of Christ's
body, the church, to worship, pray, and praise. The church
is that body which believes and bears witness to the coming
of God's kingdom by the power of God's unconditional grace.
Precisely in that light the church engages in its activity in and
for this world. Perhaps one can say, the church is the macrocosm of Luther's formula: "Conscience in the gospel, flesh in
the law." Knowing the unconditional gospel, the church bears
witness to and incarnates the proper use of the law in the world.
This is the basis for its political activity. The law and politics are
for taking care of people. "The sabbath was made for man, not
man for the sabbath" (Mark 2:27). In the light of unconditional
grace, the church cannot separate itself from political concerns,
but must look on itself as the witness to the proper use of God's
creation and God's law, in taking care of God's creatures.

How does the church which has heard decide what to do? It
uses its head and its heart in the concrete situation, to attempt

to incarnate the commandment of God. In this task the church can and must utilize all the wisdom of its own tradition and experience as well as the wisdom of the world. In seeking answers in concrete situations to the question "What should we do?" the church can draw on the work of the wise of all ages, the specialists who can help in seeking to apply the commandment of God to take care of the earth and the neighbor in complex and changing situations.

From this vantage point, we can also make better sense of Paul's injunction to "be subject to the governing authorities" (Rom. 13) and of the Reformation's derivation of respect for civil authority from the fourth commandment ("Honor your father and mother that it may be well with you and you may live long upon this earth"). Because of the promise given to faith, we are sent into this world with respect for the authority God has established there under the law. The point of the injunction is not to make Christians into reactionary conservatives or subservient slaves to the status quo. It would hardly have occurred to Paul (or to Luther and the reformers) that anyone grasped by the power of the eschatological promise would be such. Only centuries of attempted synthesis between "eternal law" and the gospel have eroded the eschatological vision and turned Christians into reactionaries. The point of the injunctions is quite the opposite. Christians are likely to be impatient enthusiasts, who think the gospel gives them the right to rebel against and flaunt all existing order. The injunctions remind that this is not so. God is still God—in this world as well. Redemption is not against creation. If Christians are not reactionary conservatives protecting the status quo, neither are they in principle revolutionaries thinking to bring in the eschaton by force. Their concern is for the proper use of law and authority to care for human beings and to foster truly human existence and just societies. The Christian aim is to support causes, laws, and authorities that give promise of justice, whatever form (conservative, liberal, or even revolutionary) these may take at a given time, always remembering that God's kingdom comes by God's power alone in God's good time.

The gospel as the unconditional promise of the kingdom humanizes and naturalizes the law. No doubt we can say even that it "contextualizes" the law—as long as we realize that the gospel does this and not just the passage of time or historical expediency. The distinction between the two kingdoms or kinds of rule is made precisely to foster such humanization. God's rule in the gospel is the rule of unconditional grace, and as such is the limit and ultimate goal of the rule of this age, which is a conditional rule of law. The tendency is always to project the rule of law into God's eternity and thus tyrannize people rather than care for them. The distinction between the rules is made both to give the rule of law its proper place and to protect the world from the tyranny of the religions which have become a substitute for eschatology (which is what most political ideologies have been and are, including the Marxist dream of the "withering away of the state"). The distinction must be made also (and perhaps especially) for biblical and Christian religions that have succumbed to a false eschatology. The criticism must begin at home. Before rashly plunging into political adventure, we must get our eschatology straight, lest we just add to the tyranny. Centuries of church history do not breed confidence that Christians are immune from destructive religious ideologies.

Separation of church and state, of religion and politics, is an impossible move from the eschatological standpoint. The church as a sociological organization is not an eschatological vestibule into which one can prematurely escape from politics. The distinction makes that clear. Such separation is therefore not to be identified with necessary "two kingdoms" teaching. But church people and theologians should not forget that the actual separation we now have is a political expedient necessitated by bad theology: The world had to take steps to protect itself from false eschatology and its tyranny. If the political and social activity of the church just means imposing bad eschatology, the world is no doubt better off without us. The political activity of the church will be properly executed when the church acts in the faith that God's kingdom comes by God's unconditional grace and that for the time being we are to care for God's creatures and God's creation.

CHAPTER FOUR

Justification Today

> *The doctrine of justification is always and everywhere relevant because it speaks of God's judgment on our existence and drives to the direct declaration of that judgment itself. For that reason justification language is dogmatically primary and is the plumb line for the church's proclamation: the article by which the church stands or falls. Its relevance for individual life is that it delivers from the prison all construct for themselves in the fear and denial of death. Its larger relevance for the life of the world derives from the vision it inspires, in contrast to competing visions. It directs our vision beyond absolutism and relativism to the hope that God's will be done "on earth as in heaven."*

The Question of Relevance

Is what we have said about justification "relevant" today? Arguments about relevance are somehow always elusive, mostly depressingly dull and finally inconclusive. Probing for the "modern" person, to whom one is supposed to be relevant, has become more and more like shooting at a moving target. As Karl Barth put it, one seems always to be running after the train that has just left. Perhaps part of the problem is that we mistake relevance for topicality. The topical is peculiar to a particular *topos*, a restricted time and place, as are styles which come and go, or "topics" of current interest expatiated on in television talk shows. The topical is here today, gone tomorrow. To be *relevant*, the matter in question must be lifted above the merely topical to the status of that which always and everywhere applies. It is thus redundant to inquire about the relevance of something "today." If it is relevant at all, it is always so.

To be precise we should therefore put our question thus: Is justification by faith as we have described it relevant, or was it only of topical interest? Is it always and everywhere applicable, or does it answer only to certain restricted states and needs of the human psyche? More specifically, Does talk of justification carry credence only for those afflicted by a guilty conscience produced by excessive legalism and penitential practice? Does justification language depend too much on metaphors drawn from legal and juridical spheres?

Arguing for the relevance of justification by faith is perhaps like making an apology for marriage in a brothel. Those who have some inkling of what is involved will not need to be convinced, and those who do not will hardly be convinced by such an exercise. But there is utility in such argument nevertheless, since dogmatics is intended as aid and instruction to teachers and preachers. Thus we can make a beginning by reiterating some of the points made in the note at the end of the first chapter of this *locus*. Speaking in terms of justification is dogmatically necessary and relevant (always and everywhere), because such speech deals directly with God's judgment on our existence. It deals directly with the concrete structures of law and justice under which we live. It is a mistake to say that such language is restricted to Paul, Augustine, Luther, and a few others who had some problem with "the law." Everywhere in Scripture God is the judge, the ultimate judge over human existence. The "last judgment," the ultimate sentence, is certainly of some relevance. Justification deals directly and conclusively with that judgment. It says what the judgment *is*: You are justified for Jesus' sake.

No doubt there are other metaphors, other pictures and images, for our relationship to God which are important and enlightening and instructive for our communication of the gospel: love, light, truth, meaning, reconciliation, redemption, and so on. They lack the dogmatic importance accorded to justification language, however, because they tend to remain just metaphors, describing the relationship rather than creating it. "Justification" and related concepts like "imputation," "reckoning," and "forgiveness of sins" maintain their relevance because they point to a quite specific use of language, a use consonant with the eschatological character of the event: *doing* the deed, *delivering* the judgment. Justification language, when properly spoken, does not just talk *about* the relationship to God, it decides the issue. It speaks simply and directly: "I forgive you all your sins for Jesus' sake," "I pronounce you just by virtue of Christ's righteousness." It tells us, in effect, why the apology for marriage is not likely to work in the brothel: One cannot merely describe the marriage, one has to give the bridegroom.

Dogmatically speaking, the reason for the priority and abiding relevance of justification language lies just here: It stipulates what kind of communication is supposed to take place in the proclamation of the church. If justification is an unconditional eschatological pronouncement, then it has simply to be pronounced. There may no doubt be all sorts of ways to do that without using the actual terminology of "justification," but this language remains the dogmatic plumb line for the church's proclamation. Thus the article on justification is that by which the church stands or falls. When the church forgets this use of language it has lost its reason for being.

The question whether justification appeals to this or that state of the human psyche or answers to this or that need or consciousness of guilt is dogmatically secondary. Indeed, one can well ask whether justification by faith is strictly speaking relevant to the old Adam at all. It spells the *end* of the old Adam.

In that sense it does not cater to our needs as old beings at all; it makes *new* beings. It puts to death and raises up. The relevance of the justification proclamation therefore does not depend on guilt feelings or the "introspective conscience." These may, no doubt, be one "point of contact"—a more persistent one than many moderns think—but there are others. The justification proclamation is an attack on the old being, on whatever folly it happens to be engaged in. It attacks the proud, the secure, the super-religious, as much as it attacks and attends to despair. Indeed, Paul seems to apply the message more to secure super-Christians and Judaizers than to the despairing. Justification as unconditional gift is relevant always and everywhere because it means the end of whatever selfish folly we have gotten ourselves into, be it despair, pride, plain boredom, sloth, or the attempt to stave off thoughts of tomorrow by filling our barns today. Justification for Jesus' sake is good news for all. It grants newness of life, life in the Spirit.

Relevance: The Life of the Individual

The Epistle to the Hebrews sets forth for all time a basic statement about the relevance of the Christian message in what we have called the microcosm of the life of the individual: Jesus partook of our nature, "that through death he might destroy him who has the power of death, that is, the devil, and deliver all those who through fear of death were subject to lifelong bondage" (Heb. 2:14–15). Ernest Becker's recent study, *The Denial of Death*, can explicate for us what this means in contemporary terms.[1] Unlike other animals, we, as human beings, know we are going to die, and we cannot bear it. We cannot bear our finitude. Our life project is the denial of death. As the serpent whispered, "You shall not die, you shall be as gods!" We embark on our own cause (*causa sui*) and build our own defenses against death—and necessarily so. We need protection against death; thus we build the lie—the vital lie—of character and maturity. Exactly as we have been saying, this quest is to be a person of substance and virtue, who will supposedly survive death. But the very project we are engaged in becomes our prison. We are trapped by our own lie. Becker says:

> The defenses that form a person's character support a grand illusion, and when we grasp this we can understand the full drivenness of man. He is driven away from himself, from self-knowledge, self-reflection. He is driven toward things that support the lie of his character, his automatic equanimity. But he is also drawn precisely toward those things that make him anxious, as a way of skirting them masterfully, testing himself against them, controlling them by defying them. As Kierkegaard taught us, anxiety lures us on, becomes the spur to much of our energetic activity: We flirt with our own growth, but also dishonestly. This explains much of the friction in our lives, we enter symbiotic relationships in order to get the security we need, in order to get relief from our anxieties, our aloneness and helplessness; but these relationships also bind us, they enslave us even further because they support the lie we have fashioned. So we strain against them in order to be more free. The irony is that we do this straining uncritically, in a struggle within our own armor, as it were; and so we increase our drivenness, the second-hand quality of our struggle for freedom. Even in our flirtation with anxiety we are unconscious of our motives. We seek stress, we push our own limits, but we do it with our *screen against despair* and not with despair itself. We do it with the stock market, with sports cars, with atomic missiles, with the success ladder in the corporation or the competition in the university. We do it in the prison of a dialogue with our own little family, by marrying against their wishes or choosing a way of life because they frown on it, and so on. Hence the complicated and second-hand quality of our entire drivenness. Even in our passions we are nursery children playing with toys that represent the real world. Even when these toys crash and cost us our lives or our sanity, we are cheated of the consolation

that we were in the real world instead of the playpen of our fantasies. We still did not meet our doom on our own manly terms, in contest with objective reality. It is fateful and ironic how the lie we need in order to live dooms us to a life that is never really ours.[2]

That is an almost perfect modern statement about "all those who through fear of death were subject to lifelong bondage." Becker's quote from Otto Rank sums up the matter "once and for all, for all future psychoanalysts and students of man: 'Every human being is . . . equally unfree, that is *we . . . create* out of freedom, a prison.'"[3]

The story of Howard Hughes is a modern parallel to the parable of the rich fool in this vein. He was so afraid of death that it killed him! He retreated into seclusion with his hoards of wealth, fearing all who might make some claim on him or "contaminate" him with their touch. He would not even wear clothes and sat alone in darkened rooms watching movies. In the end, when help was needed the self-made prison was too secure. Extreme, no doubt, but parabolic of the prison we all construct. Parabolic also of a world so bent on self-preservation that it is choking on its own refuse.

The proclamation of justification—of daily renewal in the unconditional promise—is relevant always and everywhere because just by its very unconditionality it is the "death of death." Justification brings the death which we fear so much forward to meet us, and through it grants new life, and thus deliverance from bondage. It is relevant always and every-where because bondage to the fear of death is universal. It is relevant because its unconditionality absolutely forestalls and rejects categorically any attempt to synthesize or connect it with the self-made prisons, with the projects we set up in our futile attempts to deny finitude and death. It is relevant because it gives us back our lives as God's creatures and sets us free.

"For *freedom* Christ has set us free; stand fast therefore, and do not submit again to a yoke of slavery" (Gal. 5:1).

From this vantage point, the perennial protests against unconditional justification must be seen as protests put from within the prison of our *causa sui* projects. As old beings we fear the death such justification brings. The cries, questions, and protests are the death rattle of the old being, who knows that the prison wall has been breached and that the end of all his pet projects draws near. "But don't we have to do *something*?" "Is not *unconditional* grace dangerous?" "Who will be good if *nothing* is demanded?" "Is not such grace 'cheap'?" and so on and so on. The old being can hope to rescue something from the threatening disaster to its *causa sui* projects only by claiming some little bit to do or by casting doubts on the wisdom or propriety of an unconditional gift. The questions are designed to put anyone who proclaims justification by faith alone on the defensive. And most generally, alas, the strategy succeeds. One says, "Well, yes, now that you mention it, there *is* a little something. . . ." Or one tries to forestall the danger by hedging grace about with certain minimal conditions, raising the price just a little—perhaps at least to the level of the bargain basement. Thus, though the prison has been broken into, we stay in our cells.

When that occurs, when the death rattle of the old being frightens us onto the defensive, the battle for relevance is lost. Then justification indeed becomes of merely topical interest, to those prisoners who perhaps can make use of it in further sealing themselves in. If justification by faith is to be relevant at all, one cannot go on the defensive. The questions must be met squarely and offensively. Is not such grace "cheap?" No, it is not cheap; it is priceless; it is *free*. "Is not unconditional grace dangerous?" Of course. God takes a great risk to get what he wants. "To him who has, more will be given; from him who has not, even that which he has shall be taken away." One can take offense at the unconditional gift and lose everything. But God, apparently, does not want just a little something. He is out to get everything: all the heart, soul, mind, strength, and love of others. "But don't we have to do *something*?" How like us in our last extremity piously to hold out for a little "something"! It demonstrates our true intent: That is all we had ever planned to do. "Don't we have to do something?" No. Simply be still for once and listen. Faith, Luther insisted, arises out of the absolute passivity of listening to God's justifying word. Out of that death, that passivity, life comes, life born by the divine Spirit.

The question must then be put in an entirely different way. Paul put it, "Shall we sin the more that grace may abound?" That is the only question left to ask. "What are you going to do now that there is nothing you *have to* do?" "What's the matter? Don't you *want* to do good?" "How can you who died to sin still live in it?" Paul's question reflects incredulity: How can you manage sin once you have heard the unconditional word? Put this way, the questions often bring the shock of surprise and sometimes even a smile to the lips. That smile is just the point. In it is hidden the entire relevance of the doctrine of justification.

Relevance: The World Vision

The wider relevance of justification by faith, in the macrocosm, the world and its future, consists in the kind of vision, the basic hope in life, that it inspires. What we have already said in the previous sections has laid the foundation and needs only to be explicated more pointedly.

Justification by faith fosters a hope that "endures all things" in unreserved service of this world, because of the unconditional promise of eschatological fulfillment. It fosters a hold on life which believes that the world will progress most surely toward its appointed goal precisely when it believes that the goal will be granted by God alone in God's good time. The world will progress most surely, that is, when it ceases building its own prisons in its denial of death and begins to behave as though God justifies sinners. The doctrine promotes a vision that does not, therefore, "abolish the law," but hopes for the ultimate fulfillment of God's will, the ultimate doing of God's commandments—indeed, the inscription of God's law in the heart. It believes that the will of God is the ultimate good of truly human existence—that the sabbath, the final eschatological rest, was made for man, and not man for the sabbath. Thus it does not find it necessary to alter one iota of the law, but looks to the day when the law will end because what it points to will be realized. Having a foretaste of things to come in justification by faith, the believer hopes and serves in this world.

It is important to say this because the vision will be quite different when justification is not understood as bringing an end and new beginning into our present by faith. The church will then falter—as it does today—between a legalistic absolutism on the one hand and an accommodating relativism on the other. In the past, the most common failing has no doubt been legalistic absolutism (though not without casuistic accommodation where necessary). Where justification is not the end and telos, law becomes absolute and eternal. Man is made for the sabbath. People become expendable for the sake of the absolute (usually identified with the status quo or the desires of the rulers). Pretensions to political power, tyranny, and inquisition in the history of the church testify to the evil outcome of such a vision.

Instructive in this regard is the Jansenist movement in seventeenth-century France, perhaps one of the last attempts to reassert a kind of pristine theological and legalistic absolutism in the face of casuistic compromise with the modern world. For many Jansenists such absolutism simply meant denial of and retreat from the world. For someone like Pascal, however, escape was impossible. There is no place here where one can escape to achieve the absolute. Humans are caught between the "grandeur and the misery" of created existence. Held by the absolute and yet knowing it is unattainable leads to a "tragic vision."⁴ Nowhere can one escape the demanding voice and searching eye of God. One can only remain in the world and try ones strength, even though one knows the task is hopeless. "Christ will be suffering the torments of death to the very end of the world; for all that time we must not sleep."⁵ Such tragic vision imagines no further change or transformation. The absolute is given and is unattainable, and one cannot go back to the world of compromise. Jesus is on the cross to the end of time.

> In this eternal and intemporal moment which lasts to the very end of the world, tragic man remains alone, doomed to be misunderstood by sleeping men and exposed to the anger of a hidden and absent God. But he finds, in his very loneliness and suffering, the only values which he can still have and which will be enough to make him great: the absolute and rigourous nature of his own awareness and his own ethical demands, his quest for absolute justice and absolute truth, and his refusal to accept any illusions or compromise.⁶

The tragic vision is, perhaps one can say, a disappointed absolutism. The absolute is not surrendered, but the hold on life is tenuous. Perhaps one could say that an atheistic existentialism is the secular counterpart to that vision. The tragic vision holds onto God but finds life a tragedy; the existentialist surrenders God, and finds life absurd. Both are disappointed or disillusioned absolutists.

The predominant modern replacement for the absolutism of the past has been relativism, the idea that truth (or, in our case, law) is relative to its historical context. As a protest against absolutism there is some right in the assertion, but a theology based on justification must raise questions about the antinomianism and ultimate destructiveness of the vision. Dogmatic theology must pay attention to the manner in which this vision evolves and the effect it has on the world today.

Relativism is a human attempt to domesticate the law. Where law has no eschatological end, this is perhaps the only recourse. Relativism evolved out of the failure of theology to assert the eschatological vision of the end and goal, death and resurrection. Kant took the absolute out of its metaphysical heaven and placed it within the pious heart, to protect and ensure the autonomy of the individual vis-à-vis the law. Hegel found even "the law within" too "heteronomous" and dissolved it in the dialectic of history: the "concept" by which the present is grasped only to be challenged by the new antithesis and taken up into a higher synthesis. The "law" is constantly negated to be taken up in "higher" synthesis, and is thus entirely relative to its place in the dialectical movement of history. Marxism takes the dialectic and uses it to change the course of history, not merely to understand it. But the result of the relativism is that right and wrong can then be evaluated entirely in terms of our own vision. Human beings can be sacrificed quite easily for the sake of the cause.[7]

From the point of view of a theology of justification, the significant thing in this development is that it involves a kind of eschatology, a doctrine about the end, carried by the idea of negation. But what is false is that it is always *the law* that is negated, not the old Adam. The old Adam escapes unscathed and appears on the stage of history as the one who embodies, understands, and eventually carries out the negation. Unnegated themselves, old beings appear now in the role of archnegators, revolutionaries, the arbiters over the lives and deaths of other beings. The truth, the law, is relative to their vision. Human beings are expendable. The result is, if anything, worse than absolutism. If the absolutist was a wolf, the relativist is a wolf in sheep's clothing. Who knows when or where the knife of the relativist will strike?

Today a relativism that pronounces a benediction on all our vices seems to be threatening. A theology of justification must consider carefully what it means by the claim to uphold the law in the light of its hope. Threatened by relativisms and puzzled by "liberation" movements, the church seems to halt, if not to incline toward reversion to old absolutisms. The church seems unable to handle either the relativism or the egoism and narcissism in many liberation movements, not being able to put its finger on what is wrong. As protests against the tyranny of past absolutisms, the liberation movements are most often quite justifiable. But the difficulty is that like Marxists, liberationists are too often revolutionaries who have taken the right to negation into their own hands, presiding over questions of life and death. Absolutist tyranny and injustice must be resisted, but it is no gain for the church if it simply falls prey to a relativism that once again justifies arbitrary destruction of human life—whatever the age, creed, sex, or color. Neither absolutist nomism nor relativist antinomianism will save or liberate us. Neither circumcision nor uncircumcision matters, but a new creation and "faith working through love" (Gal. 6:15; 5:6).

The vision and the hope inspired by justification can help us find our way between the tyranny of yesterday's absolutisms and today's relativisms. The vision is not absolutist: The sabbath was made for man, not man for the sabbath. Nor is the vision the "tragic vision" of the disillusioned absolutist. Christ is not on the cross until the end of time. Having died once to sin, he dies no more. He is risen and is the end of the law to all who believe. The "revolutionary" move to put the world on the cross until the dawn of its secular vision is no better. *Christ* has died for us, once for all, that the law of God might be fulfilled in us, "who walk not according to the flesh but according to the Spirit" (Rom. 8:4). The Christian vision leads into the world, to suffering for and with others in the expectation of God's will being done on earth as it is in heaven. The aim is not to gain one's own holiness or to bring in the kingdom by force or tyranny, but to care for God's creatures and God's creation. "The creation waits with eager longing for the revealing of the sons of God" (Rom. 8:19).

Notes

Part 1

Introduction

1 Smalcald Articles, Part II, Article I, *BC* 292.
2 Augsburg Confession, Article III, *BC* 29–30.
3 H. Richard Niebuhr, *The Kingdom of God in America* (New York: Willett, Clark & Co., 1937), p. 193.
4 Gustaf Aulén, *Christus Victor*, trans. A. G. Hebert (New York: Macmillan Co., 1931).
5 See Osmo Tiililä, *Das Strafleiden Christi*, AASF 48 (Helsinki, 1941).
6 J. W. C. Wand, *The Atonement* (London: SPCK, 1963), p. 1.
7 Ibid., p. 9.
8 Hans Kessler, *Die theologische Bedeutung des Todes Jesu*, Themen und Thesen der Theologie (Düsseldorf: Patmos Verlag, 1970), p. 16.
9 Martin Hengel, *Crucifixion in the Ancient World and the Folly of the Message of the Cross* (Philadelphia: Fortress Press, 1977), p. 90.
10 From Iwand's unpublished *Christologievorlesung*, cited in Jürgen Moltmann, *The Crucified God*, trans. R. A. Wilson and John Bowden (New York: Harper & Row, 1974), p. 41.
11 Ibid., p. 36.

Chapter 1

1 Martin Hengel, *Crucifixion in the Ancient World and the Folly of the Message of the Cross* (Philadelphia: Fortress Press, 1977).

2 See the discussions in Hans Kessler, *Die theologische Bedeutung des Todes Jesu*, Themen und Thesen der Theologie (Düsseldorf: Patmos Verlag, 1970), pp. 227ff.; and Sam K. Williams, *Jesus' Death as Saving Event: The Background and Origin of a Concept*, Harvard Dissertations in Religion 2 (Missoula, Mont.: Scholars Press, 1975), pp. 203ff.

3 See Williams, *Jesus' Death*, esp. pp. 59–135, 165–202, for an account of the use of this material.

4 Ibid., passim.

5 See Morna Hooker, *Jesus and the Servant* (London: SPCK, 1959).

6 Williams, *Jesus' Death*, p. 230.

7 Hengel, *Crucifixion*, pp. 89–90.

8 Friedrich R. Hasse, *Anselm von Canterbury*, vol. 2 (Leipzig: Verlag von W. Engelmann, 1852), pp. 608–9. Cited in Kessler, *Die theologische Bedeutung des Todes Jesu*, p. 84.

9 Kessler, *Die theologische Bedeutung des Todes Jesu*, p. 84.

10 Ibid., p. 35

11 Ibid., p. 55

12 See below, and Kessler, *Die theologische Bedeutung des Todes Jesu*, p. 75.

13 Ibid., pp. 75ff.

14 Ibid., pp. 139ff.

15 Anselm, *Cur Deus Homo*, preface.

16 Kessler, *Die theologische Bedeutung des Todes Jesu*, p. 145.

17 Anselm, *Cur Deus Homo*, i, 11.

18 Ibid., i, 12.

19 Ibid., i, 13.

20 Ibid., ii, 20.

21 Kessler, *Die theologische Bedeutung des Todes Jesu*, p. 63.

22 One should not drive this too far, since Anselm did work with the more aesthetically tinged Augustinian concept of *order* rather than strict justice and law. The fact remains, however, that Anselm did make the concept of justice determinative for his entire soteriology and that one can therefore speak of a juridicizing of the Augustinian *ordo*. See ibid., pp. 130, 136.

23 Ibid., pp. 130ff.

24 Ibid., p. 134. Cf. Anselm, *Cur Deus Homo*, i, 24.

25 See John McIntyre, *St. Anselm and His Critics* (Edinburgh: Oliver & Boyd, 1954).

26 *Cur Deus Homo*, ii, 14.

27 Kessler, *Die theologische Bedeutung des Todes Jesu*, p. 168. Also W. Kasper, *Jesus the Christ* (New York: Paulist Press, 1976), p. 220.

28 *Cur Deus Homo*, i, 8. This remains a standard—and the best—refutation of exemplarist theories. Protestant orthodoxy later turned it against the Socinians. It would be absurd for God to go to such lengths merely to provide an example of what everyone knew already. See Hans Emil Weber, *Reformation, Orthodoxie und Rationalismus*, part 2, "Der Geist der Orthodoxie" (Gütersloh: Gerd Mohn, 1951), p. 190, n. 5.

29 *Cur Deus Homo*, i, 12; cf. i, 24.

30 See R. S. Franks, *The Work of Christ* (New York: Thomas Nelson & Sons, 1962), p. 145; and Kessler, *Die theologische Bedeutung des Todes Jesu*, p. 167.

31 Cited in Franks, *Work of Christ*, p. 365. Usually the emphasis on the freedom of God in Socinus and followers is attributed to the influence of Duns Scotus.

32 Osmo Tiililä, *Das Strafleiden Christi*, AASF 48 (Helsinki, 1941), pp. 67–68.

33 Weber, *Reformation, Orthodoxie und Rationalismus*, p. 185.

34 See Lauri Haikola, *Studien zu Luther und zum Luthertum*, UUA 2 (Uppsala: Lundequistska Bokhandeln, 1958), pp. 9, 106.

35 Weber, *Reformation, Orthodoxie und Rationalismus*, p. 198; also Heinrich Schmid, *The Doctrinal Theology of the Evangelical Lutheran Church*, 3d ed., trans. Charles A. Hay and Henry E. Jacobs (Minneapolis: Augsburg Publishing House, 1899), p. 347.

36 Schmid, *Doctrinal Theology*, p. 347.

37 Leonard Hutter, *Loci communes theologici*, 415, cited in ibid., p. 348.

38 John Andrew Quenstedt, *Theologica didactico-polemica*, iii, 227, cited in ibid., p. 348.

39 In this regard they were following Luther, who also dispensed with the distinction between satisfaction and punishment. For Luther it was quite pointless, since as we shall see he reversed the direction. If Anselm feared punishment because it would mean destruction, Luther said that is just what happens. Jesus is "destroyed" *for us* and yet conquers. Orthodoxy, however, legalized the punishment and tended to miss Luther's point.

40 Schmid, *Doctrinal Theology*, p. 359.

41 John Gerhard, cited in ibid., p. 356.

42 Ibid., pp. 340ff. The doctrine of the threefold office, though quite prominent in the older dogmatics—even among liberals (who, however, generally reinterpreted it to fit their particular scheme)—is not treated kindly by contemporary dogmaticians. It did have the

advantage of stressing that Christ was carrying out a mandate
from God through the office and not doing something randomly from
mere human caprice. Also, it attempted to encompass the whole of
Christ's life and death in one convenient scheme. Nevertheless, it
seems to be an artificial scheme that does not contribute essentially
to the understanding of Christ's work. It can even distort when the
abstractions begin to crowd out the actualities of his life by specu-
lations about whether and when he used his kingly powers while
on earth, and so on. Werner Elert's criticism exposes the problems.
He sees the idea of the threefold office to be a classic misapplication
of the promise-fulfillment scheme. The fulfillment is taken captive
by the expectation. Jesus tends to get "imprisoned" in the Old Testament offices. What is new and better in Christ is precisely what
distinguishes him from the offices, not what he has in common with
them. (*Der Christliche Glaube*, 2d ed. [Berlin: Im Furche-Verlag,
1941], pp. 405ff.) As Prophet he did not merely speak the word; he
was the Word. As Priest he did not offer selected "spotless lambs" in
a temple ritual; he was killed himself "outside the camp." As King
he was not a despot in a theocratic dynasty; he came to serve, to
suffer, to die. There is something of a cruel irony in decking Jesus
out in the offices which he resisted and which eventually destroyed
him. He was not any of those. The law and the prophets were until
John, "grace and truth came through Jesus Christ" (John 1:17). Thus
it does not seem useful for dogmatics to continue using this scheme.
For this reason we pay little attention to it in subsequent treatment.

43   Franks, *Work of Christ*, p. 145.
44   Ibid., pp. 370ff.; Weber, *Reformation, Orthodoxie und Rationalis-
     mus*, pp. 186ff.
45   Friedrich Schleiermacher, *The Christian Faith*, ed. H. R. Mackintosh
     and J. S. Stewart (Edinburgh: T. & T. Clark, 1928), pp. 431–38.
46   Ibid., pp. 425–31.
47   Albrecht Ritschl, *The Christian Doctrine of Justification and Rec-
     onciliation*, ed. H. R. Mackintosh and A. B. Macaulay (Edinburgh:
     T. & T. Clark, 1902); cf. intro, pp. Iff. See also Albrecht Ritschl, *The-
     ologie und Metaphysik* (Bonn: Adolph Marcus, 1881). Later in life
     Ritschl used the idea of independent value judgments to character-
     ize the peculiarity of religious perceptions (*Justification and Recon-
     ciliation*, pp. 204–5).
48   *Justification and Reconciliation*, IV, 27, pp. 193ff.
49   R. Schäfer, *Ritschl* (Tübingen: J. C. B. Mohr [Paul Siebeck], 1968),
     pp. 112ff.
50   Ritschl, *Justification and Reconciliation*, pp. 477ff.
51   Ibid., p. 455.

52 Ibid., pp. 455–56.

53 Ibid., p. 477.

54 Ibid., p. 457.

55 Schäfer, *Ritschl*, pp. 59–62.

56 Ibid., p. 63.

57 H. J. Iwand, "Wider den Missbrauch des pro me als methodisches Prinzip in der Theologie," *ThLz*, 7/8 (1954): 454–58.

58 Ibid., p. 455.

59 The list is seemingly endless: J. McLeod Campbell, R. C. Moberly, Robert Dale, James Denney, Hastings Rashdall, Robert Franks, to name but a few. For a good survey of the arguments, see Robert S. Paul, *The Atonement and the Sacraments* (Nashville: Abingdon Press, 1960), pp. 162–281.

60 See, e.g., P. T. Forsyth, *The Person and Place of Jesus Christ* (London: Hodder & Stoughton, 1909), pp. 7–8.

61 P. T. Forsyth, *The Work of Christ*, FL (London: William Collins Sons, 1965), p. 85.

62 Ibid., p. 107: "He could will nothing against his holy nature. . . . Nothing in the compass of the divine nature could enable him to abolish a moral law, the law of holiness. . . . If God's love were not essentially holy love, in the course of time mankind would cease to respect it, and consequently to trust it. . . . What love wants is not simply love in response, but respect and confidence. . . . God's holy law is his own holy nature. His love is under the condition of eternal respect. It is quite unchangeable."

63 Forsyth, *Person and Place of Jesus Christ*, p. 222.

64 Forsyth, *Work of Christ*, pp. 113, 114.

65 Ibid., p. 181.

66 P. T. Forsyth, *The Cruciality of the Cross* (London: Independent Press, 1948), p. 41.

67 In the idea of the "confessional obedience of Christ" to the divine holiness, Forsyth modified currents in British thinking on atonement. McLeod Campbell had suggested that the atoning work be understood as a perfect and vicarious confession of sin before God. R. C. Moberly had suggested the idea of vicarious penitence offered to God. The criticism of both was that neither confession of sin nor penitence can be offered vicariously for another, nor could a sinless Christ do either. Forsyth modified these suggestions by saying that Christ as the sinless one neither confesses sin nor does vicarious penitence, but precisely as the sinless one in solidarity with the world of sin and in his obedience confesses the divine holiness in his death. He "who knew no sin" was "made to be sin" and in obedience

confesses the rectitude of divine judgment on sin. Only the sinless one could do that.

68 Forsyth, *Work of Christ*, p. 165.
69 Ibid., p. 155. Emphasis added.
70 Ibid., pp. 107–9.
71 Ibid., p. 168.
72 Ibid., p. 170.
73 Ibid., p. 173.
74 Ibid., p. 178.
75 Ibid., pp. 162ff. Forsyth was already conscious of the different aspects (as he called them) of Christ's atoning work (the triumphant, the satisfactionary, and the regenerative) and of the need to draw them together into a unity. The first, the triumphant, must be seen as the condition of the second, the satisfactionary, and the second of the third, the regenerative, so that they all condition one another in a "living interaction." "This one action of the holy Saviour's total person was, on its various sides, the destruction of evil, the satisfaction of God, and the sanctification of men. And it is in this moral medium of holiness (if I may so say) that these three effects pass and play into each other with a spiritual interpenetration." (*Work of Christ*, p. 163.)
76 Rudolf Otto, *The Idea of the Holy* (London: Oxford University Press, 1923).
77 John H. Rodgers argues that Forsyth does not intend to moralize holiness and that he understands it rather as a total claim on human existence, embracing all one is, thinks, feels, and does. The response to divine holiness is not morality but the obedience of faith which thereafter affects one's conduct. No doubt that is true. But would not Schleiermacher and Ritschl have said just the same? The question is whether one can really repair the damage of liberal theology in this fashion. Even Rodgers has to admit that Forsyth himself is not consistent and repeatedly complicates matters by identifying the moral with the holy. John H. Rodgers, *The Theology of P. T. Forsyth* (London: Independent Press, 1965), pp. 35ff.
78 Emil Brunner, *The Mediator*, trans. Olive Wyon (Philadelphia: Westminster Press, 1947).
79 Ibid., pp. 470, 456.
80 Ibid., p. 456.
81 Ibid., p. 458.
82 Ibid., p. 488.
83 Gustav Aulén, *Christus Victor*, trans. A. G. Hebert (New York: Macmillan Co., 1931).
84 Ibid., p. 5.

85 Ibid., pp. 4–5, n. 1.

86 John of Damascus, *Against the Arians*, ii, 68, cited in ibid., p. 45.

87 Aulén, *Christus Victor*, p. 45.

88 Ibid., p. 46.

89 Ibid., p. 48.

90 Ibid., p. 48.

91 Ibid., pp. 49–50.

92 Ibid., p. 51. The same idea is found in Augustine and in Luther, as Aulén notes. In Luther it is most often the law which overreaches itself in condemning Christ and loses its tyrannical power.

93 Gregory of Nyssa, *Great Catechism*, chap. 24; cited in ibid., p. 52.

94 Aulén, *Christus Victor*, p. 129.

95 Ibid., p. 155. Emphasis added.

96 Tiililä, *Das Strafleiden Christi*, p. 65 and passim.

97 Some interpreters find this move a fortunate one. Robert S. Paul, for instance, says: "Aulén not only revived the note of victory in the ancient images, but he liberated theology from the categories of logic and unimaginative rationality in which the doctrine of the Atonement had often been incarcerated and showed that the Church has been most reasonable and most logical when it has expressed the drama of the work of Christ in the pictures and images of the drama itself. He re-emphasized . . . that the fact of the Atonement is ultimate and that our theories about it are relative" (*Atonement and Sacraments*, p. 257).

Chapter 2

1 Signaled, e.g., by Walther von Loewenich's classic study *Luther's Theology of the Cross*, trans. H. Bouman (1929; Minneapolis: Augsburg Publishing House, 1976); and E. Vogelsang, *Der Angefoehtene Christus* (Berlin: Walter de Gruyter, 1932).

2 A claim similar to Aulén's had been made almost a century before by J. C. K. von Hofmann and had actually led to a similar debate among Lutherans. The debate was inconclusive, however, largely because they had not come so far as to discover the theology of the cross. Conservative Lutherans were too leery of liberal views, and vicarious satisfaction still seemed the only alternative. See Gerhard O. Borde, *The Law-Gospel Debate* (Minneapolis: Augsburg Publishing House, 1967).

3 Theobald Beer, *Der Fröhliche Wechsel und Streit* (Leipzig: St. Benno Verlag, 1974), p. 213 and passim.

4 Gustaf Aulén, *Christus Victor*, trans A. G. Hebert (New York: Macmillan Co., 1931), pp. 107–8.

5 Ibid., pp. 111ff.

6 Paul Althaus, *The Theology of Martin Luther*, trans. Robert C. Schultz (Philadelphia: Fortress Press, 1966), pp. 218–19. Tiililä is another objector. The roots of the objection often go back to the previous debate (n. 2, above) and base themselves on the work of Theodosius Harnack. Harnack's work is questionable both because of its polemical intent in the debate and because it was done before the critical edition of Luther's works.

7 Althaus, *Theology of Martin Luther*, p. 193.

8 Ibid., p. 202.

9 See the following passages: "All such [atonement] cannot happen for nothing or without satisfaction of [God's] righteousness . . . ; righteousness must first be satisfied to completest perfection" (*WA* 101/1:121, 16–19). "If God's wrath is to be taken from me and I am to receive grace and forgiveness, it must be earned from him by someone: for God cannot be kind and gracious to sin, not remove punishment and wrath, unless payment and satisfaction is made" (*WA* 21:259, 9–12). "For Christ is the Son of God, who gave himself out of sheer love to redeem me. In these words Paul gives a beautiful description of the Priesthood and work of Christ, which is to placate God (*placare Deum*)" (*LW* 26:177). "We should comfort ourselves with Christ's suffering and death as the complete payment and propitiation (*Versöhnung*) of God" (*WA* 52:643, 39).

10 *WA* 21:264, 27. Note that Luther is not interested in a one-time act but in the ongoing effect, the *new* thing brought about by the cross.

11 *WA* 51:487, 29. Cf. Carl F. Wisløff, *Abendmahl und Messe*, AGTL 22 (Berlin: Lutherisches Verlagshaus, 1969), pp. 97ff.

12 Aulén claims that whenever Luther uses "Latin" terminology he gives it a different meaning. Ragnar Bring says Luther uses Latin terminology as a way of expressing the *sola gratia* (See Vilmos Vajta, *Theologie des Gottesdienstes bei Luther* [Göttingen: Vandenhoeck & Ruprecht, 1959], p. 192). Others maintain that Luther uses the terminology only as a concession to the tradition and then abandons it when he wants to set forth his own view. There is probably some truth to all the opinions, but if they do not reveal the basic reason behind the use or nonuse, they are of little help to us.

13 *LW* 31:40, theses 19–22.

14 *WA* 8:442, 30. Emphasis added.

15 *WA* 302:291, 34ff. Emphasis added.

16 Wisløff, *Abendmahl und Messe*, pp. 97ff.

17 Ibid., pp. 99–100.

18 *WA* 5:603, 34; *WA* 56:392, 8. Cf. Wisløff, *Abendmahl und Messe*, p. 99.

19 It seems to make little difference for Luther whether the assailant is the law, sin, death, the curse, or the devil. The law attacks Jesus and kills him (*LW* 26:280). Likewise, sin "attacks Christ and wants to devour him as he has devoured all the rest. . . . It is necessary for sin to be conquered and killed . . ." (ibid., 281). Or death: "The almighty empress of the entire world . . . clashes against life with full force and is about to conquer it and swallow it; and what it attempts, it accomplishes. But because life was immortal, it emerged victorious" (ibid., 281). And the curse: "clashes with the blessing" (ibid., 281–82). All these assailants can be spoken of in virtually the same breath.

20 *WA* 3:426, 34–36.

21 *WA* 4:33, 33–37.

22 *LW* 26:283.

23 *LW* 26:284.

24 *LW* 26:287: "The speculation by which Christ is grasped is not the foolish imagination of the sophists and monks about marvelous things beyond them; it is a theological, faithful, and divine consideration of the serpent hanging from the pole, that is, of Christ hanging on the cross for my sins, for your sins, and for the sins of the entire world. . . . Hence it is evident that faith alone justifies."

25 *WA* 1:183, 39–84, 10 (1517).

26 *LW* 26:284. Emphasis added.

27 *WA* 31 1:249, 16–250, 1 (1530).

28 *WA* 10 111:162, 10. Cf. Wisløff, *Abendmahl und Messe*, p. 98, n. 47.

29 See Beer, *Der Fröhliche Wechsel und Streit*, pp. 264ff., for a good summary of such criticism; also Yves M.-J. Congar, *Chrétiens en Dialogue*, UnSa 50 (Paris: Editions du Cerf, 1964), pp. 453ff.

Chapter 3

1 Martin Luther, *The Bondage of the Will*, trans. J. I. Packer and O. R. Johnston (Westwood, NJ.: Fleming H. Revell Co., 1957), p. 107. Also, *LW* 33:70.

2 We may protest that without what we call free will we cannot be held responsible for our sins. That is a common move, but it is only a clever diversionary tactic. We use accountability for our peccadilloes as protection against having to confess to sin itself: the fact that we have taken God's place and will not give it up. "Scripture sets before us a man who is not only bound, wretched, captive, sick and dead, but who, through the operation of Satan his lord, adds to his other miseries that of blindness, so that he believes himself to be free, happy, possessed of liberty and ability, whole and alive" (Luther, *Bondage of the Will*, p. 162). To the degree we claim such

freedom and will not confess to our bondage we are not responsible. We can be made so only by having our eyes opened. Responsibility is not something we *have* as fallen creatures. We *become* responsible when we are addressed by God in Christ and we begin to realize how lost we are.

3 Martin Luther, Disputation on Scholastic Theology, Thesis 17 in *LW* 31:10.

4 That is why Luther could make statements that have gotten him into trouble ever since, such as the following: "If then we are taught and believe that we ought to be ignorant of the necessitating fore-knowledge of God and the necessity of events, Christian faith is utterly destroyed, and the promises of God and the whole gospel fall to the ground completely; for the Christian's chief and only comfort in every adversity lies in knowing that God does not lie, but brings all things to pass immutably, and that His will cannot be resisted, altered or impeded" (*Bondage of the Will*, p. 84). For Luther it is the promise of the gospel, the actual coming of God to us, that is destroyed by attacks on God's immutability and "necessitating foreknowledge." If God's will is not done in the preaching and the sacraments, then it may just be chance that I was baptized. *God* never comes, never acts. We only hear "ideas" about God. The wrath then never ends.

5 Karl Barth, *Church Dogmatics*, 5 vols. in 14 (Edinburgh: T. & T. Clark, 1936–77).

6 H. Berkouwer, *The Triumph of Grace in the Theology of Karl Barth* (Grand Rapids: Wm. B. Eerdmans, 1956), p. 317.

7 Cf. Robert W. Jenson, *God after God* (Indianapolis: Bobbs-Merrill, 1969).

8 Luther, *Bondage of the Will*, p. 170.

9 Jürgen Moltmann, *The Crucified God*, trans. R. A. Wilson and John Bowden (New York: Harper & Row, 1974), pp. 145–46.

10 See the classic statement in Luther's Small Catechism: "Jesus Christ . . . is my Lord . . . who has redeemed me, a lost and condemned creature—not with silver and gold but with his holy and precious blood and with his innocent sufferings and death, in order that I might be his . . ." (*BC* 345). Christ purchases and wins (redeems) *me* to be his own; he does not purchase God.

11 D. M. Mackinnon, "Subjective and Objective Conceptions of Atonement," in *Prospect for Theology: Essays in Honor of H. H. Farmer*, ed. F. G. Healey (London: James Nisbet & Co., 1966), p. 175.

Chapter 4

1 F. C. N. Hicks, *The Fulness of Sacrifice*, 3d ed. (London: SPCK, 1946), p. 26.
2 Frances M. Young, *Sacrifice and the Death of Christ* (Philadelphia: Westminster Press, 1975), p. 91.
3 Ibid., p. 95.
4 Ibid., p. 96.
5 Ibid., p. 111.
6 René Girard, *Violence and the Sacred*, trans. Patrick Gregory (Baltimore: Johns Hopkins University Press, 1977).
7 Ibid., p. 102.
8 Ibid.
9 Ibid., p. 103.
10 Ibid., p. 161.
11 Ibid., pp. 103–4.
12 Ibid., pp. 15ff.
13 Martin Luther, *Lectures on Romans*, trans. and ed. W. Pauck, LCC 15 (London: SCM Press, 1961), p. 199.
14 Roy A. Harrisville, "The New Testament Witness to the Cosmic Christ," in *The Gospel and Human Destiny*, ed. Vilmos Vajta (Minneapolis: Augsburg Publishing House, 1971), p. 57.
15 Dietrich Bonhoeffer, *Christ the Center*, trans. E. H. Robertson (New York: Harper & Row, 1978), p. 29.
16 *WA* 1, 28, 25–32.

Part 2

Chapter 1

1 Petro B. T. Bilaniuk, "The Mystery of *Theosis* or Divinization," in *The Heritage of the Early Church; Essays in Honor of Georges Florovsky*, ed. David Neiman and Margaret Schatkin, Orientalia Christiana Analecta 195 (Rome: Pontifical Institute, 1973), p. 352.
2 Ibid., p. 355, n. 62.
3 Thomas Aquinas, *Summa Theologica*, 1, 2ae, q. 113, art. 6., in *Nature and Grace*, ed. A. M. Fairweather, *LCC* 11 (Philadelphia: Westminster Press, 1954), pp. 192–93.
4 Ibid.
5 Eric W. Gritsch and Robert W. Jenson, *Lutheranism: The Theological Movement and Its Confessional Writings* (Philadelphia: Fortress Press, 1976), p. 39.

6 Novatian provoked a schism (251) because the church was ready to forgive "mortal" sins. The Donatists (fourth century) rebelled against the validity of sacramental acts done by priests guilty of mortal sins. Montanists, like most "spiritualists," became essentially a "holiness" sect after the enthusiasm wore off.

7 The recent penchant for combining grace and faith into the formula "justification by grace through faith" is perhaps understandable given certain modern developments, but (in spite of words suggesting such a formula in the Augsburg Confession IV) it is strictly speaking at best redundant and at worst compounding a felony. When one misses the complete interdependence of grace and faith (grace *is* the gift of faith; faith alone lets grace *be* grace), one turns faith into a "subjective response" and can then only cover one's tracks by saying, "Of course, it comes by grace!" *Faith* then simply takes the place once occupied by "works" or "merit" in the medieval system and all the problems repeat themselves. Given such misunderstanding it is clear that one cannot use the formula "justification by faith" today without careful work of reclamation.

8 Martin Luther, *Lectures on Romans*, trans. and ed. W. Pauck, *ICC* 15 (Philadelphia: Westminster Press, 1961), pp. 124, 125. Cited hereafter as Luther, *Romans*. Also *LW* 25:257ff.

9 Ibid., p. 4.

10 Ibid., p. 128.

11 For an excellent recent treatment of this, see Leif Grane, *Modus Loquendi Theologicus: Luthers Kampf um die Erneuerung der Theologie (1515–1518)*, trans. E. Groetzinger (Leiden: E. J. Brill, 1975).

12 WA 40¹: 280, 3–6; 280, 9–281, 4, 11–13. Translation and emphasis mine. *LW* 26:165ff.

13 Luther, *Romans*, p. 179. *LW* 25:310.

14 Hans Joachim Iwand, *Nachgelassene Werke*, vol. 5, *Luthers Theologie*, ed. J. Haar (Munich: Chr. Kaiser, 1974), p. 197.

15 Wilfried Joest, *Gesetz und Freiheit*, 2d ed. (Göttingen: Vandenhoeck & Ruprecht, 1956), p. 59.

16 Exegetes who maintain that Paul had a distorted or jaundiced view of the law mostly fail to understand the radical nature of the eschatological gospel that had grasped Paul and its effect on the law. Whether Paul was influenced by late rabbinic "distortions" of authentic "Torah" has little or nothing to do with the matter. Precisely the *gospel* determines Paul's attitude toward the law, not the rabbis or his own "conscience" or psyche—exactly as he himself says (Phil. 3:6ff.). The new sets off and determines what is *old*. Though "blameless" under the law, Paul says, "For [Christ's] sake I have suffered the loss of all things, and count them as *skubala* (dung)

in order that I may gain Christ and be found in him, not having a righteousness of my own, based on the law, but that which is through faith in Christ."

17 The literature is extensive. See, e.g., Ragnar Bring, *Gesetz und Evangelium und der dritte Gebrauch des Gesetzes in der lutherischen Theologie*, Zur Theologie Luthers: Aus der Arbeit der Luther-Agricola Gesellschaft in Finnland 1 (Helsinki, 1943); Lauri Haikola, *Usus Legis*, UUA (Uppsala: Lundquistska Bokhandeln, 1958); Werner Elert, *Zwischen Gnade und Ungnade* (Munich: Ev. Pressverband, 1948).

18 Apology of the Augsburg Confession, Article IV, 38, *BC* 112.

19 Karl Holl, *Gesammelte Aufsätze*, vol. 1, 2d and 3d ed. (Tübingen: J. C. B. Mohr [Paul Siebeck], 1923), pp. 35ff. Cf. Iwand, *Luthers Theologie*, pp. 176ff.

20 *WA* 40 1:285, 5. *LW* 26:168.

21 This accounts for Luther's seemingly ambiguous stand on *synteresis* and conscience. It is there, but in and of itself it does no good—now. Cf. Iwand, *Luthers Theologie*, p. 187.

22 Iwand, *Luthers Theologie*, 129, *WA* 24:140, 2iff.

23 *WA* 19:126, 16ff.

24 Does one appeal to "conscience" in preaching? No doubt, as Luther often said, one would preach in vain if there were no conscience. But one must preach, perhaps we can say, as though conscience were the empty house of Jesus' parable, now occupied by seven more demons. One must not preach in such fashion as to solidify their tenure in the house. One assumes indeed that people live and suffer "under the law," but that what they are suffering from is the *misuse* of the law, the assumption that law, in conjunction with conscience, *is* the way. Many today like to say that we do not need, therefore, to preach "the law," but only the gospel. That is a mistake. The "law" that must be preached is the absolute offense of the unconditional gospel, the "letter" which kills, so the spirit can make new—the kind of law which destroys the illusions about law as the way and thus drives the demons from the house.

25 Gerhard Ebeling, "Erwägung zur Lehre vom Gesetz," in *Wort und Glaube* (Tübingen: J. C. B. Mohr [Paul Siebeck], 1960), p. 291 (translation mine). The Luther quotation is from *WA* 40 11:18, 4ff.

26 This is the reason one cannot, as Barth would have it, preach gospel before law. The word addresses us always as letter which kills first, and through that the Spirit makes alive.

27 Gritsch and Jenson, *Lutheranism*, pp. 42, 43.

Chapter 2

1 Perhaps it was too radical for the young movement to absorb. The threat of moral chaos no doubt made it difficult to make clear what was involved. But something of that sort seems always to be the fate of Christian eschatology. It is sacrificed for the sake of expediency and continuity, with the result that the gospel gets buried. Moral chaos we always have with us—maybe just because we bury the gospel!

2 Hans J. Iwand, *Um den rechten Glauben*, Gesammelte Aufsätze, ed. K. G. Steck (Munich: Chr. Kaiser, 1959), pp. 17ff.

3 Lauri Haikola, *Studien zu Luther und zum Luthertum*, UUA (Uppsala: Lunde-quistska Bokhandeln, 1958), pp. 9ff.

4 Heinrich Schmid, *The Doctrinal Theology of the Evangelical Lutheran Church*, 3d ed., trans. Charles A. Hay and Henry E. Jacobs (Minneapolis: Augsburg Publishing House, n.d.), pp. 424–25.

5 One brave but bumbling soul, Nicholas von Amsdorf, had the temerity to suggest that good works were detrimental to salvation. Taken at face value, the statement is of course preposterous. Yet in his own way, on the practical level fostered by centuries of timid semigospel preaching, Amsdorf was right. Much of the good work done by church people, the little bit one has defined as necessary, *is* detrimental to salvation. The good works resulting from preaching their necessity turn out to be mere tokens, a pittance that insulates and excuses from deeper involvement. All the attempts to mediate between those who held out for necessity and those who claimed good works detrimental resulted mostly in much tinkering with the language (see Formula of Concord, Article IV), which only masks the real problem: Forensic justification simply will not fit with the traditional scheme. Afraid that such justification goes too far, one takes back with the other hand what one has given with the one and gets mired in the question of the necessity of doing good works "too."

6 Wilhelm Dantine, *Justification of the Ungodly*, trans. Eric and Ruth Gritsch (St. Louis: Concordia Publishing House, 1969), pp. 32–33.

7 Cf. Jaroslav Pelikan, "The Origins of the Subject-Object Antithesis in Lutheran Theology," *CTM* 21 (1950): 94–104.

8 Schmid, *Doctrinal Theology*, p. 407.

9 Ibid., p. 408.

10 Dantine, *Justification*, p. 18.

11 Wilfried Joest, *Gesetz und Freiheit*, 2d ed. (Göttingen: Vandenhoeck & Ruprecht, 1956), pp. 60ff.

12 "Proficere, hoc est semper a novo incipere." *WA* 56:486, 7.

13 Joest, *Gesetz und Freiheit*, p. 62.

14 *WA* 40²:351, 27ff.

15 Martin Luther, *Lectures on Romans*, trans. and ed. W. Pauck, LCC 15 (Philadelphia: Westminster Press, 1961), p. 129. *LW* 25:262.

16 Karl Holl, largely on the basis of his interpretation of the famous illustration of the patient believing the promise of the doctor and like images used in the lectures on Romans, came to the judgment that justification for Luther was "analytic." The passage is important enough to bear repeating: "It is similar to the case of a sick man who believes the doctor who promises him a sure recovery and in the meantime obeys the doctor's orders in the hope of the promised recovery. He abstains from those things which have been forbidden him, so that he may in no way hinder the promised return to health or increase his sickness until the doctor can fulfill his promise to him. Now is this sick man well? The fact is that he is both sick and well at the same time. He is sick in fact, but is well because of the sure promise of the doctor, whom he trusts and who has reckoned him as already cured, because he is sure that he will cure him; for he has already begun to cure him and no longer reckons to him a sickness unto death" (*LW* 25:260). Careful reading reveals that Holl misses the point. Everything hinges on the patient's belief and trust in the doctor and his promise. The promise makes the patient well (already cured, "just") at the *same time* as he is sick ("sinner"). The doctor's promise *is* the cure which takes the patient away from the sickness unto death and produces a different way of life. F. Brunstäd was right in opposing Holl by insisting on a *synthetic* justification. Cf. Karl Holl, *Gesammelte Aufsätze*, vol. 1, 7th ed. (Tübingen: J. C. B. Mohr [Paul Siebeck], 1948), pp. 119, 125; vol. 3, p. 532; F. Brunstäd, *Theologie der lutherischen Bekenntnisschriften* (Gütersloh: Bertelsmann, 1951), p. 76.

17 Joest, *Gesetz und Freiheit*, p. 70.

18 Ibid., p. 93.

19 Luther, *Romans*, p. 194.

20 Ibid.

21 Joest, *Gesetz und Freiheit*, p. 93.

22 Ibid., p. 98.

23 *WA* 10¹ 2:431, 6ff.

24 Ibid., 430:30ff.

25 Hans Joachim Iwand, *Nachgelassene Werke*, vol. 5, *Luthers Theologie*, ed. J. Haar (Munich: Chr. Kaiser, 1974), p. 137. The quote is from *WA* 10¹ 2:431, lff.

26 *WA* Br 2:372, 83ff.

27 *WA* DB 7, 8:30ff.; *LW* 35:370–71 (Preface to Romans).

28 Cf. Iwand, *Luthers Theologie*, pp. 141ff.; *WA* 36:360, 22ff.

Chapter 3

1 Cf. Martin Werner, *Die Entstehung des christlichen Dogmas*, 2d ed. (Bern: Verlag Paul Haupt, 1941), pp. 197ff.

2 The controversy started over the tricky issue of whether law preaching or gospel preaching leads to "true" repentance.

3 Formula of Concord (Article VI) vacillates on the issue. On the one hand, it speaks of a third use of the law to be applied to the regenerate, but then it goes on to say it is necessary because regeneration is incomplete in this life. It is an attempt to have it both ways and thus threatens only to obscure the issue.

4 Wilfried Joest, *Gesetz und Freiheit*, 2d ed. (Göttingen: Vandenhoeck & Ruprecht, 1956), pp. 190ff.

5 See ibid., pp. 76ff., 998–99.

6 *LW* 44, 243ff. See Hans Joachim Iwand, *Nachgelassene Werke*, vol. 5, *Luthers Theologie*, ed. J. Haar (Munich: Chr. Kaiser, 1974), pp. 147ff.

7 Iwand, *Luthers Theologie*, 150.

8 Cf. Gerhard Ebeling, "Die Notwendigkeit der Lehre von den zwei Reichen" in *Wort und Glaube* (Tübingen: J. C. B. Mohr [Paul Siebeck], 1960), pp. 407ff.

9 See ibid., esp. pp. 420ff.

Chapter 4

1 Ernest Becker, *The Denial of Death* (New York: The Free Press, 1973).

2 Ibid., p. 56.

3 Ibid., p. 62.

4 Lucien Goldmann, *The Hidden God: A Study of Tragic Vision in the Pensées of Pascal and the Tragedies of Racine*, trans. Philip Thody (London: Routledge & Kegan Paul, 1964), esp. pp. 62ff.

5 Quoted in ibid., p. 80.

6 Ibid., p. 81.

7 The Hegelian idea of the "cunning of reason," according to which even the worst of wrongs are used in the progressive self-realization of Spirit in the dialectic of history, is one of the most dangerous and destructive of modern ideas. The fall becomes a blessed event and everything is potentially justifiable—from the murder of millions of Jews to abortion on demand and Afghanistan. One's own vision of tomorrow justifies whatever murder, killing, and tyranny one might see fit to inflict today, all in the name of "justice." The church cannot accept such antinomianism—however subtly disguised.